COST-BENEFIT ANALYSIS IN ADMINISTRATION

COST-BENEFIT ANALYSIS
IN ADMINISTRATION

TREVOR NEWTON

for the

ROYAL INSTITUTE OF PUBLIC ADMINISTRATION

LONDON

GEORGE ALLEN & UNWIN LTD
Ruskin House   Museum Street

First published in 1972

© George Allen & Unwin Ltd 1972

ISBN 0 04 336043 2 hardback
0 04 336044 0 paper

Printed in Great Britain
in 10 point Plantin type by
Alden & Mowbray Ltd
at the Alden Press, Oxford

FOREWORD

This book is the twelfth in the series of major research projects sponsored by the Royal Institute of Public Administration. It stems from work undertaken in the Institute during the period October 1967 to September 1969 by Mr N. J. Kavanagh of the University of Birmingham and by Mr Trevor Newton of the Treasurer's Department of the County Borough of Teesside. Part of the book consists of material derived from surveys and experimental studies carried out during that period. It also contains, however, descriptions of studies undertaken in central and local government in recent years, and of a study by the Institute's Local Government Operational Research Unit. In addition, there is a chapter on the use of cost-benefit analysis by the Roskill Commission on the Third London Airport, whose report was issued in January 1971.

The research from which much of this book is derived, was made possible by a grant from the Nuffield Foundation for which the Institute expresses its very sincere appreciation.

To assist with this research the Institute formed a Steering Committee consisting of the following members upon whom it could call for advice.

Sir Alan Hitchman, K.C.B., *Chairman*, formerly Deputy Chairman, United Kingdom Atomic Energy Authority; previously Permanent Secretary, Ministry of Agriculture, Fisheries and Food

Professor M. E. Beesley, Professor of Economics, London Graduate School of Business Studies

R. Brain, C.B., Deputy Secretary, Department of the Environment

R. Davis, Director of Economic Planning, the Gas Council

C. A. French, Financial Adviser to the Electricity Council

R. H. Gandy, Deputy Treasurer to the Greater London Council

Dr John Green, Deputy Director, Local Government Operational Research Unit

J. D. Hender, Chief Executive and Town Clerk, Coventry

B. McLoughlin, formerly Director, Leicester and Leicestershire Sub-Regional Study

R. L. W. Moon, County Treasurer, Wiltshire

P. J. Searby, Economics and Programming Officer, United Kingdom Atomic Energy Authority

William Henry Tee, Town Clerk and Chief Executive Officer, Reading

R. Turvey, formerly Deputy Chairman, National Board for Prices and Incomes

Professor A. Williams, Professor of Economics, University of York

The Institute is most grateful to the members of this Steering Com-

7

mittee. They are not, however, reponsible individually or collectively for the accuracy of information that the book contains or for the views it expresses. This responsibility resides with Mr Newton and his fellow authors.

The Institute is particularly indebted to Mr Trevor Newton for his general authorship of this book, as well as for the part he played in the research which preceded it. The Institute also wishes to thank Mrs G. T. Banks of the Treasury for contributing the section on applications of cost-benefit analysis in the public sector.

Grateful acknowledgement must be made to Mr Ronald Wraith for his assistance in a number of ways, including the contribution of the chapter on the third London airport; to Mr N. J. Kavanagh and Mr R. J. Smith of the University of Birmingham for work on which the chapter on Recreation is based; and to Dr Richard Carter, formerly of the Institute's Local Government Operational Research Unit, for the work on Flood Relief which was the origin of the chapter on that subject.

Mrs Banks would like to express appreciation to colleagues in a number of government departments who helped in preparing her contribution. The views she expresses are her own, and do not necessarily reflect those of the Treasury.

October 1, 1971

PREFACE

This project was initiated by the Royal Institute of Public Administration and financed by the Nuffield Foundation, and to both those bodies I am grateful for the opportunity to do this work.

The research was facilitated by many organizations and individuals in both central and local government. The assistance of the following bodies was particularly valuable: the former Ministry of Housing and Local Government (now the Department of the Environment); the Metropolitan Police; the London Fire Brigade; the London Borough of Haringey; the Coventry Transportation Study Group; the Water Resources Board; the Local Government Operational Research Unit.

On a more personal level, my thanks are due to Raymond Nottage and Ronald Wraith, without whose help and encouragement the book could not have been written. My thanks are also due to the staff of the RIPA, particularly to Mrs Easterling for typing assistance and to Ivor Shelley who prepared the manuscript for publication.

The help I received from my colleagues in the Teesside Treasurer's Department was of particular importance in the later stages of the work, and I am especially grateful for their forbearance in reading numerous drafts. Special thanks are due to the Borough Treasurer, Mr J. B. Woodham, who made it possible for me to continue the research after leaving the RIPA.

Finally, my thanks are due to my wife, whose patience was more than I deserved.

While the responsibility for all statements, opinions and defects in the book is mine, I cannot claim more than part of the responsibility for any merits it may have.

T.N.

Teesside
October 19, 1971

CONTENTS

PART I

INTRODUCTION

CHAPTER I

THE BASIC PRINCIPLES OF
COST-BENEFIT ANALYSIS

In recent years public administration has been greatly helped by science. The 'art of the possible' now has a wider scope as a result of the development of skills which enable policies to be formulated and decisions made on a basis of fact more fully identified than has hitherto been possible. The techniques that have brought this about have assumed something of the character of academic disciplines. Their proponents dispute their boundaries and interrelations and these can probably never be defined with precision, but at least the outlines of a science of management are emerging. The principal disciplines of social science – economics, sociology, politics – have many subdivisions from which new disciplines may seek to establish their right to recognition – econometrics, anthropology, public administration. The principal discipline of management science, if one accepts its existence, may be said to be operational research, which is broadly concerned with the analytical approach to management and the development of a scientific rationale. Like social science it too has its 'subdisciplines'. Cost-benefit analysis, with which this book is concerned, is basically a discipline in its own right, but it is a technique which may be profitably used in conjunction with operational research.

This book is primarily concerned with practical applications of cost-benefit analysis in public administration. It has been written for the reader who wishes to understand the nature of cost-benefit analysis but who does not have a grounding in the economic theory that underlies it. On this there are many learned publications, most of which for the working administrator will not be easy reading, and perhaps not very meaningful. References to these are included in bibliographies at the end of each chapter. In order, however, that the lay reader may more readily understand the framework within which cost-benefit studies are undertaken, this first chapter describes the salient ideas on which the technique is based and the terminology that its practitioners use. It also indicates the general relationship between cost-benefit analysis and operational research.

Cost-benefit analysis is about choice, or to be more correct, about *economic choice*. As individuals, we are all faced every day with situations which force us to select one course of action rather than another. The 'iron law' of economics is that in the *real* world nobody has sufficient resources to enable him to do everything he wants to do, own everything he wants to own, or go everywhere he wants to go. Some have more wealth (resources) than others, and their range of choices is correspondingly less restricted, but even the Greek shipowner and the American oil millionaire cannot go through life without making economic choices about the disposal of their wealth.

The typical situation in which we all find ourselves is that we never have enough money (i.e. command over resources) to do everything we would like to do. In the jargon of the economist, we all have a *resource constraint* which limits our choice. In its widest sense, cost-benefit analysis is the basis of the whole process of decision-making under resource constraints. The objective of cost-benefit analysis in this wide sense is to secure 'value for money' in economic life and this is achieved by simply adding up the costs and benefits of alternative economic choices and selecting the alternative which offers the largest *net* benefit, i.e. the highest margin of benefit over cost.

CHOICE AND RESOURCE ALLOCATION IN THE PUBLIC SECTOR

The technique of cost-benefit analysis has been developed for use in the public sector (encompassing central and local government) in an attempt to provide better solutions to the problems of resource allocation. A public body has basically the same resource allocation problem as any individual, i.e. how to get the most for what it spends. Like the individual, local and central government must operate within resource constraints, although these constraints tend to depend upon what is politically acceptable as much as what is economically feasible. Furthermore the problems of decision-making and resource allocation are obviously extremely complex in the public sector and it is necessary to identify at the outset the limits within which cost-benefit analysis can legitimately operate.

It is possible to identify three levels of decision-making in the public sector. At the highest level, resource allocation decisions are guided by political ideals and moral philosophy. The problem of allocating resources between defence on the one hand, and education on the other is not one which can be solved by analytical techniques: the solution is rather to be found by examining political objectives and priorities. No economist would claim that resource allocation decisions at this level are simply a matter of economics. Political decision-making is an art rather than a science: it does not wholly rely on quantification of costs and benefits, but rather on more diffuse criteria ranging from political ideology to administrative expediency. At the other end of the decision-making spectrum there are resource allocation problems which involve consideration of alternative 'technical' choices. For instance, whether to hire or buy a service vehicle of a particular type or whether to check all invoices or just a sample. Decisions on these questions are guided by technological and financial criteria which are *wholly* quantifiable – cost-benefit analysis is not relevant here. Between these two extremes exist the problems of resource allocation *within* political objectives. Any given objective may be achieved by alternative methods* involving alternative costs and benefits, some of which can be quantified. The aim of cost-benefit analysis is to assist in this type of decision-making problem by bringing a more rational approach to resource allocation based on consideration of *all* the relevant costs and benefits.

COST-BENEFIT ANALYSIS EXPLAINED

The best definition of cost-benefit analysis is probably the one given by Prest and Turvey. They defined it as

'a practical way of assessing the desirability of projects, where it is important to take a long view (in the sense of looking at repercussions in the further, as well as the nearer, future) and a wide view (in the sense of allowing for side-effects of many kinds on many persons, industries, regions, etc.), i.e. it implies the enumeration and evaluation of all the relevant costs and benefits.'[1]

This definition focuses attention on the main features of cost-benefit analysis. The remainder of this section is an attempt to expand on the definition covering five distinct issues:

(1) assessing the desirability of projects in the public, as opposed to the private sector;
(2) identification of costs and benefits;
(3) measurement of costs and benefits;
(4) the effect of *time* in investment appraisal;
(5) presentation of results – the investment criterion.

Assessing the Desirability of Public Investments (Taking a 'Wide View')
Why do we need cost-benefit analysis to make investment decisions in the public sector? In the private sector of the economy the businessman uses the market price mechanism to assess the desirability or 'efficiency' of alternative investment proposals. In economic theory, the value of all activities and the allocation of resources among these various activities is decided by the use of a system of market prices. Briefly, the theory

---

*Although alternative ways of achieving a given objective may exist, they seldom emerge in practice unless the management process is specifically designed to encourage creative thinking about viable alternatives.

states that if all exchangeable goods and services are traded at prices which are mutually acceptable to buyers and sellers, and if there is an organized system of markets open to all (and if a number of other assumptions are met!) then resources will be allocated in a way which can be called 'efficient' in the sense that the *welfare* of consumers is *maximized* (crudely, this merely means that everybody is satisfied). In practice of course there are imperfections in the market price mechanism; however, it does enable businessmen to rank alternative investment projects in terms of efficiency or profitability by comparing the payments and receipts attributable to each alternative project.

The problem is, of course, that this market price mechanism does not operate in many parts of the public sector. In order for a market to operate, goods and services bought and sold must be identifiable and *appropriable* in the sense that the product can be supplied to some people and withheld from others. Where this is the case, an individual producer can sell his product to consumers willing to pay the market price, whilst other people who choose not to purchase this product do not enjoy its use. Food, clothing, furniture and so forth, are all examples of appropriable commodities. There is, however, an important class of goods called *collective* goods or sometimes *public* goods, which are not appropriable. In the strict sense, collective goods are those of which enjoyment cannot be confined to individuals who are prepared to pay for them. In other words, an investment which produces goods of this type yields benefits to everyone, whether or not they make any payment for them. As a result, it is not usually possible for a private *entrepreneur* to capture the value of such benefits through user charges; consequently it will not be profitable for him to undertake the investment. Police, defence, roads, flood protection and street lighting are all examples of collective goods which cannot easily be marketed on the basis of willingness to pay. Air pollution control is another type of activity which produces a collective good since everyone is free to enjoy clean air.

It is clear from these examples that collective goods may be of immense value, and that if each individual were accurately to reveal the value to him of having such a good, total benefits could far exceed total costs. However, as he can usually expect to receive the benefit of the good whether he pays for it or not, he is likely to decide not to pay and receive the benefits free of charge. As it would be impossible (or certainly un-profitable!) for a private *entrepreneur* to operate in this situation, the government steps in to supply collective goods and recovers the costs through taxation. To summarize, in the case of collective goods, socially desirable investments in general have to be undertaken *socially* rather than privately, because the nature of these goods causes a divergence be-tween the benefit captured by the *entrepreneur* (the private benefit) and the correct measure of total benefit which is usually called *social* benefit.

The concept in cost-benefit analysis which distinguishes it from all other techniques of investment appraisal is described by Prest and Turvey as taking 'a wide view'; basically this means two things. First, it recognizes the general point that a decision taken in one area of the public sector will affect many other areas. For instance decisions taken on the siting of a new local authority housing development will clearly have implications for the provision of roads, sanitation, schools, community facilities, etc. These 'external' or 'spillover' effects are obviously relevant to the original housing decision and have usually been taken into account as a matter of course because they impinge directly on the resources of the local authority. However, there are some spillover effects which traditionally have not been taken into account – these can be broadly described as *social* repercussions. As long ago as 1920, the British economist, A. C. Pigou, emphasized that decision-making involved matters of private and public welfare, that divergences between the two were possible, and that where conflicts existed public action would be required to eliminate them. This distinction between private and social cost is the very core of cost-benefit analysis. The example of the factory chimney has been widely quoted but illustrates the point well enough. A private industrialist building a new factory is only concerned with the financial cost he incurs and the revenue produced by selling the manufactured goods. He is not concerned with the fact that the smoke from his chimneys imposes costs on nearby residents, because he does not have to bear these costs. Yet such costs are real enough! They may take the form of higher laundry bills, or even hospital bills because the smoke could have serious long-term effects on health. So long as the industrialist has an objective expressed in terms of *private* profit or loss he can legitimately ignore these external costs. However, the goal of decision-making in the public sector is expressed not in terms of private profit or loss, but rather in terms of *social* profit or loss. For many years, decision-makers have not taken into account the extra-market effects of many decisions. By ignoring these social effects they have in fact contributed towards many of the problems of our time, especially so far as the physical environment is concerned. The social pathologies of slum housing, the poisoning of the atmosphere and water resources and the despoliation of the countryside might all have been avoided if the decision-makers had contemplated hard and long the possible consequences of their decisions. Even today, the lesson has not been comprehensively learned and it is often left to benevolent pressure groups to further the cause of rationality in the use of the environment, although the increasing pressure of opinion seems at last to be paying off in terms of government action in many industrialized countries. In Britain, for example, we now have a government 'Department' of the Environment, set up in order to facilitate administrative procedures for ensuring that investment spillovers receive adequate consideration in the decision-making process. In the United States, the recent decision to abandon the SST project, partly for fear of serious environmental side effects, reinforces the view that the trend is gathering momentum.

Identification of Costs and Benefits
The first task in a cost-benefit analysis is to identify all the relevant costs and benefits of the investment project under consideration. Many alternative classifications of costs and benefits have been suggested to assist this exercise: 'private', 'social', 'secondary', 'indirect' are all adjectives which have been used to describe different types of cost and benefit. However, it now seems to be generally accepted that only two types of distinction need to be made: (a) between efficiency and non-efficiency benefits and costs, and (b) between efficiency benefits and costs measured in terms of Gross National Product and other efficiency effects. Cost-benefit analysis is primarily concerned with the efficiency effects of public investment projects. It is of little relevance in evaluating other effects, e.g. the equity benefits of income redistribution policies, although it can help by identifying the sectors in the community which are affected by a project. Within the category of efficiency benefits and costs, it is possible to discern two basic types – those which impinge directly on GNP, often (though not always) measured in terms of market price, and those which cannot be related to GNP, e.g. a loss of visual amenity. The identification of all relevant effects may be an extraordinarily complex process, because the effects of a project in a major policy area may well be infinite. In practical terms, it is impossible to identify (let alone measure!) *all* the relevant costs and benefits, but an attempt will usually be made to build a model which includes all of what are considered to be the major effects (see p. 31).

The first problem in a successful formulation of a cost-benefit appraisal is to identify the 'cut-off' points in the analysis. For instance, the geographical cut-off is likely to be a fundamental issue when considering local authority projects. A major urban motorway scheme is likely to provide benefits not only for inhabitants of the local authority undertaking the project, but also for road users who do not reside within its jurisdictional area. A major shopping redevelopment in one town is likely to impose real costs on shopowners in a neighbouring town. It is essential that geographical cut-off points should be specified in the analysis (possibly by the decision-makers themselves), in order to decide whether costs and benefits of this type should be included.

Another type of cut-off relates to the range of different sectors of the community for which costs and benefits should be included. The study by Foster and Beesley on the Victoria Underground Line in London[2] illustrates the possible significance of determining this cut-off point.

The aim of the study was to measure the benefits to travellers in terms of time saved and increased comfort and convenience. The main impact of these benefits was found to fall *not* upon travellers using the new line but on *road users* who benefited from reduced vehicle congestion as a result of passenger traffic being diverted on to the new underground route. In this case, it was found that these benefits were measurable in monetary terms. However, as we shall see later, measurability is *not* a relevant criterion so far as the definition of cut-off points is concerned. If only measurable items are included in the analysis there is a danger that a project with serious social disadvantages may be selected.

Although it is important to avoid the omission of any important class of costs or benefits, it is equally important to avoid *double-counting*. Many of the earlier cost-benefit studies fell into the trap of including more than one measure of the same benefit in the analysis. For instance, an irrigation project will increase the value of crops grown on the irrigated land in future years; as a result, the market value of the land itself will increase. It is important that some measure of the contribution of the irrigation scheme to the productivity of the land should be included in the calculation, but it would be *wrong* to include a direct measure of the increased output of crops and *also* the associated rise in land value.

Measurement of Benefits and Costs
Having enumerated all the relevant costs and benefits the next problem is how to measure them. This appears to be the limiting problem so far as the development of cost-benefit analysis is concerned. There are numerous complex issues involved in the problems of measurement and in this introduction the aim is merely to provide a simple outline of the most important issues. Methodologies designed to measure particular categories of costs and benefits are described later in the book.

It was indicated earlier that the calculation of *private* profit is a relatively straightforward matter because costs and benefits are simply derived from market prices (where 'benefit' is defined as the maximum amount an individual would be willing to pay for a good.) However, we have seen that many of the goods and services produced in the public sector are not priced in the market. Therefore, when the physical outputs of a public project have been estimated, it will be necessary to assign monetary values to many of them on the basis of other information. Since the benefit to any individual is defined as the maximum amount of money he would willingly pay for a given amount of a good, it follows that this value must be imputed for each individual. In other words, in order to evaluate benefits objectively, we need to be able to construct a demand curve for the good in question. To illustrate this, suppose we wish to value the benefits of a hydroelectric power scheme which makes electricity available in an area which was previously without electrical power. The price per unit of electricity is fixed at P, and the annual amount consumed at that price is Q (see Figure 1). The demand curve shows the relationship between the price of electricity and the quantity consumed for *all* possible prices. The total market value of the benefits produced by this project is $P \times Q$. However, the *market* value understates the true value of benefits because some consumers would still be willing to consume electricity at prices in the excess of P, i.e. those on the curve from A to C. The fact that they only have to pay the market price, P, which is uniform for all consumers means that they receive a *surplus* of value equal to the difference between what they would have willingly paid and what in fact they do

Figure 1

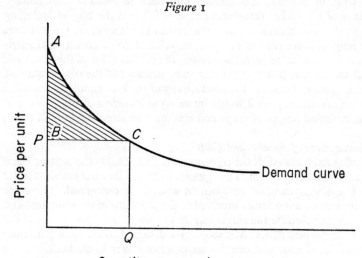

Quantity consumed per annum

pay in the market. This is called the *consumers' surplus* and is represented by the shaded area under the demand curve. The correct measure of project benefits is, therefore, the sum of market value *and* consumer surplus (this is discussed again in Chapter 2), but market price may often be used as a first approximation.

Where there is no *organized* market but where the behaviour of individuals indicates that they would buy a benefit if it were offered for sale, it may be possible to discover what they would be prepared to pay by examination of indirect evidence. There are, for instance, many opportunities for individuals to save time by travelling by more expensive means, in effect, by paying higher fares. It is therefore possible to deduce how they value time spent travelling by examining aggregate travel behaviour ('modal split'). Thus, by deriving what is in essence a demand curve, it is possible to impute a valuation for goods not directly valued by the market. This computed price is often called a *shadow price*. It may also be necessary to impute a shadow price for goods and services which are priced in the market but whose price does not reflect their true social cost. In times of balance of payments crises for example, the foreign exchange value of the pound sterling may not reflect the true *social* cost of using investment resources which require foreign exchange. In these circumstances, it may be more correct to impute a different (i.e. higher) price for foreign exchange than that assigned by the market – this is also a *shadow price*. Wherever it is possible to study trade-offs (exchanges) between a good which is normally valued in money terms and one which is not, it is possible to compute a shadow price for the latter. Several examples of this approach exist and have met with varying degrees of success; the validity of pricing road space and recreational facilities using this approach is now generally accepted, but attempts to measure amenity benefits such as reduction of noise and air pollution have been less successful.

An alternative approach to measuring benefits of this type which is worth mentioning is to use systems of arbitrary weights or trade-offs, often termed 'planners weights'. Where the trade-off is between an unvalued effect and real resources measured in money terms, this will generate a 'planners price'. However, although such a system will ensure consistency in project selection, it is often difficult for decision-makers to justify the weights used in objective terms, and where a project serves multiple objectives the determination of multiple weights is a complex process requiring a great deal of analysis, and sufficient time and manpower may not be available or justified by the potential pay-off.

The whole question of measurement of 'intangible' costs and benefits is one which has dominated the analytical development of cost-benefit analysis. When we talk of 'intangibles', what we are really saying is that a cost or benefit cannot be measured. Non-measurability may mean that a benefit or cost cannot be quantified in physical terms, for example, the aesthetic value of unspoilt countryside; or it may mean that, although quantifiable, no *monetary* value can be placed upon it – the example often quoted here is the saving of human life due to a road project. Most of the social costs and benefits of public projects were originally considered to be intangible. However, it is important to note that what was considered to be an intangible yesterday may be tangible today. Developments in the measurement of time savings, accident costs and recreation benefits testify to this. Weisbrod has summarized the debate as follows:

'To say that such benefits cannot be quantified or valued is to becloud an important issue: does "cannot" mean that it is in some sense logically *impossible* to value these benefits, or does the word only mean that in a particular case, at a particular point in time, and with the data then available we are unable to value them. In short, what is tangible or intangible, measurable or non-measurable is less a matter of what is abstractly possible than what is *pragmatically and at reasonable cost*, feasible. Therefore, the use of terms like tangible and intangible to refer to measured and non-measured effects is simply a source of unnecessary confusion. In the Middle Ages and earlier, surely it must have been argued by some that one's feeling of warmth or cold was intangible, unmeasurable and so on. Fortunately, Gabriel Fahrenheit did not agree.'[3]

Much of the recent work in cost-benefit analysis has concentrated on measuring reductions in social costs associated with public projects. In some cases it is now possible to measure social benefits and costs in monetary terms, but there remain large gaps in our knowledge. Although some writers have insisted that cost-benefit analysis is useless unless all costs and benefits can be measured in terms of money, administrators in the public sector have experienced some success without 'going all the way'. Until recently, the usual approach to public decision-making has been to concentrate attention on those items which could be measured with some degree of accuracy in monetary terms. It is now, however, generally accepted that the use of index numbers and other crude measures of the magnitude/importance of benefits can contribute in no small way to improvements in resource allocation. The identification of possible costs and benefits is, in itself, a worthwhile exercise if it is associated with some attempt at *subjective* judgement, so long as this is made explicit in the analysis. However, it should be stressed that the aim of cost-benefit analysis is to make decision-making more *objective*, and subjective evaluation of intangibles should be approached with caution.

Clearly there is no easy answer to the problems of measuring the benefits of public projects. Moreover, the measurement of cost in public resource allocation problems is also an issue which warrants a brief word of explanation. The concept of cost used in this context is that of *opportunity cost*, that is, the value of resources in their best alternative uses. For example, the opportunity cost of land to be used for a motorway is the value of the land in its 'highest' alternative use (probably agriculture). Where resources are used and paid for in cash but involve no sacrifice in terms of goods or services foregone, then they must be regarded as having zero cost. Thus, the use of labour which would otherwise have been unemployed has virtually zero social cost because production in other areas of economic activity is not foregone. In fact, many cost-benefit studies use money cost as a first approximation to opportunity cost; this is not surprising since many goods and services used by government are bought from private industry and much of the labour used on public projects is hired in competition with private firms.

The Effect of Time and Uncertainty in Investment Appraisal
Most of the other features of cost-benefit analysis do not differ in essence from techniques of investment appraisal in the private sector. The Prest/ Turvey definition stresses the importance of taking a *long view* of investment decisions because the benefits (and costs) of an investment, be it public or private, do not occur immediately; they accrue *over time*, and time affects project evaluation in three ways:

(1) changes in the market prices of benefits and costs;
(2) the relatively greater desirability of consumption in the near future to consumption in the more distant future;
(3) the possibility of alternative productive investment of the funds used in a public project.

Changes in the absolute level of prices due, for example, to inflation, can be safely ignored. However, changes in *relative* prices (*differential* inflation) should be taken into account as far as possible, although methods of achieving this will probably be rather hit or miss.

Assuming that allowance has been made for future changes in relative prices, we can now consider the problem of consumer time preference. Given the choice of £100 now or in 10 years time, most people would choose to have it now. In general, we prefer consumption in the near future to consuming something of the same value in the more distant future, i.e. we *discount* future values when comparing them with those of today. It is reasonable, therefore, for society as a whole to show the same preference in making public investment decisions – in other words, to discount (give smaller and smaller weights to) benefits as they occur in the more distant future by applying *a rate of discount* to gross benefits calculated by reference to *social time preference* as determined by the political system.

The third way in which time impinges upon investment appraisal in the public sector relates to the fact that when resources are spent on a public project, we give up the opportunity of making other productive investments in the public or private sectors of the economy. It is usually agreed that cost-benefit analysis should attempt to take this into account by means of what is called a *social opportunity cost* rate of discount.

For these reasons, the benefit and cost streams associated with any investment should be discounted back to *present value* in order to give a true comparison of benefits and costs on a time basis. Some progress has been made towards solving the problem of making different time flows comparable (known to most people as DCF). Mathematically, the solution is fairly straightforward: if we assume that a project's benefits are spread over ten years, thus

$$B_1 + B_2 + B_3 + B_4 \ldots + B_{10} = \sum B$$

then we can write the *present value* of the benefit stream as

$$\frac{B_1}{1+r} + \frac{B_2}{(1+r)^2} + \frac{B_3}{(1+r)^3} + \ldots \frac{+B_{10}}{(1+r)^{10}} = \sum \frac{B_t}{(1+r)^t}$$

where r is some rate of interest which operates to reduce the value of B with the passage of time. (Fortunately for those of us who have to use the technique of discounting, the formula can be safely forgotten because most books of financial tables give the values of discounting factors for many different interest rates for periods up to a hundred years.) However, the value of r to be used in discounting is a problem which is by no means satisfactorily resolved. There is disagreement among economists as to whether the discount rate should be based on social time preference or considerations of social opportunity cost, or both, and this difference of opinion is accompanied by a wide divergence in the rates used in actual cost-benefit studies, from as low as 2 per cent up to 15 per cent; but a consensus seems to be emerging in Britain somewhere in the range 8 per cent to 10 per cent (the current 'test' rate of discount for nationalized industries is 10 per cent). Many cost-benefit studies have acknowledged the problem of deciding a reasonable discount rate by applying several different rates to the cost and benefit streams of alternative investments. This practice is part of what is known as *sensitivity analysis** and it can be useful if it shows that the choice of interest rate is of little or no importance in the choice between investment projects. However, this will not be the case when there are significant differences in the *timing* of costs and benefits between alternative projects.

After adjusting costs and benefits to take account of the effect of time there is one further adjustment to be made. This is to take account of the effects of *uncertainty* and *risk* on investment expenditure. Risk and uncertainty are not the same thing. Risk relates to situations where, although the outcome is not known with certainty, it is possible to know what the range of probable outcomes will be and to assign a value to the probabilities involved. Uncertainty usually relates to a unique situation where no basis exists for estimating the probability of various possible outcomes. Various types of risks and uncertainties are associated with large projects – technological, economic and political – and the greater the risk and uncertainty involved the more important it is not

*This is a general term for computing a *range* of values in order to assess the significance of a variable within the analysis. It is especially valuable when presenting decision-makers with estimates of 'intangible' costs and benefits.

to accept estimates of cost and benefit at their face value. Some risks are predictable with some degree of certainty – for example risks of delay in a project due to weather or strikes. Allowances for such predictable risks can be made by adjustments in project costs and benefits as originally estimated, based upon an objective assessment of the probability of their occurrence. Many other types of risk, such as changes in the level of economic activity or major technological change, cannot be predicted with certainty. In many cases it is not even possible to assign objective probabilities and it may be necessary to use subjective probabilities (guesswork!) in order to estimate expected values. It is now fashionable to suggest that it is the subjective probabilities of the *decision-maker*, not the analyst, which are relevant here. One device which has often been used to take account of risk and uncertainty is to add a premium to the discount rate used in the analysis in order to reduce the weight given to benefit estimates incorporating a high degree of uncertainty. However, the rationale of discounting is to allow for the effect of *time* in the analysis and the practice of tampering with the interest rate to adjust it for risk now seems to be universally condemned, mainly because it allows the analyst to avoid a serious consideration of risk and uncertainty.

Presentation of Results: the Investment Criterion
The final stage in a cost-benefit analysis is to collate all the relevant information in a form which is useful in decision-making. Assuming that all the relevant costs and benefits of a number of alternative projects have been identified, measured in monetary terms, discounted for time and adjusted for uncertainty (and this is a very big assumption!) we need an investment criterion which uses the information available to rank the alternatives in terms of 'social profitability'. The criterion to use is intuitively obvious – the project which offers the highest *net* present value of benefits (i.e. present value of benefits minus present value of costs) should be ranked highest and the others ranked accordingly. However, many studies have ignored this criterion in favour of the benefit/cost ratio. When benefits and costs are expressed in this form, a ratio higher than unity indicates a relatively attractive investment and less than unity an unattractive proposition. The main advantage of benefit/cost ratios is that they can be used in cases where benefits and costs, although quantifiable in *numerical* terms, cannot be measured in *monetary* terms; in this case, the net present value criterion cannot be used. Take the case of traffic noise which clearly imposes costs upon those who endure it. Although the costs are real, the evaluation of noise in monetary terms poses severe problems. Yet quantification of noise (e.g. in terms of decibels) is a very precise business. Nevertheless, it is not possible to subtract 10 decibels from £100 and arrive at a meaningful answer. It has been found that benefit/cost ratios, like any other ratio, can be

seriously affected by the magnitudes of the costs and benefits involved and their adoption as a decision criterion in some cases could lead to a serious misallocation of resources. Consider two projects A and B. Their benefits and costs are set out in Table 1. Using the benefit/cost ratio criterion, project A would be selected because it has the higher benefit/cost ratio. However, using the net present value criterion, project B would be selected because it offers more in terms of net benefits. The question of selection of investment criterion in fact depends to a large extent on what *resource constraints* are in operation.

Table 1.

	Project A	Project B
Present value of benefits	£50m.	£100m.
Present value of costs	£25m.	£60m.
Benefit/cost ratio	2.00	1.67
Net present value	£25m.	£40m.

In practice, the final presentation of a cost-benefit analysis will usually not take the form of a simple tabulation of measured costs and benefits because many of the social costs and benefits will not be capable of measurement. In these circumstances it will be necessary to supplement the numerical analysis with a descriptive statement of the relative social repercussions involved in alternative projects. It is then the task of the decision-makers to make a value judgement based on the evidence available. It will also be useful to identify the relative *incidence* of costs and benefits in many cases. Although a certain project may appear to be socially efficient from a *global* standpoint, it may affect different groups in the community in different ways. Cost-benefit analysis identifies the most 'efficient' result, but decision-makers may wish to achieve objectives *other* than economic efficiency. For instance, the national policy on location of industry may not be *efficient* in economic terms, but the government may not be pursuing an efficiency goal. Its objective might be expressed in terms of *redistribution of income* in favour of the populations of development areas. Social decisions in the public sector cannot be concerned solely with a global view-point, they need to incorporate assessments of which groups in the community stand to receive benefits and which groups are likely to bear costs. In presenting the results of a cost-benefit analysis, this type of information should, where possible, be shown. The 'balance sheet' approach used by Lichfield* in evaluating alternative schemes for town centre development sets out in tabular form the costs and benefits accruing to the various parties (e.g. shopkeeper, developer, local authority, motorist, pedestrian, etc.), and is an extremely effective method for dealing with this type of problem.

* See Chapter 9.

THE ORIGINS AND DEVELOPMENT OF COST-BENEFIT
ANALYSIS

The development of cost-benefit analysis may be looked at in three stages: (a) its origins as an administrative tool in a particular activity of the United States Federal Government; (b) the development of the economic rationale of the technique; (c) contemporary applications of the technique.

Cost-benefit analysis originated as an administrative tool in the field of water resources development in the USA, and one form of the technique was being used by the Corps of Engineers in connection with river and harbour improvements as far back as the beginning of this century. Hammond, in his historical survey,[4] remarked that 'its formulation was purely American, and it was in origin an administrative device owing nothing to economic theory'. Basically, the technique was used by different agencies to compete for the limited supply of Federal funds available. Indeed, the 1936 Water Resources Act opened up the era of cost-benefit analysis with its crucial phrase that the Federal Government should sponsor flood control projects 'if the benefits to whomsoever they accrue are in excess of the estimated costs'. The subsequent use of the technique was not without controversy and abuse in application, much of which seems to have stemmed from the piecemeal fashion in which it developed.

The early fashioners of the technique wished to bring objective appraisal into the process of the allocation of resources in particular activities in the public sector, the objective being based upon a notion of economic efficiency. Without the depression of the inter-war years, this notion might have been more clearly defined, thereby reducing the area of misunderstanding and diminishing the abuse in the application of the method. The advent of the depression shifted the focus of economists away from the goal of efficiency in the allocation of resources to the goal of full employment in the national economy and, in particular, to the role of public expenditure as a means of expanding employment. The outcome of interest in problems of unemployment was the development of tools to be used in regulating the economy *as a whole* rather than *particular* areas of it. The period following the Second World War has been, by and large, a period of 'full' employment compared with conditions in the inter-war years. In most Western-style mixed-economies, full employment has been associated with a growth in public expenditure. The efficiency of such expenditure began to be questioned as also was the appropriateness of the concept of efficiency as a relevant criteria for resource allocation in the public sector.

In the USA the water resources programmes of the Federal Government attracted the attention of economists, partly on account of the volume of expenditure which they involved and partly because of the technical means developed by a number of public agencies for project appraisal. Eckstein in his book on water resources development[5] observed:

'The expenditures of the Federal Government have become correspondingly large, and in the fiscal year 1955, over $800m. were spent. This sum represents much the largest share of all the civil public work activities carried on at the Federal level of government. It is important, therefore, that these activities are carried on with efficiency, that the needs of the country are met and that the money is well spent.'

The focus was again moving towards an efficiency objective in resource allocation, and public decision-making was required to take into consideration the social nature of public expenditures. To this end the Federal Government devised benefit/cost ratios which public agencies had to take into account in project appraisal.

The early sixties saw the beginning of serious attempts to develop the techniques of cost-benefit analysis in Britain. In recent years there have been several notable applications involving the appraisal of various types of transport projects. The pioneering economic assessment of the London–Birmingham Motorway by Beesley and Reynolds[6] was an attempt to determine whether the huge financial costs involved in constructing and maintaining the motorway could be justified in terms of the expected social benefits of the road to the community. The most important benefit was found to be a reduction in the time spent in travelling between the two cities and this was supplemented by an expected reduction in the accident rate for the journey. It is clear that time spent in travelling and road accidents fall into the category of social costs, and that a reduction in such factors will constitute tangible social benefit. The complex problems involved in measuring such benefits will be examined at greater length in Chapter 2.

THE RELATIONSHIP BETWEEN COST-BENEFIT ANALYSIS AND OPERATIONAL RESEARCH

A strong bond has formed between economics and mathematics through the connection of cost-benefit analysis with operational research. We have seen that there are two basic steps in all cost-benefit studies: first, the measurement or evaluation of benefits, and then the allocation of limited resources to selected projects so as to obtain maximum net present value. Both processes may make use of models.

The term 'model' covers a host of technical niceties that it would not be profitable for us to explore. Sufficient for our purposes is the idea that a model is a number of statements, often highly interrelated, about how the world and the people in it are expected to behave when subjected to various changes. All models are abstractions from reality and inevitably miss some of its subtleties. However, much effort goes into testing the truth of a model's basic statements by observation and experiments – hence the use of the word 'scientific' – so that it will simulate reality as well as it can. The purpose of the model is to enable us to manoeuvre and combine its minor truths in such a way that a greater truth is revealed or verified. Since this can be best done with unambiguous symbols and clearly laid down rules, we end with a *mathematical* model.

Mathematical models are the life blood of operational research which, like cost-benefit analysis, also has a preliminary phase of measurement or 'data collection'. The difference between the two disciplines is ultimately a matter of degree. In cost-benefit analysis the measurement or evaluation of benefits is difficult and demanding. It often requires a sensitive understanding of complex social issues, especially where the trade-off of one benefit for another is concerned. The identification of the effect of 'cut-offs' is also a technical question of some intricacy. The resulting models, whose job it is to predict the size of the benefits that can be obtained, are correspondingly complex. In contrast, the models used for the allocation procedure are often no more than a simple calculation of the net present value of each of a limited number of projects of which one and only one is to be finally selected.

Operational research, on the other hand, has tended to work with measurements – often financial – that are wholly quantifiable and obtainable without the need for an understanding of the nuances of human behaviour. The models required to absorb and process this data are, however, frequently very complex indeed. Complexity is clearly not sought as an end in itself, and the reason for it is two-fold: first, for the model to be capable of absorbing a very wide range of information ('taking account of all the factors'), and second, for it to be able to analyse a wide range of eventualities (risk analyses, sensitivity analysis, etc.). For example, suppose that, having completed the first stage of a cost-benefit analysis, we are required to choose not one but several projects which are to be undertaken either wholly or in part and at different times. The calculation of the answer to this problem – namely the choice of projects or part-projects that gives maximum net present value, different answers being given for, say, different interest rates – is an established technique of operational research. Thus the second stage of analysis is operational research.

The inevitable merging of the two spheres of interest is a progressive process which is already well advanced. Purists may occasionally dispute a nice point of demarcation, but many practitioners are keenly aware of the advantages of collaboration.

The remainder of the book is chiefly concerned with surveying what has happened in the last 10 years or so. Analytical and methodological developments in the key areas of transportation, urban development and recreation are described, together with studies undertaken by the Institute's research team. The next section of the book is concerned mainly with the application of cost-benefit techniques by central government in Britain. The last chapter presents some general guidelines for administrators and others in the public sector who may at some stage be involved in a non-technical role in cost-benefit analysis.

REFERENCES

1 Prest, A. R. and Turvey, R., 'Cost-Benefit Analysis: A Survey', *Economic Journal*, Vol. LXXV (December 1965), No. 300.
2 Foster, C. D. and Beesley, M. E., 'Estimating the Social Benefit of Constructing an Underground Railway in London', *Journal of the Royal Statistical Society*, Vol. 26 (1963), Part 1.
3 Weisbrod, B. A., *Economics of Public Health: Measuring the Economic Impact of Diseases* (London, Oxford University Press, 1962).
4 Hammond, R. J., *Benefit-Cost Analysis and Water Pollution Control*, Miscellaneous Publication 13 (Stanford, Calif., Stanford University Food Research Institute, 1960).
5 Eckstein, O., *Water Resource Development: The Economics of Project Evaluation* (Cambridge, Mass., Harvard University Press; London, Cambridge University Press, 1958).
6 Beesley, M. E., Reynolds, D. J. and Coburn, T. M., *The London/Birmingham Motorway: Traffic and Economics*, Road Research Laboratory Technical Paper No. 46 (HMSO, 1960).

FURTHER READING

Dorfman, R. (ed.), *Measuring Benefits of Government Investments* (Washington, DC, Brookings Institution, 1965; London, Allen and Unwin, 1968).
Feldstein, M. S., 'Cost-Benefit Analysis and Investment in the Public Sector', *Public Administration*, Vol. 42 (Winter 1964).
Frost, M. J., *Values for Money: the Techniques of Cost-Benefit Analysis* (London, Gower Press, 1971).
Hender, J. D., 'The Uses and Abuses of Cost-Benefit Analysis in the Public Sector', *Cost-Benefit Analysis in the Public Sector* (London, IMTA, 1971).
Institute of Municipal Treasurers and Accountants, *Cost-Benefit Analysis in Local Government* (London, IMTA, 1969).
Krutilla, J. V. and Eckstein, O., *Multiple Purpose River Development*, 2nd ed. (Baltimore, Md, Johns Hopkins Press; London, IBEG, 1970).
Maass, A. et al., *Design of Water Resources Systems: New Techniques for Relating Economic Objectives Engineering Analysis, and Governmental Planning* (London, Macmillan, 1962).
McKean, R. N., *Efficiency in Government through Systems Analysis* (London, Chapman and Hall, 1958).
Marglin, S. A., *Public Investment Criteria: Benefit-Cost Analysis for Planned Economic Growth* (London, Allen and Unwin, 1967).
Merret, A. J. and Sykes, A., *The Finance and Analysis of Capital Projects* London, Longman, 1963).
Mishan, E. J., *Cost-Benefit Analysis* (London: Allen and Unwin, 1971).
O'Donoghue, M., 'Cost-Benefit and the Analysis of Government Expenditure', *Administration*, Vol. 13 (Winter 1965), No. 4.

Peters, G. H., *Cost-Benefit Analysis and Public Expenditure*, 2nd ed., Eaton Paper, No. 8 (London, IEA, 1966).

Walsh, H. G. and Williams, A., *Current Issues in Cost-Benefit Analysis*, CAS Occasional Papers, No. 11 (HMSO, 1969).

Williams, A., *Output Budgeting and the Contribution of Micro-Economics to Efficiency in Government*, CAS Occasional Papers, No. 4 (HMSO, 1967).

Wilson, A., 'The Uses of Cost-Benefit Analysis in the Local Government Sector', *Local Government Finance* (August and September 1966).

PART II

SELECTED SURVEYS

CHAPTER 2

ROAD TRANSPORT: THEORETICAL CONSIDERATIONS

INTRODUCTION

Transport, perhaps more than any other field except water resources, has aroused the attention of economists and others concerned with the appraisal of public investment projects. Spectacular advances in transportation technology during the twentieth century have led to increasing demands for public investment in roads, airports, docks and railway systems. The impact of this progress on the physical and social environment has stimulated research into the conceptual and methodological problems of using cost-benefit analysis to evaluate transport projects in terms of their economic and social consequences. Most of the research has concentrated on defining and measuring the benefits and costs associated with major urban and rural motorway projects, and relatively little work seems to have been done on other forms of transport. (Many of the more significant British studies are described in Chapter 5.) The weightiest piece of cost-benefit research involving transportation issues is, without doubt, that undertaken by the Roskill Commission to investigate alternative sites for the third London Airport. This is described separately in Chapter 4. This chapter will go on to discuss the theoretical nature of the benefits of motorway projects and the identification and measurement of benefits and costs. The pioneering study of the MI motorway[1] will be described to illustrate some of the issues involved.

THE NATURE OF BENEFITS

A road is a classic example of a public good because the benefits it provides are not (in the first instance) capable of being measured in monetary terms by reference to market prices. In assessing rail and air travel investment projects it is possible to argue that the fares charged to passengers may be used as an approximation of benefits. However, user charges for road transport are usually part of the general tax structure (fuel tax, road fund licences, etc.), and are not useful as measures of the benefits which the users of a particular road may be expected to enjoy. There are of course exceptions to this general rule, e.g. user charges on the Italian autostrada, tolls on the 'turnpikes' in the United States, and tolls on certain bridges in the United Kingdom.

If information about the structure of prices which consumers are willing to pay for the use of roads were available, then the parameters of the demand function could be estimated and measures of the benefits of a particular road project could be made by estimating the consumers' surplus associated with the project. Assuming that the effect of a motorway scheme is to reduce the price per vehicle-mile of road transport on a particular route, and given the demand curve $D'D'$ for road transport on this route, we can measure the gain in consumers' surplus as shown in Figure 2. At price P_0, the demand for road transport (measured in

Figure 2

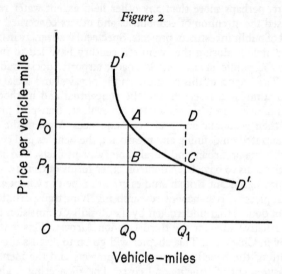

Vehicle–miles

vehicle-miles) is OQ_0. At the reduced price P_1, consumers can maintain the same level of transportation and pay less for it, and are therefore enjoying a 'surplus' measured by the area of the rectangle P_0ABP_1. Because of the reduced price, the original consumers will tend to increase their vehicle mileage, and additional demand from *new* consumers will be generated, increasing total demand to OQ_1. Thus a further 'surplus' is apparent, measured not by multiplying P_0P_1 by Q_0Q_1, but by the area under the demand curve within the rectangle $ABCD$. The total consumers' surplus associated with this reduction in price is therefore measured by the area P_0ACP_1, which expresses what consumers would be *willing to pay* to enjoy additional road transport Q_0Q_1. In order to calculate accurately the gain in consumers' surplus, it is necessary to know the shape of the demand curve between A and C. Many studies, including the M1 appraisal, make an important distinction between benefits to *diverted* traffic and benefits to *generated* (new) traffic on the basis of consumer surplus. The so-called '50 per cent rule' rates the benefits per vehicle-mile to generated traffic as half as great as those accruing to diverted users (this implicitly assumes that AC in Figure 2 is a straight line). The justification for this differential is simply that as generated traffic is now undertaking journeys which were not previously worth the cost involved, then these additional units of transportation must be valued by those who undertake them at less than the unit values for existing traffic.

The theory of consumers' surplus underlies many attempts to provide a general theoretical framework for the evaluation of road projects. However, although many economists accept consumers' surplus as a valid *theoretical* basis for the measurement of motorway benefits, severe difficulties are usually experienced when trying to put the theory into practice. The main stumbling block concerns the question of what determines the 'price' of transport, and how far changes in price reflect the true value of benefits. Many studies measure the reduction in price P_0P_1 (see Figure 2) following a road project in terms of savings in costs, usually vehicle operating costs and travel time costs. However, such benefit estimates may only be rough approximations because these savings may not represent true *social* benefit. The question of identifying (and measuring) *all* the relevant costs and benefits of road projects is taken up in the next section.

THE IDENTIFICATION AND MEASUREMENT OF BENEFITS AND COSTS

Table 2 sets out the items which have generally been regarded as the main costs and benefits of road projects, although their significance may

Table 2

Benefit-Cost Framework for an Inter Urban Motorway Project

Benefits	Costs
1. Travel time savings	1. Project costs
2. Vehicle operating cost savings	(a) opportunity cost of land
	(b) site clearance costs
3. Reduction in accident costs	(c) construction costs
4. Other benefits from reduced congestion. e.g. less mental and physical strain on drivers and passengers	(d) cost of ancillary equipment (traffic signs, etc.)
	(e) road maintenance costs (including police and accident control)
	(f) administrative costs (e.g. cost of raising funds)
	2. Environmental and amenity cost (or benefit)

vary in different studies. The costs of motorway investment may be defined as all the identifiable negative effects caused by a project, and are considered separately from the *cost-savings* which constitute the benefit function. Project costs (1(a)–1(f)) do not, as a rule, present serious measurement problems. However, little attention has been given until recently to the rather diffuse *environmental* costs (and possibly benefits) arising from a highway development. Certain aspects of highway disbenefit, e.g. disturbance to shopkeepers and severance, are explicitly taken into account by including a sum for compensation in the purchase price of land for highways purposes under compulsory purchase law in Britain. It is more difficult, however, to assess the cost to the community when a new motorway spoils the natural beauty of a rural area or splits in two an existing town, with a consequent reduction in amenity. The *valuation* of such despoliation will usually be subjective, but with the increasing impact of roads, airports, electricity lines, etc., on the modern environment, attempts are now being made to value such factors as noise, air pollution, and visual amenity. Some of this work is discussed in Chapters 3 and 4.

The benefits of highway projects generally fall into the category of savings in costs, i.e. in individual user costs and collective or *social* costs. The benefits listed in Table 2 are all clearly associated with reduced traffic congestion and travel times, which are usually the major objectives of any motorway project. In fact, *time-savings* are usually the most significant item on the benefit side, and because of the special problems they pose they are treated separately below.

Savings in the operating costs of vehicles affected by a road project are typified by savings in fuel consumption, tyre wear, brake wear, engine and other maintenance, and possibly (in the longer term) in insurance and other fixed costs. The importance of such savings to road users will depend on the nature of the project in question and is a matter which is primarily determined by first estimating traffic speed/flow relationships on the new road and on existing routes. The placing of monetary values on these savings presents few problems because of the continuing research into these matters by the Department of the Environment and the Road Research Laboratory.

Benefits derived from a reduction in motor accidents due to a road project are more difficult to measure. First, an estimate of the number and type of accidents is required. Once this is available, a *monetary* evaluation has to be made and this has caused some controversy. The M1 study estimated accident savings in terms of loss of output, medical expenses, property damage and administrative expenses, but the authors admitted their inability to place a *money value* on such factors as personal suffering and sense of loss. Some writers have expressed distaste for the view that accident *money* benefits should be included in a benefit-cost estimate. They argue that it is not the analyst's job to convert human life and health into monetary terms because this would inevitably involve the introduction of personal feelings and value judgements into the analysis. This school of thought would prefer to present estimated accident figures as addendae to the calculations of monetary costs and benefits, so allowing the decision-makers to exercise their own value judgements in making trade-offs between monetary cost and human life. This view has been questioned by other writers in the field who argue that, although no one would claim to be able to value personal suffering, it is feasible to value human life in terms of lost production and some inherent worth of person. They argue that valuations on this basis are being made in the civil courts every day and they are perfectly acceptable for the purposes of cost-benefit analysis. Perhaps the best justification for attempting to value accident savings was given in a statement by the 11th International Road Congress:

'Decisions on highway construction attribute unconsciously in each case a value to human life and suffering. It seems preferable to make this more conscious and systematic.'

In a study published in 1967,[2] Dawson took the M1 work further and also considered the subjective cost associated with pain, grief and loss of life. Court awards were examined, but it was found to be impossible to distinguish pecuniary and non-pecuniary damages, and awards were not always consistent. Dawson therefore recommended the arbitrary figure of £5,000 as the subjective cost of a fatal accident. This ensured that the life of older people would still have a positive value even though their future consumption might exceed their output, representing a net economic cost to the community. Smaller sums were suggested for suffering in serious and slight accidents. These arbitrary values are reasonably satisfactory for ranking schemes which produce similar benefits, but clearly will have to be reviewed when conflict arises between time and safety or between different types of accidents.

Item 4 on the benefits side of the cost-benefit framework is probably the most difficult of all to quantify, although it is no less a real benefit for that. Increased mental and physical well-being as a result of less congested road conditions may, to some extent, be accounted for by reduced accidents, but it is more conveniently linked with the problem of time valuation which is discussed below.

The Valuation of Time Savings
A major objective of road investment is to save the time of those travelling, i.e. either as private individuals or as drivers responsible for the conveyance of goods or passengers. The value of time saved by a transport project is therefore usually central to any judgement as to whether

or not the expenditure of public funds is worthwhile. Most studies agree that such savings constitute a substantial proportion of highway benefits and it is apparent that any value used to convert time savings into monetary terms should be reliable and defensible. However, although the problems of time valuation have provoked a great deal of theoretical and methodological discussion, earlier road project appraisal studies often tended to assign them rather arbitrary money values. There are several distinct areas where major problems have arisen, notably the valuation of working time, the valuation of commuter time, the valuation of leisure time, and the value of very *small* time savings. It is proposed to review here some of the main issues associated with these questions by referring to some of the empirical studies which have been undertaken in recent years in Britain.

The valuation of working time is relatively straightforward – most studies have simply taken the average gross wage rate (including overtime) for the category of working time saved. It is difficult to imagine any alternative approach, although this particular item caused some controversy in the Roskill exercise (see Chapter 4).

The problems of valuing non-working time, i.e. commuter time (the journey to work) and leisure time, are, however, manifestly more severe. It is possible to assign a value for working time directly from the labour market, but in the case of non-working time, no such market exists and it is necessary, therefore, to consider situations in which people make choices which *imply* values for time. For instance, many cities offer a choice between various modes of transport (bus, underground, private car). Each mode of transport has different speed/cost characteristics, and observation of modal split (choice between travel modes) allows some inference to be drawn about the preferences of users for a more expensive but quicker mode of travel for the journey to work.

Beesley was one of the first to analyse time/cost trade-offs in choice between public transport and the private car for the journey to work.[3] He examined data from a sample of employees of the Ministry of Transport in London with the aim of establishing the price people may be willing to pay to minimize the 'disutility of travel'. The sample was divided into two income groups and, on the assumption that overall travel time and cost were the only relevant factors, values for time were derived which minimized the number of apparently 'bad' choices in each group. This assumed that it is possible to explain modal choices in terms of overall *travel* time and cost alone. In fact Quarmby has shown that differences in walking and waiting times (which may have a different value to travel times) may, in part, account for choice of travel mode.[4] Using a sample of car owners working in central Leeds, he tested a model using up to seven variables to explain modal choice, and produced evidence of a strong relationship between the value of time and income.

The results also suggested that the cost of bus travel time was more highly valued than car travel time, and that walking and waiting time were valued at 2–2½ times travel time. (One interesting application of this may be in the design of bus routes; it may be worth sending buses a longer way round in order to reduce walking time to bus stops, even if *overall* travel time is thus increased.) Another journey to work analysis has been carried out using a sample of employees working at County

Table 3

Values of Time Indicated by Modal Choice Studies of the Urban Journey to Work

1. Beesley	Mean hourly income (n.p.)	Value of public transport time (n.p.)	% of income
	45	16	39
	33	10	31
		Value of car	
	45	22	49
	33	10	31
2. Quarmby	Mean hourly income (n.p.)	Value of time (n.p.)	% of income
	115	24	21
	74	unreliable	—
	53	13	25
	36	9	25
3. County Hall	Mean hourly income (n.p.)	Value of time (n.p.) (averaged over all modes)	% of income
	195	20	14
	100	15	15
	65	15	23
	45	10	33
	35	10	28

Hall in London. Two methods were used, broadly similar to Beesley's. In all three studies there was evidence that values of time increased with income (see Table 3). Clearly, these studies have produced a range of values which are quite close to each other and were therefore probably fairly accurate at the time they were derived. Other studies in this field have produced similar results and the former Ministry of Transport felt justified in adopting a figure of 25 per cent of income for valuing time on the journey to work in connection with their own economic appraisals. However, these studies were all concerned with the measurement of *commuting time* and it must be questioned whether numbers in this range can be valid as valuation of *leisure time*.

It may be argued that the marginal value of leisure can be equated with the wage rate on the grounds that the number of hours spent working is such that the marginal hour's effort is just worth the wage rate, and the next hour has the same marginal value. This seems reasonable as an average applied to all workers because if all employees in a firm wanted a longer or shorter working week, this would eventually come about. Thus, it is not unreasonable to suppose that the number of hours worked must in some way reflect (on average) the wishes of the workers, leading to the conclusion that the average person values his last hour's work at the wage rate. In fact, most writers on the problem would probably disagree with this approach. Recent commuter studies indicate that commuter journey time is valued at around one-quarter of the wage rate, and there is no empirical evidence to assume that 'pure' leisure travel time is valued at any more than this. There are three reasons to support this view:

(1) some leisure trips (e.g. to cinema or theatre) are closer in their nature to commuting trips;
(2) time saved during the week may allow certain activities to be carried out which saves 'leisure' time at weekends;
(3) time saved at one part of the day (e.g. on journey to work) is often interchangeable with time spent at other parts (e.g. on leisure activities).

The Ministry therefore decided that it would be sensible to adopt the journey to work figure for *all* leisure time. However, it is apparent that this assumption might break down, for instance, if travel time was spent eating, sleeping or working, or was regarded as a pleasure in itself. This point caused controversy during the Roskill inquiry.

The problem of how to value the time of non-earners, e.g. children and housewives, has not been the subject of much empirical research and has usually been ignored in cost-benefit analysis studies (although, once again, some of the problems were raised during the Roskill inquiry).

So far, we have ignored the size of time savings. Little empirical evidence is so far available to answer the question – does the value of 60 separate minutes saved equal the value of 1 hour saved? It is often argued that savings of a few minutes are valueless. However, if these are ignored, a whole series of changes in journey time, each small in itself, will be valued at zero, even though the cumulative effect is large. Moreover, whilst some people may not be able to use an extra 5 minutes, others may find that this just enables them to do something requiring considerably more time. For instance, small time savings may permit major adjustments in vehicle schedules which already have some slack in them. The conclusion is, therefore, that on average small time savings should be allotted the same value per unit of time as large ones.

One other problem to be touched upon is the difficulty of valuing time *per se*. It may be questionable to assume that people are indifferent to travelling by private car or public transport *at the same speed*. Such factors as bodily comfort, mental and physical strain must also influence the choice of mode. However, it seems reasonable to include these 'residual' elements in time valuations, not attempting to distinguish them from the 'pure' time element, so long as this is recognized and possibly adjusted for in special cases.

One final important point to note is that, in assessing road schemes, the Ministry use a single value for leisure time of all adults, based on 25 per cent of the *national average wage*. The reason for this is an equity consideration. Using a higher value for higher income groups would divert public investment towards schemes used by such groups, and since road space is not priced, this would have distributional, social and regional effects which might be politically undesirable.

The M1 Study

The economic assessment of the London–Birmingham Motorway was carried out by Beesley and Reynolds and published almost 10 years age. It has served as a model for the economic appraisal of major motorway projects, although certain improvements in techniques have since taken place. The study was undertaken *after* a decision had already been made to go ahead with the project. Its purpose was to test methods of forecasting and valuing the effects on traffic, using data from experience of motorways abroad. The main cost-benefit table is summarized in Table 4. This table is very similar in content to the benefit/cost framework outlined earlier in Table 2, although no attempt was made to assess the value of possible environmental and amenity cost, and the possibility of a reduction in physical and mental strain was also ignored.

Users were divided into two categories – those diverted from other routes and those who would otherwise not have made the journey at all (i.e. generated traffic). For the former, the effect of the motorway would be to speed up their journey, reduce vehicle operating costs (except in so far as diverting on to the motorway increased overall mileage), and reduce the number of accidents. Changes in vehicle operating costs and benefits from reduction in accidents were calculated as described earlier. Savings in working time were also calculated as previously described, i.e. by reference to average wage rates. These savings are by far the largest item on the benefit side, accounting for between 60 per cent and 78 per cent of net annual savings.

However, no values were imputed for non-working time saved: instead, a range of values was considered and the rates of return on the funds

Table 4

Estimated Savings (−) and Increases (+) in Annual Costs Resulting from
Construction of the M1 Motorway

	Changes in £000 per annum		
	1st assignment*	2nd assignment*	3rd assignment*
1. Savings in working time by traffic transferring to motorway	−453	−624	−766
2. Reduction in vehicle fleets	−80	−161	−227
3. Changes in fuel consumption for vehicle-mileage transferred to motorway	−117	−84	−18
4. Changes in other operating costs for vehicle-mileage transferred	−200	−200	−200
5. Costs of additional vehicle-mileage incurred in transferring to motorway	+229	+307	+375
6. Reductions in cost to vehicles remaining on old roads	−128	−128	−128
7. Total vehicle costs	−749	−890	−964
8. Reduction in accidents	−215	−215	−215
9. Maintenance costs of motorway	+200	+200	+200
Net annual measured savings	−764	−905	−979

* Assignments relate to different assumptions about average speeds
on the motorway.

Table 5

Rates of Return* Including Average Values for Non-Business Time Saved

Average value of non-business time (n.p.)	1st assignment Rate of return (%)	2nd assignment Rate of return (%)	3rd assignment Rate of return (%)
10	4.6	5.4	5.9
20	5.4	6.4	7.1
30	6.2	7.4	8.3
40	7.0	8.3	9.4
50	7.8	9.3	10.5

* Expressed as a percentage of total capital cost, £23.3m.

invested were shown to be quite sensitive to different values of non-working time within this range (see Table 5). A further aspect of time savings is reflected in item 2 (Table 4) – reduction in vehicle fleets. Because of the savings in time of vehicles, it was argued that the same volume of commerce could be carried on with fewer vehicles.

SUMMARY AND CONCLUSIONS

The technique of cost-benefit analysis has made only a minimal impact on many areas of the public sector involving the allocation of investment expenditure of millions of pounds every year. However, the research effort which has been concentrated for some years on cost-benefit analysis in road transport now, at last, seems to be paying off. The Department of the Environment is engaged in cost-benefit type appraisals of various policies and projects, some of which are described in Chapter 5. Some local authorities, notably the GLC, have also made contributions in this field.

However, the methodological debate continues. The nature of the benefit/cost framework for transport projects is fairly well established, but further progress needs to be made on the problems of valuing time, accidents, and most of all, the impact of transport modes on the environment. The data needed for cost-benefit studies have often been lacking or inadequate in the past, but the increasing use of land use and transportation studies will inevitably produce more and better data. Without these data, the only alternative methods of allocating investment in the transport field is guesswork. However, as more information becomes available, cost-benefit analysis will become a better tool in the sense that it will become more capable of discerning small differences between schemes. Transport technology is developing at a frightening pace; supersonic air travel and eight-lane motorways are already with us. Without a sound appraisal of their economic and social consequences, we may leave an unwanted legacy to future generations more damaging than that bequeathed to us by the Victorian railway enthusiasts.

REFERENCES

[1] Beesley, M. E., Reynolds, D. J. and Coburn, T. M., *The London/ Birmingham Motorway: Traffic and Economics*, Road Research Laboratory Technical Paper No. 46 (HMSO, 1960).

[2] Dawson, R. F. F., *The Cost of Road Accidents in Great Britain*, Road Research Laboratory Report LR 79 (HMSO, 1967).

[3] Beesley, M. E., 'The Value of Time Spent Travelling: Some New Evidence', *Economica* (May 1965).

[4] Quarmby, D. A., 'Choice of Travel Mode for the Journey to Work: Some Findings', *Journal of Transport Economics and Policy* (September 1967).

FURTHER READING

Beesley, M. E. and Kain, J. F., 'Urban Form, Car Ownership and Public Policy: an Appraisal of "Traffic in Towns" ', *Urban Studies*, Vol. 1 (November 1964), No. 2.

Bos, H. C. and Koyck, L. M., 'Appraisal of Road Construction Projects', *Review of Economics and Statistics*, Vol. 43 (February 1961).

Brownlee, O. H., 'Optimal Expenditure for Highways', *Public Finance*, Vol. 17 (1967), Nos. 1-2.

Charlesworth, G. and Paisley, J. L., *Economic Assessment of the Returns from Roadworks* (Institute of Civil Engineers, November 1959).

Foster, C. D., *The Transport Problem* (London, Blackie, 1963).
   'Economics of Roads: Surplus Criteria for Investment', *Bulletin of the Oxford Institute of Statistics*, Vol. 22 (November 1960).

Foster, C. D. and Beesley, M. E., 'Victoria Line: Social Benefits and Finances', *Journal of the Royal Statistical Society*, Series A, Vol. 128 (1965), Part 1.

Friedlaender, A., *The Interstate Highway System: a Study in Public Investment* (Amsterdam, North–Holland Publishing Co., 1965).

Gilhespy, N. R., 'The Tay Road Bridge: a Case Study in Cost-Benefit Analysis', *Scottish Journal of Political Economy*, Vol. 15 (June 1968), No. 1.

Glassborow, D. W., 'Road Research Laboratory's Investment Criteria Examined', *Bulletin of the Oxford Institute of Statistics*, Vol. 22 (November 1960).

Haning, C. R. and Wootan, C. V., 'Value of Commercial Motor Vehicle Time Saved', *Highway Research Record* (1965), No. 82.

Harberger, A. C., *Cost-Benefit Analysis of Transportation Projects*, paper prepared for a conference (unpublished).

Johnson, M. B., 'Travel Time and the Price of Leisure', *Western Economic Journal*, Vol. 4 (Spring 1966), No. 2.

Kuhn, T. E., *Public Enterprise Economics and Transport Problems* (Berkeley, Calif., California University Press, 1962; London, Cambridge University Press, 1963).

Little, A. D. (Inc.), *Cost Effectiveness in Traffic Safety* (New York, Praeger Press, 1968).

Millward, R., 'Road Investment Criteria', *Journal of Transport Economics and Policy*, Vol. 2 (May 1968), Part 2.

Ministry of Transport, *Road Pricing: the Economic and Technical Possibilities*, Smeed Report (HMSO, 1964).

Proposals for a Fixed Channel Link, Cmnd 2137 (HMSO, 1963). See also Chap. 10 in Munby, D. (ed.), *Transport* (Harmondsworth, Penguin, 1968).

Mohring, H., 'Land Values and the Measurement of Highway Benefits', *Journal of Political Economy*, Vol. 69 (June 1961).

Urban Highway Investments, in Dorfman, op. cit.

Mohring, H. and Harwtiz, M., *Highway Benefits: An Analytical Framework* (Evanston, Ill., Northwestern University Press, 1962).

Moses, L. N. and Williamson, H. F., 'Value of Time, Choice of Mode, and the Subsidy Issue in Urban Transportation', *Journal of Political Economy*, Vol. 71 (June 1963).

Munby, D. L., 'Investment in Road and Rail Transport', *Institute of Transport Journal*, Vol. 29 (March 1962).

Nelson, J. R., 'The Value of Travel Time', in Chase, S. B. (ed.), *Problems in Public Expenditure Analysis* (Washington, DC, Brookings Institution; London, Allen and Unwin, 1968).

Reynolds, D. J., 'The Cost of Road Accidents', *Journal of the Royal Statistical Society*, Series A: Vol. 119 (1956), No. 4.

Road Research Laboratory, *The Assessment of Priority for Road Improvements*, Road Research Laboratory Technical Paper No. 48 (HMSO, 1960).

Schelling, T. C., 'The Life You Save May Be Your Own', in Chase, op. cit.

Sharp, C., 'Congestion and Welfare: An Examination of the Case for a Congestion Tax', *Economic Journal*, Vol. 76 (December 1966), No. 304.

Wilson, F. R., *Journey to Work* (London, MacLaren and Sons, 1967).

Winch, D. M., *The Economics of Highway Planning* (Toronto, Toronto University Press, 1963).

Wohl, M. and Martin, B. V., 'Methods of Evaluating Alternative Road Projects', *Journal of Transport Economics and Policy*, No. 1 (January 1967).

CHAPTER 3

THE ENVIRONMENT

INTRODUCTION

Pollution and conservation – two 'in-words' of the seventies – could possibly be the make or break test of cost-benefit analysis as a tool of decision-making. If cost-benefit is concerned with identifying and evaluating the externalities or spillovers of public expenditure decisions, then, to be successful and acceptable to the sceptical layman in public administration, it is important that the technique should be developed further in order to tackle the most difficult and complex set of problems facing humanity today.

The serious dangers of polluting and destroying man's environment have not always been so clearly recognized by the administrative and political bureaucracy. Amenity groups, conservation societies and other 'middle-class liberal' pressure groups have been pointing out some of these effects for years – the neglect has been due more to the feeling of politicians and administrators that there were more important social and economic problems to deal with. Generations of students, now decision-makers, have been brought up to regard natural resources such as air, water, trees and grass as free goods of nature requiring no economic management. The consequences of increasing population pressures, material affluence and the technological explosion have overcome this complacency. Yet the tools of environmental planning and natural resource management are still relatively crude. Apart from applications to water resource developments in the United States, little research had been undertaken on environmental economics by the mid-sixties. This chapter will summarize some of the later work and will speculate on how far cost-benefit analysis might develop to undertake the evaluation of investment proposals designed to preserve and improve the environment.

A SKETCH OF THE PROBLEM

The concentration of the population into urban communities has been a feature of British society since the beginning of the last century. Today, nearly eight out of every ten inhabitants live in an urban environment compared with three out of ten in 1801. However, the character and quality of urban life today differs markedly from that enjoyed in the 'dark satanic' towns of the last century, which in many cases persisted right up to the Second World War. The urban society we live in today is more affluent – real income per head is £480 per annum compared with £250 per annum in 1900 (1958 price levels); people have more leisure time – the average working week in industry is 43 hours compared with 50 hours a generation ago. Even more striking is the increase in personal mobility due to the growth in car ownership – in 1908 there were 8,000 private car licences current; by 1938 this number had risen to 2m., and now the number is over 9m.

Urbanization today is associated with many benefits unknown to earlier generations, and with continued economic growth and full employment it can safely be predicted that even greater benefits will be forthcoming by the end of this century. The portents are that there will be increasing affluence combined with more leisure time and higher travel mobility, and under the pressure of these forces and the forward march of 'big' industry it is easy to see why the quality of the environment will be prone to deterioration.

There are many ways in which this deterioration might occur. The increase in production and distribution of electrical power, for example, involves just two aspects. First, the generation of electrical power requires power stations with cooling towers located near rivers – the effects of the discharge of millions of gallons of hot water can be disastrous for a river's eco-system, resulting in the loss of a valuable recreational facility. Further, the distribution of electricity by the cheapest method (financially) requires lines of unsightly pylons and cables strung out across the countryside. In many cases these cause a loss of visual amenity which results in the destruction of a natural beauty spot. Thus, satisfying the needs of some affluent urban dwellers who spend their wealth on household durable goods (and the electricity to power them) is likely to cause a conflict with other urban dwellers who choose to spend their wealth on outdoor recreation such as picnics in the countryside or fishing on the banks of a river.

In a recently published preliminary report,[1] the Royal Commission on pollution gave a classic exposition of the economic reasons for, and consequences of, pollution. This is reproduced (in part) below:

'15. The economic reason why society may not strike the right balance between economic output and the quality of the environment is that costs of many kinds of pollution are not borne by the polluters, but by somebody else. As a result these "external" costs will not, in general, be taken fully into account by firms, individuals or other bodies who cause pollution. The other side of the coin is that those who spend money on reducing pollution may not always be the people who gain from the resulting improvement in the environment. This applies to both "tangible" pollution, such as poisoning of fish in polluted waters, and to "intangible" pollution, such as unpleasant smells and ugly landscape.

16. This characteristic of pollution has three main consequences:
(a) Output of goods and services which give rise to pollution tends to be pushed beyond the socially optimum point. Also, expenditure to reduce pollution will often be inadequate. This is true not only for private firms or individuals: it is true also for public authorities. . . .
(b) There is generally not enough incentive to reduce the amount of pollution per unit of output of the goods and services responsible, so that not enough resources and effort are devoted to this objective. . . .
(c) In so far as pollution costs are not borne by those who cause pollution or by the purchasers of their products, but by people who happen to be the victims of pollution, some of the total welfare resulting from the economic activity of the community is being redistributed away from the victims of pollution in favour of other groups in the community. . . .'

It is within this sort of economic framework that solutions to the problems of pollution will eventually be found.

Evidence of public awareness about trends in pollution and conservation is easily obtained. Recent spectacular accidents (e.g. the Torrey Canyon and the Rhine fish incidents) and equally spectacular but deliberate acts of pollution (the dumping of nerve gas at the bottom of the Atlantic, 160 miles from the Bahamas) have sparked off mass agitation on the pollution issue. What people do not seem to realize (or accept) is that pollution can be contained – *but at a cost*. From the economic point of view the increasing pressures of population, affluence and technology lead to increasing social costs in an urban society. This raises the question – how should such costs be avoided or at least minimized? Here, we are concerned with some facets of urban life where social costs occur – specifically, water pollution, air pollution, and noise. The final part of this chapter speculates on the use of cost-benefit analysis by public bodies to guide conservation policies.

WATER POLLUTION

A modern urban-industrial complex produces waste in enormous quantities and traditionally disposes of it in three ways – burying it, burning it, and dumping it into rivers and the sea. This final method is by far the biggest source of pollution. A developing urban economy requires continuous quantities of water for its survival in order to dispose of the effluent it produces. However, as well as being effluent drains, water resources – inland (rivers, lakes and canals) and the sea – are also actual or potential sources of potable water supply. Clearly, it is essential to secure an adequate supply of 'pure' water if society is to survive and historically the potable water supply in Britain has been of very high quality. The major problem for the future is to find sources of water supply to meet the growing demands of people and industry in the face of competing demands for other uses of land and resources available for the building of new reservoirs and river systems. Estimates for domestic consumption today and projections for the year 2000 show a significant increase in consumption, mainly associated with increased usage of durable goods which might be correlated with higher levels of affluence (see Table 6).

Table 6

Estimation of Future Water Demands in Britain

	Estimate of present average consumption (gal./hd/day)	Estimate of possible average consumption AD 2000 (gal./hd/day)
1. Drinking and cooking	1	1
2. Dishwashing and cleaning	3	4
3. Laundry	3	5
4. Personal washing and bathing	10	13
5. Closet flushing and refuse disposal	11	14
6. Car washing	—	1
7. Garden use and recreation	1	6
8. Waste in distribution	5	8
Total	34	52

Source: Sharp, R. G., 'Estimation of Future Demands on Water Resources in Britain', *Journal of the Institute of Water Engineers*, Vol. 21 (May 1967).

To domestic demand must be added industrial demand and the requirements for agriculture. It is more difficult to predict demand for industry in an era of changing technology, but trends suggest that the new technologists are more intensive users of water. How are such demands to be met? The flooding of Welsh valleys to create reservoirs cannot go on forever. Recent decisions suggest that alternative methods of supply are being given serious consideration – rivers can be cleaned up, estuarial barrages built, desalination plants constructed; it may even, some economists suggest, be necessary to introduce some form of price constraint to bring demand into line with supply. Each method has its own benefits and costs with implications for the social use of natural and human resources. The destruction of valley farm-land cannot simply be valued as the loss of agricultural production – some notion of loss of community life with its own intrinsic value must be built into the equation. Cost-benefit analysis has not made much impact here.

A practical example of a cost-benefit approach to water pollution is provided by a large-scale research study on the River Trent. The Trent and its tributaries flow through the densely populated and industrial centres of the landlocked Midlands. Stretches of the river are deteriorating in quality as the effluent of households and industry is poured into the river at such a rate that it can no longer be cleaned by natural flow. Basically, the water supply problem in the Midlands has two solutions: (a) rely on alternative sources of supply – the Welsh valleys again! or (b) rely on the Trent and its tributaries. The economic and social costs of the first alternative have not seriously been investigated, but the political consequences of such a course of action have manifested themselves in an often violent fashion in recent years. In order to avoid these economic, social and political consequences, the other alternative has to be seriously considered. To rely on the Trent and its tributaries as a source of supply would require treating and controlling effluent disposal so as to raise water quality to potable levels. Apart from the technical feasibility of accomplishing this, the financial cost is likely to be very high. However, there are social benefits to be gained, especially in terms of recreation which can be, and are being, evaluated so that they can be incorporated in the policy decision matrix. The situation occurring in the Trent brings home a feature of water resources which has often been neglected in the past, i.e. their multiple use potential. If this potential is recognized and evaluated, the interests of a wide section of the community can be served.

If cost-benefit analysis is not used to appraise alternatives in the field of water pollution, the longer-term effects of allowing a river to become and remain a sewage and chemical drain might be disastrous. American experience points the way: Lake Erie is the most frightening example of what can happen – it is now described as a dying lake, its end being advanced by discharge into it of sewage and industrial waste. One of the rivers flowing into it from Cleveland is reported to be 'the only body of water ever classified as a fire hazard'.[2] This is undoubtedly an extreme example, but it is a warning that man's activities in an urban-industrial concentration can shorten the life of a natural resource with concomitant effects on health, recreation and commercial activities.

AIR POLLUTION

Air pollution, unlike water pollution, has been recognized as a problem for many centuries and there are early records of efforts to contain it. In 1273, coal, perhaps the most common generator of air pollution, was prohibited in London because it was considered to be prejudicial to health, whilst in 1306 there is a record of an execution for a violation of a royal proclamation prohibiting artificers from using sea coal in furnaces. The nuisance value of coal as a fuel was the subject of a Commission of Inquiry in 1307 and it is recorded that Queen Elizabeth I 'found herself greatly grieved and annoyed with taste and smoke of sea coalers'.[3]

Considering that coal received this bad publicity in Britain seven centuries ago, it seems surprising, on the face of it, that nothing was done to eliminate the problem before 1956. The villain in the piece was, of course, the Industrial Revolution. The development of steam technology based on coal laid the foundation of Western industrialization but, although atmospheric pollution worsened considerably, too much was at stake for radical antipollution measures which would have reduced private profit margins. However, throughout the nineteenth century, air pollution was the subject of parliamentary inquiry and legislation. The Public Health Act of 1875 contains a section on smoke abatement, and much of today's legislation on this subject stems from this Act. After the war, smoke abatement societies gathered strength and the concept of smokeless zones was developed. In 1956 the Clean Air Act was passed, based on the smokeless zone concept. However, the nature of the air pollution problem is changing and many people consider that the legislation needs updating.

Most of the early development of pollution control was concerned with the problem of coal-based pollution. In 1952, in London, occurred an event which was to bring home dramatically to the community the horror of atmospheric pollution. The event was a fog in London which lasted for 2 weeks in December of that year. This fog proved lethal – over 4,000 excess deaths were estimated to be due to it, and because of its special characteristics it was given a special name – smog. Smog struck again in London in 1962 with an estimated death roll of 750 people.

The control of coal-based pollution is technically a relatively straightforward matter – because such pollutants as coal smoke (primary pollutants) are easy to trace in the atmosphere and as an energy source coal is steadily being ousted by newer gaseous and liquid fuels. The shift to newer fuels has, however, led to the generation of what are known as secondary pollutants. Generally, these pollutants are more intractable and their effects less predictable. Primary pollutants are created by men's activities in business and in the home, but secondary pollutants arise

55

from interactions between primary pollutants and the atmosphere. The chemistry of the problem need not detain us here, but London smog is an extreme example of secondary pollution. Another example is the Los Angeles smog which is caused by unburned automobile fuel being irradiated in stagnant air by sunlight. It has been estimated that motor vehicles emit some 8,050 tons of carbon monoxide and almost 1,650 tons of hydrocarbon in Los Angeles each day. The effect of this is to produce an atmosphere which can be eye-irritating, unsightly and literally breath-taking.

Trends in control of primary pollutants in Britain are encouraging but there is still a long way to go before the air of Britain can be said to be truly clear and pure. Research into the problems of pollution has been undertaken by the Warren Spring Laboratory of the former Ministry of Technology. However, most of this work is concerned with the physical measurement of air pollution and little work has been done to measure the social and economic benefits of reducing air pollution levels. The *identification* of possible sources of benefit of achieving such a reduction is conceptually straightforward. These may take the form of savings in cleaning expenditure, increased crop yields, improved health and 'amenity'. In addition there may be wider climatic effects. However, to measure these effects *as a function of the pollution level* is much more difficult, for both theoretical and practical reasons.

As a general proposition it seems reasonable to assume that an increase in the level of atmospheric pollution will increase the amount of dirt in the atmosphere and therefore also increase the use of cleaning materials. However, research carried out by the Programmes Analysis Unit and by Ridker does not confirm this because no correlation could be found between expenditures on cleaning products and pollution levels. However, this may simply mean that the efficiency of cleaning materials such as detergents increases in proportion to the level of dirt, or that people do not take account of higher dirt levels. In their attempt to estimate the social costs of air pollution, the Beaver Committee[4] attributed a notional cost to dirt which was measured by the amount of expenditure needed to clean highly polluted areas to the same standards of cleanliness evident in non-polluted areas.

Some research has been undertaken to assess the effects of pollution on amenity, defined in terms of property values. It is clearly a reasonable hypothesis to suppose that identical properties in polluted and non-polluted areas within a town or city will command different market prices, and that this price difference, other things being equal, will reflect a loss in utility due to pollution. This loss will include the capitalized cost of additional maintenance, painting and cleaning which may be necessary in a polluted area, but will also incorporate values for discomfort and inconvenience. Several studies have been undertaken in the

United States which attempt to provide empirical evidence of this general proposition, but they have usually come up against serious measurement and data problems.[5] Generally, it can be concluded that property values are undoubtedly affected by air pollution, but the effect is probably rather small and hidden by a series of more major factors, e.g. properties in 'black' areas tend to be older and structurally different to those in 'clean' areas.

The effects on health of atmospheric pollution have long been regarded as the major reason for the implementation of pollution control measures. Ridker has estimated the resource costs of diseases associated with air pollution for the United States and his results are shown in Table 7. The figures used are discounted over the probable life span of males and females in the USA. Subject to the limitations of the methodology and data used, these figures indicate the range of likely benefits to the community of the elimination of air pollution (although no one can say that pollution is the *sole* cause of all these diseases). One course of action the figures suggest is that an air pollution control policy should seek to eliminate those pollutants most closely associated with illness and premature deaths due to cancer, bronchitis, the common cold, pneumonia, emphysema and asthma.

The measurement of the costs associated with pollution-oriented disease takes three forms: (a) the economic costs resulting from lost production and medical treatment programmes, (b) the losses involved in the non-producing (i.e. in terms of GNP) sectors of the community such as students and housewives, and (c) the strictly *social* costs of disease and death. Loss of production is usually valued by reference to wage rates and treatment costs pose no particular problems. Where production is not included in GNP, such as the output of housewives, this may legitimately be valued at the average wage which could have been earned in alternative employment. The social costs of illness or premature death could be estimated by looking at the values attached by society as indicated by damages awarded by the courts or by considering what society is willing to pay in terms of pensions, etc., to compensate for disablement. Although it cannot be pretended that estimates made on these bases reflect true economic and social costs, they can point the way to the range of cost magnitudes associated with atmospheric pollution and enable decision-makers to grasp the scale of benefits obtainable from anti-pollution investments.

An examination of British data on disease incidence suggests a similar picture to that in the United States. According to the Beaver Committee 'death rates from pneumonia and bronchitis in 1952 in this country show a definite and consistent difference between large centres of population and rural areas'. There is no reason to suppose that this pattern has changed much since 1952. In its Interim Report, the Committee

Table 7

Resource Costs of Diseases Associated with Air Pollution (in USA) (Costs in $m. Discounted at 5 per cent per annum)

	Cancer of the respiratory system	Chronic bronchitis	Acute bronchitis	Common cold	Pneumonia	Emphysema	Asthma
Premature death	518	18	6	—	329	62	59
Treatment	35	89	—	200	73	—	138
Absenteeism	112	52	—	131	75	—	60
Total	665	159	6	331	477	62	257

Source: Ridker, R. G., *Economic Costs of Air Pollution* (London, Praeger Press, 1966).

stated that air pollution was costing the community of the order of £100–£150m. per annum. Of these estimates, the Committee said:

> 'All estimates are necessarily somewhat conjectural owing to the lack of adequate data and the great diversity of the possible items of damages or losses. Many of the items are not measurable in terms of money and for those that are, little or no precise information can be obtained. One can but make reasoned estimates of the broad orders of magnitude taking account of the specific items which can be given something of a definitive monetary value.'

However, 16 years later, cost-benefit analysis can reasonably claim to have made a little progress in measuring the social and economic costs of air pollution. It is not yet possible to claim success, or even near-success in this field, but the evidence is that the technique will play an ever increasing role in the allocation of resources to combat atmospheric pollution in Britain.

NOISE

Noise may be defined as unwanted sound. This definition is very wide since it can range from the repugnance experienced by a Mozart purist on hearing a pop tune, to the chagrin of local inhabitants whose sleep is being disturbed by the night arrivals and departures of aircraft at a nearby airport. Provided the Mozart devotee and the pop enthusiast can listen to their respective musical sounds to the exclusion of the other, any complaint about nuisance sound is likely to be regarded as a variety of cultural snobbery or intolerance and can be ignored without great social repercussions. The problem of aircraft and vehicle noise, however, is more serious and the solution less tractable.

There are many sounds generated by activities within an urban community which are regarded by many sections of the community as having a negative value. These are generally produced as unwanted by-products of human activities, e.g. motor traffic and factory noise. In this sense, noise is conceptually similar to the other sources of pollution discussed earlier, i.e. water and air pollution, and it clearly affects the quality of the environment in which people live. For this reason, demands for some form of social regulation have been steadily increasing and have led to a recent Act of Parliament which makes it an offence for certain classes of motor vehicles to exceed specified noise levels.

The first problem encountered in attempts to measure the social cost of noise is to define the limits of what constitutes a noise nuisance. Generally, this has been achieved by postulating 'reasonable' noise levels which should not be exceeded for more than a specified period of time. The Wilson Committee[6] suggested that the noise levels shown in Table

8 should not be exceeded for more than 10 per cent of the time. However, to measure the impact of noise in physical terms does not provide us with estimates of its social cost. Only by measuring noise impact in an economic sense is it possible to determine whether investment expenditure designed to reduce noise levels is worthwhile. This is another task for cost-benefit analysis, and it is a field where the technique is still in its infancy.

Table 8

Situation	Day (dBA)*	Night (dBA)
Country areas	40	30
Suburban areas away from main traffic routes	45	35
Busy urban areas	50	35

* dBA = A weighted decibel – a physical measure of noise which measures the amount of annoyance caused by noise in terms of sound pressure on the human ear.

Vehicle noise, as stated earlier, is an unwanted by-product of the transport system which pollutes the environment. Several alternative methods exist to reduce noise levels, e.g. noise created by vehicle engines may be reduced, or traffic flows along certain roads may be controlled to achieve noise reductions. However, such forms of social regulation may be *politically unacceptable* (car owners constitute a substantial proportion of the electorate) and *economically undesirable* (the transport industry is a vital sector of the national economy). Any form of acceptable regulation must be based on some conception of balancing the loss of benefits of an activity to individuals against reductions in social cost to the community. It is not enough to impose some standard of physical control but to identify a form of control which is *socially optimum*. There are other alternative methods of reducing vehicle noise impact which are concerned not with the transmission of noise but with its reception. These consist of providing 'noise belts' (strips of land left clear at the side of roads within which residential development is not permitted) and soundproofing buildings by such methods as double-glazing. However, these methods also impose resource costs on society and we need to know whether the benefits obtainable from noise reduction can justify them.

Some research into the evaluation of noise-reduction programmes is taking place[7] but the problem is an extremely complex one and does not seem capable of easy or rapid solution. However, it is encouraging to note that decision-makers now wish to take noise pollution *explicitly* into account when considering major investment prospects.

URBAN AND RURAL CONSERVATION

This short section is concerned not with the conservation of wildlife (although the need to apply some form of social cost consideration to agricultural insecticide programmes is becoming increasingly urgent), but with the wider problems of urban and rural conservation. Research into this aspect of cost-benefit analysis is just beginning and the ensuing paragraphs do nothing more than speculate briefly on how this and other techniques may be developed to meet the challenges to come.

Threats to the environment take many forms; some of them have already been discussed in this chapter. But the threat to the finer parts of our heritage take a more subtle form than do the dangers of pollution. The decision of the newly appointed Secretary of State for the Environment to overrule one of his inspectors and allow a brewery to be sited on 53 acres of 'white' land in the north-west of England is typical of the type of problem involved. The disappearance of a green belt area in one of the most industrialized parts of England clearly involves a loss in amenity (and therefore a loss in utility) to the surrounding inhabitants, and it would certainly improve decision-making in this type of case if some estimate of the social cost involved could be made.

A case where some of the benefits of conservation might be measured is by examining the relationship between amenity and tourism. Clearly, if all the historic buildings and parks in central London were destroyed and replaced by the featureless concrete and glass blocks so favoured by modern architects, there might well be an adverse effect on tourism which would be measured in terms of economic loss to the community. However, this extreme case is not likely to occur and we are faced with severe conceptual and methodological problems when attempting to analyse an intermediate case.

In what ways might cost-benefit studies assist in conservation policy? First of all, economic analysis can be used to assess the relative probabilities of redevelopment pressures in conservation areas. Redevelopment is often a profit-making activity and it would not be beyond the skills of economists and valuers to predict which areas of land might be attractive to speculative developers, and even to grade them in order of priority and risk. Such information would be invaluable since it would allow time for basic research to be carried out in advance of redevelopment applications.

Second, more sophisticated techniques for measuring the spillovers associated with conservation need to be developed and they can only be developed within the framework of cost-benefit analysis. The work of the Roskill Commission in placing monetary values on historic buildings was, frankly, disappointing (see Chapter 4). It may well be that this aspect is beyond the limits of credible quantitative analysis of any kind given the present state of knowledge. The point is that quantitative analysis is not a substitute for judgement, it is an *aid* to judgement and if cost-benefit analysis can reduce conservation policy issues to a more straightforward set of value trade-offs than is presently the case, this in itself will be a useful contribution to the problem.

CONCLUSION

The economic rationale of the control of pollution received its classic statement in the work of the English economist, A. C. Pigou,[8] who emphasized the distinction between private and social decision-making, the possibility of a divergence between them, and that the reconciliation between them was a matter for public regulation. This was a challenge to the view of Adam Smith that any divergence arising could be corrected by the *'invisible hand of competition'*. The atomistic decision-maker according to Smith

> 'generally, indeed, neither intends to promote the public interest nor knows how much he is promoting it ... and he intends only his own gain and he is in this, as in many other cases, led by an individual hand to promote an end which was not part of his intention'.[9]

Adam Smith wrote in 1776 no doubt, with the state of decision-making suitable for the small-size farms and manufacturing units of a rural society in mind. Britain at the time was basically a rural society and continued to be so into the early nineteenth century, but in an urban society the problem is different. Burstein succinctly described the situation:

> 'The atomistic-individualistic approach is especially non-viable in an urban society where massive consumption services are provided by huge lumps of socialized or naturally monopolized capital, such as water works, sewage plants, underground railways, parks, etc.'[10]

Finding a social optimum pattern of economic society is by no means an easy problem. It is certainly more complicated than in the type of society Adam Smith saw around him. Left to himself, Adam Smith's atomistic decision-maker has no inducement in an urban economy to seek a social optimum, i.e. a situation where private costs and social costs are not divergent. Even if he were inclined to do so, he would find the process far too costly. Since the writings of Pigou and under the impetus of the urban octopus, economic theorists have begun to pay more attention to the nature of the social optimum and the conditions for its existence. At a formal level the problem is one of finding an optimum pattern of economic activity in a system where there are externalities, i.e. where economic activity is associated with side-effects which are imposed on others who do not necessarily share the benefits of the activity. The existence of externalities is a matter of fact. However, the costs of externalities, which is what social costs often are, is a matter for observation, and it is painfully obvious that more observation needs to be carried out.

Where estimates of social costs have been made, they have usually suffered demonstrably from methodological limitations. Progress in the fields of air and water pollution, however, now seems to be gathering pace; research into the social cost of noise will doubtless follow; but there is an urgent need to develop techniques to analyse the social costs and benefits associated with urban and rural conservation. The Royal Commission itself has recently emphasized the need for more research on the economics of the problems because they cannot be fully resolved without estimates of the costs and benefits of changes in the levels of different kinds of pollution. Its view is that:

'we need an economic framework to aid decision-making about pollution, which would match the scientific and technical framework we already have. This economic framework should include estimates of the way in which the costs of pollution, including disamenity costs, vary with levels of pollution; the extent to which different elements contribute to the costs; how variations in production and consumption affect the costs; and what it would cost to abate pollution in different ways and by different amounts. There may well be cases where most of the costs and benefits of abatement can be assessed in terms of money. Many of the estimates are likely to be speculative, but this is no excuse for not making a start. There are other cases where most of the costs and benefits cannot be given a monetary value. In these cases, decisions about pollution abatement must not await the results of full economic calculation: they will have to be based largely on subjective judgements anyway. Even so, these subjective judgements should be supported by as much quantitative information as possible, just as decisions about health and education are supported by extensive statistical data. Further, even if decisions to abate pollution are not based on rigorous economic criteria, it is still desirable to find the most economic way of achieving the abatement.'

As the scale of the problem increases, it is probable that cost-benefit analysis will produce many of the answers; the danger is that the answers will come too late. This is why the Commission stresses the need to take action in advance of full economic appraisal being carried out.

REFERENCES

1 Royal Commission on Environmental Pollution, Cmnd. 4385 (HMSO, February 1971).
2 *Wall Street Journal* (February 1969).
3 *Clean Air Year Book*, 1968–9 (London).
4 Committee on Air Pollution, Cmnd. 9322 (HMSO, 1954).
5 Ridker, R. G., *Economic Costs of Air Pollution* (London, Praeger Press, 1966). See also Wolozin, H. (ed.), *The Economics of Air Pollution* (New York, W. Norton and Co. Inc., 1966).
6 Committee on the Problem of Noise, Final Report, Cmnd. 2056 (HMSO, 1963).
7 Foster, C. D. and Mackie, P. J., 'Noise – Economic Aspects of Choice', *Urban Studies*, Vol. 7 (1970), No. 2.
8 Pigou, A. C., *Economics of Welfare*, 4th ed. (London, Macmillan, 1932).
9 Smith, A., *The Welfare of Nations* (1776), E. Cannan's Edition (1939).
10 Burstein, M. L., *Economic Theory: Change and Equilibrium* (Chichester, J. Wiley, 1968).

FURTHER READING

Brigham, E. F., *A Model of Residential Land Values*, RM-403-RC (Santa Monica, Calif., Rand Corporation, 1964).
Nourse, H. O., 'The Effect of Air Pollution on House Values', *Land Economics* (May 1967).
Peterson, G. L. A., 'A Model of Preference: Quantitative Analysis of the Perception of the Visual Appearance of Residential Neighbourhoods', *Journal of Regional Science*, Vol. 7 (Summer 1967), No. 1.
Ridker, R. G. and Henning, J. A., 'The Determinants of Residential Property Values with Special Reference to Air Pollution', *Review of Economics and Statistics* (May 1967).
Waller, R. A. and Thomas, R. J., 'The Cash Value of the Environment', *Arena*, Vol. 82 (1967).

CHAPTER 4

THE THIRD LONDON AIRPORT

One of the criticisms of the original inquiry into the proposed airport at Stansted was precisely that the Government had not taken a 'wide view'. On the contrary their proposal was based on the narrow view of an inter-departmental committee, which had been concerned almost exclusively with aeronautical advantages; the only other consideration to which serious attention had been paid was the loss of agricultural land; none had been given to environment or regional planning; no cost-benefit analysis had been attempted, and even such vital questions as surface access and travelling time to the new airport had been the subject of estimates which the public inquiry had shown to be fallible.

The subsequent Roskill Commission more than restored the balance, for the cost-benefit study of its own research team, which formed the basis of most of its investigations, added a new dimension to such studies in the United Kingdom. In the first place the sheer scale of the project was without precedent, since it would comprise the greatest alteration to the face of England ever to be deliberately undertaken.* And secondly, instead of being restrained only by the self-imposed discipline of the researchers' study, the analysis was exposed to the glare of a major public inquiry, so that each constituent item was subjected to the expert criticism of economists of differing opinions, led by the flower of the Planning Bar. And by the time the inquiry started, the Commission had cost the Government £1,200,000, most of which had been spent on the cost-benefit research.

For the purposes of this chapter, interest lies not so much in the Commission's recommendation and the Government's final decision as in the research methodology that was employed, and the documents relating to the public inquiry. The difficulty is rather to extract from a mountain of available paper a few salient points that will illustrate the advantages and limitations of cost-benefit techniques.[1]

The research team's agenda was formidably complicated. At the Stansted inquiry the Government had been concerned to justify a particular site, though as a late concession to objectors, when the force of

---

* Even at a late stage of the inquiry, and after wide national publicity, Professor Buchanan, a member of the Commission, was giving it as his opinion that nine people out of ten had not begun to realize the magnitude of the changes that would come about.

opposition became apparent, they were allowed to propose and to attempt to justify alternative sites. The Roskill Commission, on the other hand, were from the outset concerned with four alternative sites, each raising characteristic problems of benefit and cost; there was, moreover, an important distinction between the three inland sites, on the one hand, and the coastal, marshland site, on the other. It was essentially a comparative exercise, and cost-benefit analysis was used as an aid to a choice between alternatives.

Indeed, the method by which the short-list itself had been chosen, out of all the sites in the south-east of England that were operationally possible, was deliberately designed to compel consideration of the main alternative criteria, such as noise, distance from London, disamenity, disturbance of other establishments, and to avoid prejudging their relative importance. If, *prima facie*, a site scored badly on them all it would be discarded; if it appeared weak on some but strong on another it could be retained. The selection procedure was, so to speak, a preliminary rough sketch of a cost-benefit exercise.

On the other hand, the actual way in which the four sites were compared did not in itself furnish a good example of a cost-benefit analysis, being in the main a study of disbenefits, or of cost *minimization*. Benefits were taken for granted and assumed to be of equal weight wherever the airport was sited, a point to which we return towards the end of this chapter.

Cost-benefit, in the proper sense, was better exemplified in an area of the Commission's studies that attracted less public attention, namely the timing of the need for the airport. The general assumption that it must be built by a given date in the fairly near future is an over-simplification. Doubtless the time could come when its absence would mean catastrophe, but in the meantime there is still a measure of flexibility, since no airport works at full capacity 24 hours a day. The cost of delaying the third airport is accountable in terms of congestion and delay, which could admittedly, if sufficiently acute, lead to loss of traffic, discouragement of the tourist trade, an adverse effect on the balance of payments, and a decline in national prestige; but amelioration is at least possible by spreading the peak load. The benefits of postponement, on the other hand, can be considered in terms of the alternative use of the capital investment – a figure thought to be of the order of £22m. per annum – the possibility of technological developments, either in airport or aircraft design and construction, which could make the eventual airport cheaper and more efficient, and the continued enjoyment of those benefits which an airport must inevitably destroy. The Commission attempts to 'construct a decision model which includes and quantifies all the factors .. relevant to the timing of the airport'. Although some of the elements of this very complicated calculation are of wide application – for example, the use of pricing to reduce congestion – most of them are peculiar to the airport situation, and it will be more appropriate in the rest of the chapter to concentrate on those matters which are of general interest, and which are principally found in the comparative studies of disbenefit and cost minimization for the four short-listed sites.

There are various ways in which these figures could be classified, but for our present purposes the most useful is simply a broad two-fold division. On the one hand, there are those matters in which cost-benefit techniques, developed over a long period, have reduced subjective judgement to insignificance; experts might differ over refinements of technique but would be in general agreement about the results. On the other hand, there are those in which subjective judgement is still a powerful factor, or in which techniques of measurement are still the subject of disagreement between experts.

In some of the twenty-one items in Table 9, and notably in the key items 'Passenger user costs' and 'Airspace movement' (rows 5 and 6), there is an element of each, and the main problem in evaluating the results of the research was that, in comparing the three inland sites with the coastal site, the main weight of the evidence derived from sources in which subjective judgement was still relatively important, or techniques still in an experimental stage. Incidentally, the least controversial, or most objective, items, accounting for possibly £400m. out of the total of £2,300m., were those where the resource cost would fall directly on the public sector.

The Commission was concerned with the major *differences* in cost between the four sites, and these are concentrated in a bare half dozen items; the student of cost-benefit analysis, on the other hand, may find points of interest in some of those which had the least quantitative significance, for example those included under the compendious term 'recreation'. Such commentary as space allows must necessarily be selective, and in what follows, emphasis is placed upon matters of methodological interest rather than on those which will be most likely to determine the site of the airport.

There is of course less to be said about the straightforward than the dubious. Items such as demolition and construction (for example, rows 1, 3, 8 or 9), the cost of moving fixed establishments (rows 11, 12, 13, or 15) or of serving the airport when built (rows 3, 10 or 21) do not offer points of exceptional methodological interest. Of more interest to the expert, though it is largely incomprehensible to the mathematical layman, was the research necessary to estimate the methods of air traffic control and the cost of surface access, the latter in terms of the likely split between London's airports and the traffic and infrastructure which the alternative sites would generate. These involved computer models

Table 9
Summary of Best Estimates of Cost and Benefits (£m. 1968 prices, discounted to 1975, final row discounted to 1982)

Row	Tables	Elements of cost or benefit	Cublington	Foulness	Nuthampstead	Thurleigh
1	7.20	Third London airport construction	184.0	179.0	178.0	166.0
2	para 12, 23 & 25	Extension/closure of Luton airport	-1.3	10.0	-1.3	-1.3
3	7.20	Airport services	74.6	62.9	70.7	67.2
4	10.10	Meteorology	5.0	1.6	3.0	2.0
5	12.5	Airspace movement	960.0	973.0	987.0	972.0
6	13.14	Passenger user costs	887.0	1,041.0	868.0	889.0
7	13.25	Freight user costs	13.4	23.1	17.0	13.9
8	13.22	Road capital	7.4	7.4	7.5	2.7
9	13.23	Rail capital	4.4	16.0	8.0	3.8
10	14.14	Air safety	0.5	2.5	0.5	0.5
11	15.14	Defence	66.0	20.0	52.0	73.0
12	16.1–2	Public scientific establishments	2.0	3.4	11.2	16.6
13	17.3, 6 & 7	Private airfields	8.7	3.1	9.8	12.2
14	20.6	Residential conditions (noise, off site)	9.0	3.6	19.0	5.6
15	20.6	Residential conditions (on site)	4.8	—	3.0	2.4
16	para 20.43	Luton noise costs	—	6.7	—	—

Table 9 (contd)

Row	Tables	Elements of cost or benefit	Cublington	Foulness	Nuthampstead	Thurleigh
17	21.6, 7, 13 & 16	Schools, hospitals and public authority buildings (including noise)	2.5	0.8	4.1	4.9
18	22.3	Agriculture	3.1	4.2	7.2	4.6
19	23.6	Commerce and industry (including noise)	0.6	0.1	1.2	2.0
20	24.12	Recreation (including noise)	6.7	0.3	3.6	3.8
21	25.5	Work and service journeys to airport	26.2	26.5	24.4	25.4
22		Total net costs (discounted to 1975)	2,264.6	2,385.2	2,273.9	2,266.3
23		Total net costs (discounted to 1975) expressed as differences from lowest cost site	0	120.6	9.3	1.7
24		Total net costs (discounted to 1982)	4,416	4,651	4,434	4,419
25		Total net costs (discounted to 1982) expressed as differences from lowest cost site	0	235	18	3

Note: for the convenience of the reader the costs directly attributable to noise discounted to 1975 have been extracted from rows 12, 14, 16, 17, 19 and 20, and amount to:

£14.3m. for Cublington, £22m. for Foulness, £11.1m. for Nuthampstead, £23.9m. for Thurleigh.

Discounted to 1982 they are:

£28m. for Cublington, £47m. for Foulness, £28m. for Nuthampstead, £28m. for Thurleigh.

Source: Commission on the Third London Airport, Papers and Proceedings, Volume VII, Parts 1 and 2, Stage III, pp. 490–1. Reprinted with permission of the Controller, H.M. Stationery Office.

69

of great complexity, though according to the research team itself it was the complexity rather than the methodology that was unique. These calculations are not shown as distinctive items (or separate rows) in the analysis, but form part of the build-up of items 5 and 6. Further in the background, and the necessary precursor to the whole colossal calculation, was an elaborate forecast of the whole future of air traffic itself.

AGRICULTURE

Interest of a different kind is to be found in the loss of agricultural production (row 18). The item is insignificant in quantitative terms and the problem is a familiar one in cost-benefit calculations, but the actual technique was a departure from previous practice and attracted some criticism.

The valuation distinguished between the airport site, which would result in a loss of agricultural land and would not otherwise have occurred, and the ancillary urbanization, on the ground that this would have had to take place anyway through the growth of population, and that it was merely being aggregated in one place. What was required, therefore, was to establish not the total but the differential loss of agricultural production, and the base line was taken as the least valuable land, agriculturally, at any of the four sites. The method was criticized by the National Farmers' Union on the ground that it ignored the detrimental change in farming patterns which would be forced on those farmers who survived in the vicinity, caused by the propinquity of a large town.

The agricultural value of the land was based on the current market price (including subsidy) of its produce; from this was deducted the value of transferable farm assets, including labour, leaving the residual value of non-transferable assets, such as the inherent quality and situation of the land, drainage, roads and fixed equipment. Since it then appeared that the replacement cost of the food lost would exceed the gross market value, the 'value added' factor was increased by a factor varying with each site (but roughly doubled), and a potential growth rate was calculated, also varying with each site in accordance with the standard of husbandry observed.

It was noted that the market price of land exceeded its estimated agricultural value, and the difference, representing its residential and social value, was assumed to grow at 3 per cent per annum up to the time when the land would be acquired for the airport.

The matters to which we have so far drawn attention are those in which science and human ingenuity have provided some degree of certainty. Putting it in its lowest terms (and excepting agriculture) no one at the inquiry seriously challenged what the research team had done or offered to improve upon it. We turn now to the more difficult area of the intangibles, where there is wider scope for subjective judgement or where the subject is that indefinable 'quality of life' over which people are bound to differ, namely the cost of travelling time, the 'cost' of noise and the 'price' of amenity.

Broadly speaking, those who wrestle with these elusive matters have two approaches open to them – they can start with the academic problem and bring to bear on its solution the known techniques of costing and research; or they can observe how people actually behave in order to see how they value one thing (e.g. noise) against another (e.g. convenience or employment); evidence based on such observed behaviour could be regarded with certainty; all else would be a matter for political judgement. The difference is perhaps one of emphasis rather than kind, since both approaches must at some point employ the market researcher's method of the grass-roots inquiry and the questionnaire; but current cost-benefit research, for example further research into the value of travelling time, inclines towards the latter emphasis.

THE VALUE OF TRAVELLING TIME

This was the most contentious item in the research team's analysis, and it is perhaps fitting that it should have been tried in the furnace of a public inquiry. One says this because although the bases of such valuations are still disputable – at any rate in the context of journeys to and from an international airport – the result of the work on time valuation that was actually done was a very large item in the final total – so large that it proved to be the most important influence against the choice of Foulness. The comparative figures of 'passenger user costs', of which travelling time represented the major proportion, were:

	£m.
Cublington	887
Foulness	1,041
Nuthampstead	868
Thurleigh	889

If this item were removed altogether from the calculation in Table 9, the disadvantage to Foulness of £120m. – as compared with the cheapest site – would become an advantage of £33m. If, more realistically, the value of 'leisure' passengers' time (discussed below) was reduced, the disadvantage to Foulness would proportionately diminish.

The preceding item 'airspace movement' also includes an element of the cost of passengers' time (as well as operating costs) for the comparative distances that would have to be flown.

The way in which the value of passengers' time was arrived at is therefore of the utmost importance. The method was in fact adopted from earlier research undertaken by the Ministry of Transport in respect of commuter journeys to work. This research had been expert and thorough, and there was little disposition at the public inquiry to challenge it in the context in which it had originally been undertaken; the question was whether it could sensibly be used without qualification for journeys to an international airport.

The Ministry of Transport research had shown that people tended to value their own leisure time at about 25 per cent of their gross income, which, translated into an hourly basis for the commuter, and in terms of the average income of commuters, gave a figure of 23p. an hour, compared with a national average of 16p. an hour. It appears that some 80 per cent of journeys to London's international airports are 'leisure' journeys, though the word 'leisure' is differently employed, since the commuter (who may, of course, commute either from necessity or choice) is travelling to work, whereas the airport traveller is going on holiday. The point, hotly pursued by counsel, was whether the time spent in an airport bus by a holiday-maker could be considered a 'resource cost' at all, either by a British traveller setting out on a journey abroad, who had set aside the whole day for the journey and might well regard the whole thing as part of his holiday, or by a foreign visitor who had been travelling all day and who spent the final hour to the metropolitan terminal in something of a stupor. Members of the Commission and learned counsel found themselves debating such esoteric questions as when the average man regarded his holiday as beginning and ending, to be led to such conclusions as that it began with the ritual act of closing his front door (which would suggest that the resource cost of his journey to the airport was nil), and that it ended at the point when he began worrying about the length of his grass when he got home. Whether this problem started to nag him when he was over Zurich or over the Channel could, assuming the Ministry of Transport's calculations to be relevant, make a difference of several million pounds to Table 9.

The valuation of 'business' time was on somewhat firmer ground. That is to say there had been much earlier work on the cost of business travellers to their employers, related to their salaries and the overhead cost of their employment, which gave the value of their time in terms of a resource cost at 231p. an hour; but its context contained many variables, e.g. the amount of work the traveller might be able to do in a train or bus, whether the time was broken or continuous, whether he was travelling in or out of normal office time, and so on. It was also maintained from one quarter that the correct valuation was nil, since the entire cost was in any case passed on to the overseas customer, to which the counter argument could be that this would reduce British competitiveness. And what of the businessman's wife, who might drive him to the airport? Was this at business or leisure rates? What is the business rate for a housewife? Did it make any difference if she enjoyed the journey or regarded it as a chore? These matters also were learnedly, and expensively, debated.

It is, of course, easy to ridicule such calculations, and members of the Bar, or at least those whose clients wanted the airport at Foulness, found them highly diverting. The serious point is that if millions of people are travelling annually from A to B, the time it takes them to do so ought not to be ignored in deciding where the airport should be. It is, on the other hand, arguable that it is unscientific to equate holiday-makers with commuters, or to assume that an employer is always losing 138p. worth of work if his employee spends an hour and a half getting from his office – or from his home – to the airport. What this amounts to is that if cost-benefit is to be applied to this situation, new research is needed rather than a simple adoption of previous research. It is, so to speak, a 'twilight' area of cost-benefit analysis, and it is unfortunate that both absolutely and relatively, the final valuation of travelling time bulked so large in the total sum.

THE COST OF NOISE

The problem of aircraft noise – from the point of view of cost-benefit analysis – lies partly in its pervasiveness, since it is a complicating factor in half a dozen normally straightforward cost-benefit calculations, such as those concerning dwelling houses, schools, hospitals, public buildings, commerce and industry; and partly in the fact that many people regard it as inherently unquantifiable, or at any rate destructive of a quality of life which itself cannot be quantified.

There is, however, agreement as to the method of quantifying, accepting that it can be done at all. The problem has long been studied, and a method of quantifying was generally accepted in 1963[2] by the device of the Noise and Number Index (NNI), which relates degrees of annoyance to contours on a map. Annoyance is a function of the noisiness of aircraft, on the one hand, and their frequency, on the other; they may accordingly be louder if fewer, or more frequent if quieter. A high number of 'perceived decibels' at rare intervals may be balanced against a lower number where the noise is more or less continuous. An NNI of 31 is held to cause 'little annoyance', 44 'moderate annoyance', 60 'very much annoyance'. Indeed, anything over 50 or 55 is held to be intolerable for normal life.

This method of assessing the nuisance of noise had been thoroughly examined at the original Stansted inquiry, but the attempt to place a proper value on it in relation to the proposed development was crude, and comprised no more than the hearing of conflicting evidence as to the effect on house property values of the airport at Gatwick, and the trends in north-west Essex when the extension of the airport becomes a possibility. The Roskill research team, by contrast, constructed an elaborate mathematical model which took account of consumer surplus and market depreciation within each succeeding noise contour. No one would pretend that the result could be an accurate reflection of human suffering and inconvenience; on the other hand, in a comparative exercise, the model provided as objective a statement as possible of the relative nuisance of noise at each of the four sites. Its resource cost was represented by the cost of demolishing property within the zone of intolerable noise and rehabilitating the occupants elsewhere, or of insulating against noise indoors if the nuisance was otherwise tolerable.

One of the most useful results of the research team's study of noise was that it was able to show its *distributional* effect. An airport must necessarily bring small, widespread benefits to many and severe losses to a few, and the study showed how the heavy losses could be most concentrated.

THE COST TO AMENITY

Finally the team was faced, in a severe form, with the problem of placing a value on those other factors which go towards the creation of what is called a 'quality of life' – the intangibles which cannot be bought and sold and on which, in popular thinking, no monetary value can be placed – not only peace and quiet but landscape, rural sports, historic houses, ancient monuments, wild places – in short the English rural heritage.

As an exercise in quantifying the hitherto unquantifiable, the team's research did not add greatly to existing knowledge. Although cost-benefit analysis is always – and rightly – trying to extend its frontiers into territories previously thought resistant to quantification, there are some matters which are surely beyond its reach, and the Commission did its own credibility no good by assessing ancient churches in terms of the fire insurance they carried, since this merely provided the sceptics with humorous ammunition, which was fired, somewhat monotonously, in every hostile speech and newspaper article. They were wiser when they came to historic houses, because here they simply gave up. It is unfortunate that the extravaganza over churches should have tended to disguise the Commission's more tangible achievement in the realm of the intangible, namely that, as in the case of noise, they were able to show with some accuracy the *distributional* effect of the airport on general amenity. Their meticulous plotting of every noteworthy building or site of architectural, historic, scientific, scenic or sporting interest within the range of disturbance by each alternative airport site was a valuable addition to the evidence, with or without a hypothetical money value being attached to them.

As to simple visual amenity, a value had been placed upon it at an earlier stage, when the effect of the airport on residents was being considered, in terms of consumer surplus, i.e. the value which people placed upon their houses over and above the market price because of the scenery or the peace and quiet; a calculation, incidentally, which drew the criticism that these intangibles were already reflected in some measure in the market price itself, and that the team were therefore in danger of the error of double counting.

Be this as it may, although the proposal to place a monetary value on a view, or a Norman church, or a historic mansion may invite ridicule, it is important to note that the team were fully aware of this, and of the fact that they might be considered humorless and materialistic. The point raises, in an extreme form, the problem which is common to all cost-benefit calculations beyond the most obvious and tangible, and one may therefore quote the following from the team's own statement of its general principles (*Papers and Proceedings*, p. 6), not only in relation to ancient monuments and the like, but to other and commoner hazards.

'It is assumed by some that subjective judgement properly exercised is a substitute for quantitative analysis and assessment. On this hypothesis, judgement takes over when quantitative analysis begins to weaken, and it is unwise to attempt to push quantitative analysis into the area more appropriate to pure judgement.'

This is, of course, what many people think, and the team's justification of their own view is interesting. They worked on the principle of accepting the scale of values apparently held by the people concerned, as revealed by their choice and behaviour.

'The attempt to value non-material benefits in monetary terms in no way implies a materialistic view of life. A judge has as a matter of course to make such valuations when assessing damages and this is a socially acceptable way of acting. People may assign very high values to cultural or natural phenomena; to observe and record what these values are is not to be confused with pure materialism.'

The team carefully considered, but deliberately rejected, the alternative method of evaluating, in money terms, those costs and benefits which presented no problem, and then of applying subjective judgement to each site in turn to see whether the 'materialistic' ranking was likely to be shaken by the 'imponderable' ranking. In general they believed that the comparative result of attaching monetary value was as reliable as subjective judgement, and that it had the advantage of consistency with the total calculation.

A further reason for a comprehensive, as distinct from a selective, cost-benefit analysis was suggested in evidence by Professor Lichfield, namely that while certain matters might seem obvious in the light of hindsight it should be remembered that without the findings of the analysis it would have been impossible to be sure which were really the basic issues relating to a decision, either in nature or in quantity. In the case of the third London airport the analysis suggested that by far the most important element *from the comparative point of view* was passengers' travelling time, where the difference between the highest and the lowest could be of the order of £173m. Then came the cost of moving defence establishments (£53m.),* followed by 'airspace movement' (£27m.), i.e. the comparative distances that would have to be travelled by aircraft on normal services, airport construction (£18m.), the movement of scientific establishments (£14m.) and rail capital (£12m.). Noise was the most pervasive factor, since it was an element in six different calculations, but the total differential was only £13m. Agriculture and 'recreation' were insignificant both absolutely and relatively.

The relative importance of these various considerations, even if allowance is made for very wide margins of error, would not have been by any means self-evident without the analysis. They were not evident to the Government at the time of the Stansted inquiry.

WEIGHTING

The calculations in Table 9 were not weighted but were made according to the straightforward criterion of efficiency, no account being taken of the incidence of cost/benefit upon rich or poor, or of whether more importance should be attached to one interest than to another. This is fair only if the beneficiaries pay for the benefits they receive and if those who suffer loss are fully compensated, neither of which conditions apply to an international airport, where those who benefit do so at comparatively small individual cost, while those who are affected by noise or loss of amenity receive no recompense – unless, of course, they are actually displaced from the airport site, in which case their compensation is usually less than the value they themselves attach to their property.

Accordingly figures of this kind need to be weighted before their final consideration. The general problems of weighting costs and benefits are discussed elsewhere. As applied to the third London airport weighting

---

* Many people were surprised by the relatively low figure for Foulness, but the cost of moving the well-known shore establishments, which the Ministry of Defence had held to be inviolable, was considerably less than that of replacing the military airfields which would be displaced at any of the inland sites.

could take various forms. First, there are a number of matters in which the essence of the problem is the assessment of future risk. For example, the figures could be adjusted, either by up-grading after the calculation had been made or by the use of differential discounting, in the light of the added value likely to be placed on certain items by future generations, as compared with the market price, real or hypothetical, placed on them by the present one. This would probably involve placing a higher value on those amenities – such as rural scenery, historic buildings, peace and quiet – which will automatically be diminished by the airport development and by similar developments in the future; and perhaps also on agriculture, not only because it is diminished and disturbed by urbanization but because there may be good reasons for giving agriculture a higher value in the national reckoning than that reflected in the current market price of land. Secondly, the cost of noise, the principal uncompensated loss, could be weighted as against the cost of travelling time, since the mere fact of travelling to an airport means that the traveller regards himself as benefiting, whereas the owner of a noisy dwelling house manifestly does not. Thirdly, the figures could be weighted to take account of the principal income groups among those directly affected, since £1 means more to a poor man than to a rich one.

The absence of weighting in the Commission's figures is deliberate. The research team was instructed to do no weighting, as the Commission preferred to consider how it should be done in the light of the evidence which the public inquiry would produce, rather than in the light of economists' preconceptions.

In reaching its final recommendation the Commission had also to take account of certain other intangible factors, which could not be measured in money terms. The whole investigation was conducted in the absence of a national plan for airports, but at least two of the four sites could have been considered as potentially serving the industrial Midlands as well as London and the South East, and a final decision could not have been made in isolation from the future of Elmdon (Birmingham) or Castle Donnington airports. Again, when the research team was at work the Joint South-East Planning Team had not published their report. Moreover, the possibility of a joint air–sea port at Foulness and future developments in rapid surface transport or vertical take-off aircraft, though in the background of the Commission's consciousness, were not within its terms of reference to consider. These are major problems to which space does not permit even a brief introduction; they are mentioned at this point to emphasize that the cost-benefit analysis, formidable though it was, was merely part of an even more formidable exercise in foresight.

Moreover, the analysis, though of great importance, was not in itself conclusive. The final decision which the Government made would in any case have had to be a political one, and the Chairman of the Commission was at pains to make clear that cost-benefit analysis was intended to assist, and not to determine, their ultimate recommendation to the Minister. The methodology itself came under sharp criticism and attack at the inquiry.[3] Nevertheless, the matters summarized in *Papers and Proceedings* will remain a landmark in the development of methodology and technique.

Despite its seminal importance, however, it was not, as we have said, a good example of a cost-*benefit* analysis, since benefits were assumed to be of equal weight wherever the airport was sited:

> 'No attempt is made, or could be made, to quantify the total benefits accruing to the travelling public and the country as a whole from the operation of each individual site. To set against the net costs for each site there is what might be termed a "base-load" of benefits not measured, but for the existence of which it would be wrong to proceed with a third London airport at all. *This "base-load" of benefits is approximately the same for all four sites.*' (author's italics)

The assumption contained in the last sentence was challenged from only one quarter,* but the challenge was cogent and included some interesting reflections on the research team's work in general. The Thurleigh Committee was wholly in favour of decision by cost-benefit analysis, as the method most likely to diminish subjective judgement. It could not however abolish it, and in their view the team had been falsely led to assume that the base-load of benefits was equalled by the pressure of articulate middle-class opinion which took for granted that an airport was necessarily undesirable for everyone living in its vicinity. Middle-class assumptions were inherent, for example, in the meticulous costing of the loss of field sports and cultural monuments, to the complete exclusion of the corresponding benefits of public houses, bingo halls, cinemas, dance halls and bowling alleys which an airport would bring. The base-load of benefits could *not*, in their view, be regarded as equal, because at Thurleigh the majority *wanted* the airport and the benefits it would bring in more lucrative employment, greater leisure and better prospects for their descendants; while the majority at Cublington and Nuthampstead, having other and middle-class interests, wanted to resist it. This important fact should have been reflected in the cost-benefit analysis, and should have helped to sway the decision in favour of Thurleigh.

Irrespective of the accuracy or otherwise of TECDA's claims, it would

---

* TECDA – The Thurleigh Emergency Committee for Democratic Action, representing over thirty local trade union branches (principally AEFWU), trade councils and constituency Labour Party organizations, formed to support Thurleigh as the site for the airport.

seem that they had a case in suggesting that comparative benefits as seen by the various local communities should have been measured, especially after the experience of the Stansted inquiry some years previously, when the size and strength of the pro-airport elements, which undoubtedly existed but which were slow in gathering their forces, was one of the many matters about which the real facts were never established.

The Thurleigh Committee had also some thoughts on the costing of noise which deserve serious consideration. In their view sensitivity to noise is highly subjective. If a family is deriving a good living from an airport it will tolerate noise cheerfully. Those who complain are those whose living, and childrens' prospects, are independent of the airport.

We may conclude with the Commission's own reminder of the real nature of the issue, which could easily be forgotten in a dispute which touched so many aspects of human experience, and roused such deep emotion in residents, farmers, businessmen, planners, preservationists and trade unionists:

> 'The third London airport is (many) things, but fundamentally it is a piece of transport investment, one of the biggest single pieces of transport investment this country may ever see. The most important problem in determining the infrastructure of a transport system is to get it in the right place; the transport planner's nightmare is to place the infrastructure where no one wants to use it. . . . The value to the nation of this third London airport rests on its efficiency assessed as a piece of transport investment.'

Seen thus, the project becomes comprehensible again in terms of ordinary investment appraisal; its unique feature was that the 'externalities' had tended to become the central issue.

At the end of the day, of course – or more accurately at the end of 2 years – the Commission's recommendation, based on its economic appreciation, was not accepted. The environmental case was held to be politically stronger than the economic, which led to the criticism that the inquiry had been a costly waste of time. This does the Commission in general, and its much criticized cost-benefit analysis in particular, less than justice. The million and a quarter pounds that it cost, which was also much criticized, was an insignificant sum in relation to the repercussions which the decision will have on posterity. It was obvious that the Government would ultimately have to balance one set of considerations against another, and nothing could be more important than that the weights that were to be put in each side of the scales should be as accurately known as possible. Those who will be living in 2071 would scarcely thank our own generation if we had done anything less.

What did the Government in fact have to say ?[4]

'. . . the Government have weighed with care the economic arguments identified by the Commission which indicated an inland site, and the regional planning and environmental issues which the Commission also identified. As the Commission's Report stressed, on environmental and planning grounds the Foulness site is the best, and the Government have concluded that these considerations are of paramount importance. In the Government's view the irreversible damage that would be done to large tracts of countryside and to many settled communities by the creation of an airport at any of the three inland sites studied by the Commission is so great *that it is worth paying the price* involved in selecting Foulness.' (author's italics)

The Government could not have talked of 'paying the price' if it had no idea what the price was, and in the present state of our knowledge there is no better way of trying to ascertain the price than by a cost-benefit study.

REFERENCES

[1] Commission on the Third London Airport, *Papers and Proceedings*, Vol. VII, Part 1: Proposed Research Methodology. Part 2: Result of Research Team's Assessment (HMSO, 1970).

[2] Committee on the Problem of Noise, Final Report, Cmnd. 2056 (HMSO, 1963).

[3] Self, P., 'Nonsense on Stilts', *New Society* (July 2, 1970).

[4] House of Commons Debate, April 26, 1971.

PART III

APPLICATIONS IN THE PUBLIC SECTOR

CHAPTER 5

ROADS AND PUBLIC
TRANSPORT

This section gives a brief survey of ways in which cost-benefit methods have been used by central and local government in the United Kingdom. It is divided into three chapters, dealing respectively with transport, with other public sector investment, and with research, education and training. The survey is inevitably far from comprehensive, particularly on the local government side, and studies have been selected more because they illustrate interesting points of method than because of the magnitude of the decision or the quality of the research, which both vary enormously. The description of particular studies is also highly selective; many points such as problems of demand forecasting and use of sensitivity analysis occur repeatedly, but are only illustrated from one or two cases. Many of the studies described are really concerned with cost effectiveness in that they consider alternative ways of achieving some objective which is not itself subject to scrutiny, but they have been included because secondary costs and benefits, or 'externalities', are assessed. Pure cost-effectiveness analysis, as in the defence field, is not however covered. Despite the many limitations, it is hoped that these chapters will give some idea of the range of work going on, the practical problems encountered, and the ways in which analysis can assist the decision-maker.

Obviously attempts have always been made to forecast and evaluate the effects of alternative policies, but the use of a formal cost-benefit framework has only recently been developed in this country. The first pioneering study in the transport field was that of the M1 motorway in 1960,[1] followed shortly after by Foster and Beesley's analysis of the Victoria Line.[2] This work led on to further research on valuing time and accidents, and increasing application to surface transport investment. Another early application was to urban development and the use of agricultural land. Since 1967 the range of problems tackled has increased rapidly; research was carried out to measure and value other 'intangibles' such as unemployment, noise, pollution and recreation facilities, and results obtained in the context of one type of problem sometimes opened up further uses. The study of the M1 has already been described in Chapter 2; this chapter therefore starts with the Victoria Line appraisal.

THE VICTORIA LINE

The analysis of the Victoria Line used basically similar methods to the M1 study. Forecasts were made and benefits evaluated for generated traffic and for traffic diverted from other underground lines, bus, railway, private car and walking. Leisure time was valued, at roughly two-thirds working time, on the basis of some empirical evidence mainly from America. A small study was also made of the way in which individuals behaved when faced with a choice between standing on a fast train or a seat on a slower one, and from this an estimate was made of the value attached to getting a seat (in terms of time and hence of money); this value was used to calculate the benefit from reduced overcrowding.

The major departure in the Victoria Line study was that it investigated benefits to those who did not use the new line as well as those who did; whereas in the case of the M1, effects on other parts of the transport system were thought to be small, relief of surface congestion was potentially a significant benefit from the Victoria Line. To value this benefit, an estimate was made of the increase in average speed on roads as a result of the reduction in the number of buses and cars, and savings in time and vehicle operating costs were valued in the usual way. The great problem, however, was to forecast the effect into the future. Many economists argued that the demand for road space was so great that the reduced congestion would induce more people to use their cars, until congestion reverted to almost the same level as before. Against this Foster and Beesley argued that as total traffic grew, the value of the Victoria Line would increase. In their calculations they assumed that these two effects would roughly cancel, giving a nil trend. On this basis, the present value of benefits from reduced congestion was estimated at £30m. out of gross benefits of £86m. and net benefits of £31m., using a 6 per cent discount rate (Table 10).

Table 10

Social Benefit and Loss Tables – Victoria Line

	5½ years construction plus 50 years operation					
	Interest rate 6 per cent		*Interest rate 4 per cent*		*Interest rate 8 per cent*	
	Annual amount (£m.)	*PDV* (£m.)*	*Annual amount (£m.)*	*PDV* (£m.)*	*Annual amount (£m.)*	*PDV* (£m.)*
1. *Costs:* Annual working expenses	1.413	16.16	1.448	25.07	1.391	11.14
2. *Benefits: Traffic* diverted to VL						

(a) Underground:						
time savings	0.378	4.32				
Convenience, etc.	0.347	3.96				
(b) British Rail: time savings	0.205	2.93				
(c) Buses: time savings	0.575	6.58				
(d) Motorists: time savings	0.153	3.25				
Savings in vehicle operating costs	0.377	8.02				
(e) Pedestrians: time savings	0.020	0.28				
Sub-total (2)	2.055	29.34	2.055	45.30	2.055	20.35
3. Traffic not diverted to VL						
(a) Underground: cost savings	0.150	1.72				
(b) Convenience, etc.	0.457	5.22				
(c) Buses: cost savings	0.645	7.38				
(d) Road users: time savings	1.883	21.54				
Operating savings	0.781	8.93				
Sub-total (3)	3.916	44.79	3.91	66.41	3.916	32.03
4. Generated traffic						
(a) Time savings	0.152	2.17				
(b) Fare savings	0.092	1.31				
(c) Other	0.578	8.26				
Sub-total (4)	0.822	11.74	0.822	18.65	0.822	7.91
5. Terminal scrap value		0.29		0.82		0.10
6. *Total benefits* (2+3+4+5)		86.16		131.18		60.39
7. *Net current benefit* (6–1)		70.00		106.11		49.25
8. *Value of capital expenditure*		38.81		41.14		36.68
9. *Net benefit* (7–8)		31.19		64.97		12.57

* PDVs are present values discounted at the relevant rate of interest set out in the column heading.

Source: Foster, C. D. and Beesley, M. E., 'Estimating the Social Benefit of Constructing an Underground Railway in London', *Journal of the Royal Statistical Society*, Vol. 26 (1963), Part 1, Table 2, p.49.

Another major problem arose over repercussions on public transport fares. The original study assumed that these would be the same whether the Victoria Line was built or not. However, because London Transport would only recoup a relatively small part of the total benefit in revenue from new passengers, the line would cause a financial loss, and one way of offsetting this would be a general increase in fares. This, however, would deter some travellers from switching to the Victoria Line and would also induce some existing users of public transport throughout the system to switch to the private car, thus worsening surface congestion. In a subsequent paper[3] Beesley and Foster estimated that, if London Transport stuck to its policy of average cost pricing, and if fares generally were raised enough to cover the cost of the new line, the expected social benefit might be wiped out. They also considered ways in which the pricing system might be altered to mitigate this effect.

The relationship between different parts of the transport system and the effects of pricing policy were thus shown, even at this early stage, to be critical to the evaluation of urban transport investment. The two major problems raised by the Victoria Line study have re-emerged in current discussion of urban transport in a slightly different form. Some transport economists[4] maintain that one effect of city motorways would be to divert traffic from public transport; this would lead to reduced services and higher fares (unless ever-increasing subsidies were provided to maintain standards), and this in turn would induce even more travellers to switch to the private car. This process could continue until travel by road was slower than before, despite the new motorways; in the new situation motorists would be prepared to drive through even worse jams than now because the alternative offered by public transport was even less attractive. Conversely, it has also been argued that the best way of reducing congestion on the roads is to improve speeds and reduce costs on reserved track public transport. This is an interesting restatement of Foster and Beesley's original contention that an underground line brings benefits to surface traffic.

Given these important relationships between different parts of an urban transport system, clearly the logical procedure would be to evaluate alternative systems as a whole, considering different mixes of public and private transport of different kinds, together with different policies of pricing, subsidy and restraint to decide which overall system would offer the greatest net benefit to the community. But even if the location of housing and employment is taken as fixed, and political and social considerations ignored, the problems in a large city are extremely complex; many simplifying assumptions have to be made to get a usable model which can be run on a computer sufficiently cheaply to test a worthwhile number of alternatives. Some attempts have, however, recently been made to look at transport in towns as a whole, and three of these, in Coventry, Stevenage and Manchester, are discussed later in this chapter.

The M1 and Victoria Line studies led to further research on valuing the main benefits of transport investments, savings in time and accidents. Some of this work is described in Chapter 2. On the basis of various empirical studies the Department of the Environment (then the Ministry of Transport) felt justified in adopting a set of standard values for working and leisure time and various types of accident.

The simplest application of these new results was to inter-urban road investment which did not significantly alter the pattern of travel by road or other means. The Department of the Environment worked out and gradually refined standard methods for estimating the savings in time, accidents and vehicle operating costs, assuming the same journeys were made as before, in the first year of a scheme's life. These first year benefits were then valued (net of maintenance) and expressed as a percentage of the capital cost. This figure, known as the 'first year rate of return', was used to help in ranking schemes in order of priority for inclusion in the road programme. The method was simple enough to be computed manually.

The method did not, however, take into account costs and benefits in later years, and the Department of the Environment has now developed a computer program which makes it possible to value schemes over their full economic life, discounting costs and benefits to a present-day value at the public sector discount rate, currently 10 per cent. The programme also takes into account delays to traffic at junctions in greater detail than was previously possible.

The reason for using this discount rate is that it is regarded as the opportunity cost of capital in the public sector; it is based partly on returns (in real terms, before taxes and subsidies) on low risk investment in the private sector, and it is intended to ensure that one part of the public sector does not use resources which would be more profitably invested in another part. The rate is used as a test discount rate for investment in the nationalized industries; to be acceptable, a project must have a positive net present value after costs and revenues have been discounted at this test rate. The same rate is used in cost-benefit appraisal in central government, but it is worth noting an important difference between cost-benefit and financial investment appraisal – the inclusion of consumer surplus.

Usually only one price can be charged for a commodity, OC in Figure 3, and the revenue to the producer is this price times the quantity bought at this price, or the area $ACOD$. But the value of the commodity to those who purchase it at this price will range from OC (those who just purchase) to some higher value OB (the price above which no one would want to buy). The gain to those who would have been prepared to pay more than OC is known as 'consumer surplus', and is represented by the area ABC. In cost-benefit studies this consumer surplus is counted as a benefit in addition to the revenue (if any) to the producer. Hence, ignoring other externalities (which may be positive or negative), the cost-benefit return on a project will be higher than the maximum financial return. This has to be borne in mind in considering cost-benefit assessments; for instance a 10 per cent cost-benefit return on roads is not equivalent to a 10 per cent financial return on nationalized industries' investment. The precise relationship will vary with the shape of the demand curves and pricing policy.

Figure 3

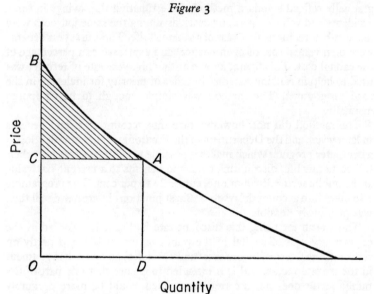

The inter-urban road programme is not in any case large enough to accommodate all projects which have a positive net present value after discounting at 10 per cent. In order to get the best value out of the programme it is desirable to select those schemes which have the greatest net value for each unit of capital used; schemes are therefore ranked by the ratio of net present value to capital cost. This is a good example of benefit/cost ratios in a capital rationing situation. The ratio is, however, only one of the factors which must be taken into account; other important points are benefits which may not have been included in the evaluation, such as regional benefits, and the extent to which a scheme will lose value by being postponed. It may happen that a good scheme, with a high benefit/cost ratio, has relatively small benefits in earlier years, and less will be lost by postponing this scheme than another with a lower benefit/cost ratio.

This method of ranking inter-urban road schemes assumes that the investment does not alter the journeys which are made. For large investments this assumption breaks down, and the Department of the Environment is therefore developing traffic models which simulate the way in which traffic flows over a whole network, taking into account road conditions, the pattern of land use, and other factors such as population, employment and income. A national network model is being developed, described in the Green Paper *Roads for the Future*.[5] The method is used for considering regional networks, for instance in the Morecambe Bay barrage study mentioned below, and is also an essential part of urban transport studies.

BRIDGES AND TUNNELS

The methods used for assessing inter-urban road schemes have also been applied to the special case of bridges and tunnels. The first major study in this group was the 1963 appraisal of a fixed Channel crossing.[6] This study, and a subsequent reappraisal[7] considered the alternatives of a road or railway bridge or railway tunnel against the base line of sea and air transport. In addition to the financial appraisal, an economic assessment was made of costs and of benefits to traffic diverted to and generated by the new link, including passengers and freight.

Another study was that of the Tay Bridge in 1966.[8] This presented a relatively simple problem, since it was an isolated improvement which would not affect the general road network. Savings in travel costs, including accidents, and benefits to generated traffic were valued, using methods based on the M1 study; there was also a discussion of the unquantified benefits of regional development and economic integration.

The appraisal of a river-crossing at Thamesmead raised rather different points of method. It was assumed that a new crossing would be built, and the question was whether to construct a tunnel or a bridge. The former was more expensive, but would take up less land at Thamesmead and would be in operation sooner, bringing earlier traffic benefits. Benefits to traffic diverting to the crossing were calculated on certain assumptions about the surrounding road network and the rate of traffic growth. The value of the land was assessed as the difference between the cost of constructing houses there and of providing them elsewhere, including the market price of alternative sites. The environmental effects on Thamesmead were discussed, but not valued. An assessment was also made of the economic and financial effects of introducing tolls.

A final example is the assessment of traffic benefits from a road along a Morecambe Bay barrage.[9] This was part of a wider study described in the next chapter. Alternative barrage sites were considered, each in conjunction with alternative complementary road systems, and an analysis was made of the effects on traffic on the whole sub-regional network, excluding holiday traffic which was assessed separately. The report discussed distributional effects, the consequences of introducing tolls, and the problem of valuing benefits in a multi-purpose project where part of the finance would come from a programme subject to capital rationing.

ROAD SAFETY SCHEMES

Many road investments are intended not to speed journeys, but to reduce accidents. The same methods of valuing costs and benefits over the life of the scheme, discounting at the public sector rate and ranking by benefit/cost ratio is applied as far as possible to these schemes, although in the case of very small improvements there is often less data available. Incidental savings in travel time and operating costs are taken into account, just as savings in accidents are included in the evaluation of time-saving inter-urban projects. Although the value of accidents is not based on objective evidence of what people would pay to avoid them – the Road Research Laboratory could not find any consistent evidence about this (see Chapter 2) – it includes the evaluation of the 'economic' costs attributable to accidents (lost output, medical treatment, damage to property and administrative costs) plus an allowance made for pain, suffering, grief and loss of life. The figures selected influence the relative importance attached to accident and time savings, and also to different types of accident. This does not affect the comparison between schemes producing these different benefits in similar proportions, but it can make a critical difference where schemes vary in their impact on different kinds of benefit. The problem became acute in evaluating crash barriers on motorways, which while preventing cross-over accidents may actually increase the number of more minor accidents; the Minister finally decided in favour of installing more crash barriers.

This case illustrates well the relationship between analysis and political judgement in cost-benefit studies. The analysis can give the decision-maker a more accurate idea of what benefits can be obtained by different schemes and at what cost; where schemes all have the same benefit, or a variety of benefits in roughly the same proportions, analysis can also show which schemes are more cost effective. But it cannot determine the relative importance to attach to life, suffering and economic benefit; this must be a matter for political decision. In the longer term it may, as Dawson suggested,[10] be possible to analyse the values implicit in expenditure on different kinds of life saving, for instance aircraft, fire-fighting and different kinds of medicine; this might produce a consensus, and, if not, the results might suggest some reallocation of resources between different life-saving programmes.

RAILWAY CLOSURES

Whilst road investments can only be appraised in cost-benefit terms, since no charge is made for using them, railway investment is normally assessed in terms of financial costs and revenues. However, the 1967 White Paper on the Nationalized Industries[11] stated that:

'Where there are grounds for thinking that the social costs or benefits do diverge markedly (from those of alternative investments offering similar financial returns) the Government will take this into account when assessing the investment.'

The same reasoning can be applied to maintaining a service, where the costs are mainly recurrent rather than capital. It was thought that some loss-making rail services might be justified on the grounds that they provide social benefits, either in relieving congestion on roads or providing a service of greater value to a community than revenue receipts suggested. In 1967 Clayton and Rees published a cost-benefit analysis of some railways in Wales.[12] A similar study of the Edinburgh–Hawick–Carlisle railway was included in the Central Borders report the following year.[13] Subsequently the Department of the Environment carried out a number of such studies,[14] which looked at various alternatives to existing services, such as keeping the line open with reduced costs and services or closing it altogether and providing a bus service. Direct costs of alternative services were estimated, together with time costs to passengers diverted to an inferior service, loss of consumer surplus for those who would no longer make the journey (using a 50 per cent rule as for generated traffic – this is explained in Chapter 2), and any increased congestion costs on the roads. These costs and benefits were valued and discounted in the usual way, and alternatives were then ranked according to their net present value; since there was little capital expenditure involved and no capital rationing problem, the aim was to find the best of mutually exclusive projects. Various other benefits were considered in different cases, such as convenience and reliability and employment and regional development effects.

PUBLIC TRANSPORT IN LONDON

Public transport in cities is also usually judged by financial criteria, but cost-benefit assessments have been made of some investments such as the Victoria Line extension to Brixton, Pimlico Station and the Fleet Line. The methods used have been developed from the original Victoria Line study, and research is being carried out into the actual effects of the Victoria Line, to check up on and improve the earlier methodology.

Cost-benefit methods have also recently been applied to the choice between alternative public transport links from London to Heathrow Airport.[15] This study was carried out by the Department of the Environment in collaboration with the GLC, British Rail, London Transport and the British Airports Authority. The alternatives assessed were an expanded coach service (taken as the base line), a British Rail link to Victoria (with or without a coach service and with or without a check-in at Victoria), and an extension of the Piccadilly Line to Heathrow. In forecasting traffic, a generalized cost modal split model was used, which was calibrated from observed behaviour on the choice between public and private transport. Direct costs, user costs and costs to others in the form of road congestion and crowding on the underground were evaluated, and various unquantifiable factors were discussed. A financial appraisal was also made. The conclusion was that, even on the least favourable of the assumptions tested, the underground extension was best in both cost-benefit and financial terms, and this conclusion was accepted.

URBAN TRANSPORT SYSTEMS: COVENTRY, STEVENAGE AND MANCHESTER

A problem on which rapid progress is now being made is the evaluation of alternative urban transport systems as a whole. A great deal of work is going on in this field; the two examples of Coventry and Stevenage have been selected because they illustrate points of theoretical interest. Both were primarily concerned with the problem of peak-hour travel.

Phase I of the Coventry study[16] was carried out by a local authority team aided by consultants and with assistance from the (then) Ministries of Transport and Housing. The study was based on the projected situation in 1981. It compared three basic alternatives: to keep to the road network already approved as part of the development plan; to increase capacity by using more local roads which otherwise would have been closed to through traffic on environmental grounds; or to undertake further road construction to cater for full motorization at peak periods without congestion. In each of the first two cases, it would be possible either to accept congestion, or to meet excess demand through commuter bus services or other public transport. Another possibility was some system of car pooling. In all, ten alternatives were considered. The traffic projections were based on detailed analysis which took into account land use, population, employment and car ownership forecasts, derived from various sources including a 2 per cent home interview survey. Capital, operating and time costs under each system were valued in money terms, and an attempt was made to rank each alternative in respect of the likely amount of damage that could be caused to the environment. This ranking was based on three factors: the number of properties affected, the volume or intensity of traffic, and the length of time for which this volume exceeded a level considered by the planners to be environmentally acceptable. These three factors were weighted to give a single index, but it was not possible to put a money value on this and hence uniquely rank the schemes. Further work on environmental aspects is being done in phase 2 of the project.

The results of the study are summarized in Figure 4. This showed the 'do nothing' alternative, with or without using local roads, as most costly; and constructing sufficient roads to cater for full motorization, even if it were physically possible, next to worst. (Had the construction of further roads been assessed simply against 'do nothing', it would have appeared worthwhile; a clear example of the need to take into account all the relevant alternatives when doing cost-benefit analysis.) On the development plan network, without local roads being used, car pooling in conjunction with buses was best on evaluated costs and amenity; it was, however, doubtful whether car pooling would be practicable, and if not, the best solution would be to use buses without car pooling (with or without rail). If local roads were used, the ranking of these alternatives was much the same. Thus the economic and environmental assessments both favoured developing commuter bus services in preference either to mounting congestion or to further road construction; these last were worse on both counts, or in the jargon 'dominated solutions'. The economic and environmental criteria to some extent conflicted when it came to the choice of using or closing local roads in combination with greater use of buses, although using local roads for buses only would also safeguard them from congestion and thus bring (unquantified) economic advantages to public transport. Since there was no objective way of putting a money value on the environmental effect, this had to be left for political decision. The nature of the choice was, however, much more precisely defined as a result of the analysis; again analysis and judgement were complementary. After seeing the report, the Policy Committee of the city council agreed that there should be an extensive public relations exercise before any decisions were taken by the council; this proved useful as a platform to explain the problem and the implications of alternative policies, and also as a way of assessing public concern and the degree to which restraint was acceptable.

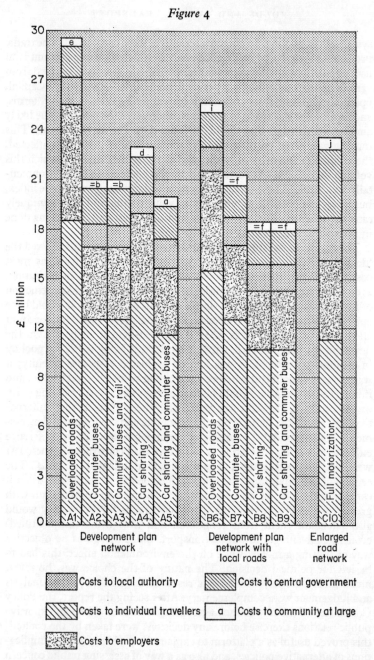

Figure 4

Comparative costs of transportation solutions 1981 – Coventry.
Source: *Coventry Transportation Study*, 1965. The assessment of the
study Team does not necessarily reflect current Council policy.

The Stevenage study[17] was carried out by Nathaniel Lichfield and Associates, assisted by a working party on which the Development Corporation, London Transport and the Ministries of Transport and Housing were represented. Again the basic alternatives considered were provision of further (elevated) roads and car parks and a residual bus service, or the development of special bus services to take a larger proportion of peak-hour traffic. This study used the 'planning balance sheet' approach developed by Lichfield (described in Chapter 9), which enumerates costs and benefits to all sectors of the community. As in the Coventry study, travel time was valued in money terms, but a points system was used to rank schemes for their effect on amenities for residents, and also comfort and convenience for travellers. On certain assumptions about modal split (which was not investigated in depth) the costs expressed in money values and the amenity considerations both favoured the special bus system. On comfort and convenience there was little to choose between these and greater use of the car, since the advantages of the car were offset by inferior bus services for those who still used public transport. One type of special bus service proved preferable to the other on most counts.

A major advantage of the planning balance sheet approach is that it shows very clearly who would bear the costs under the different alternatives. These distributional effects, which are ignored as transfers when overall costs and benefits are calculated, may nevertheless be extremely important. Thus a transport investment which gave some benefits to the less well off might be preferred to one which mainly benefited the better off (e.g. car owners) other things being equal, and a project which inflicted large costs on a few individuals to achieve small benefits for many people might be rejected even though the sum of benefits exceeded costs.

Financial effects on public bodies are also important in their own right; neither central nor local government have unlimited funds at their disposal, and a project which is socially desirable but financially costly may pre-empt some other even more worthwhile scheme. There is at present no way of putting a money value on these effects; again political judgement has an essential part to play. The Stevenage study recognized this, and in particular discussed the problem that the special bus services would make a loss. If fares were raised high enough to cover costs, there was a risk that passengers would divert to the car, and the social benefits would not be realized. The report therefore suggested that, if London Transport had to cover its costs, there would be a case for subsidies by the Ministry of Transport, the Development Corporation, local authorities and/or local employers, all of whom stood to gain financially because of the reduced need for roads and car parks. Another possibility suggested was to make a profit on car parks and use this to subsidize buses.

Recently several conurbation studies have been undertaken with

DOE help. That of South-East Lancashire and North-East Cheshire (SELNEC) is well advanced. This examines alternative combinations of investment in roads and public transport (for instance a rapid transit system or upgrading the railways) with a limited budget. The study develops Department of the Environment methods of network evaluation to take account of alternative modes and changes in trip patterns; it uses a computerized model to test a large number of alternatives.

CONGESTION, ROAD PRICING AND TRAFFIC MANAGEMENT

The Stevenage report concluded, in its discussion of wider implications, that the motorist's preference for the car might be based on inadequate realization of the costs and lack of an attractive public transport alternative. A major problem of urban transport is that vehicles do not pay the costs which their journeys create; once a person owns a car and has insured and licensed it, the only payment to the community for actually using a road is fuel tax, which comes to about 1p. a mile. In a town or city the cost of providing additional roads may exceed this several times, and congestion costs on existing roads may be even higher. The White Paper of 1968[18] on *Transport in London* suggested that the cost of an additional 15m. car trips a year at peak periods, averaging 2 miles and spread throughout London, would be nearly £13m.; this included vehicle operating costs and time costs valued in the usual way. Clearly a pricing system which brought costs to individual drivers more in line with costs to the community would lead to a more efficient use of road space, and considerable theoretical work has been done on the social benefits of road pricing.[19] One attempt to apply this theory to the London situation was a report by Thompson to the Ministry of Transport in 1967.[20] It can also be shown that, given that one commodity is supplied below cost, resources are used more efficiently if any competing commodity is also supplied below cost. Hence a case can be made out for subsidizing public transport.[21] This general theory has many other applications, and is an interesting extension of cost-benefit analysis from investment to pricing policy. Such analysis must, of course, take account of the costs of introducing a pricing system, and other less tangible damage to managerial efficiency if the discipline of making a financial profit is removed.

Pricing is not the only method of improving the use of existing road space; traffic management and parking restrictions are other possible means. Cost-benefit analysis has been applied to such policies by various local authorities; one example is a GLC analysis of a scheme designed to increase the flow of traffic through the Tower Hill area.[22] Data was collected on existing journeys and a computer model used to analyse the effect of the scheme on traffic over a fairly large surrounding network, taking account of delays at junctions. The analysis covered both peak and off peak conditions; this was important because schemes sometimes assist peak-hour traffic at the expense of longer journeys (in time as well as distance) off peak. The increase in speed was penalized to allow for the effect of traffic generated and diverted from other routes and public transport. Linked traffic lights were optimized to give minimum delays on the new network. Benefits to existing users were calculated in the usual way for the first year of the scheme, but benefits to diverted and generated traffic could not be assessed, so that the calculation was of a minimum value. These benefits were then compared to the capital cost, but no allowance was made for inconvenience during alterations.

A major problem of this type of analysis is the enormous complexity of the network which means that highly simplifying assumptions have to be made to get a manageable model; even so research costs, including data collection, can be very high in relation to the costs and benefits of the scheme itself. The analysis also ignores effects on the rest of the transport system. The generation of traffic may cause worse delays outside the network being analysed, imposing costs in excess of the benefits of the new journeys; this can be partly taken into account by enlarging the network under analysis, but there are severe practical limits to this extension. Moreover the diversion of passengers from public transport may lead to higher fares or cuts in services and hence have adverse effects on the whole transport system; the effect is small in relation to one traffic management scheme, but a series of such schemes all over a city could have a significant impact. These problems could be removed if the analysis were in the context of an optimal strategic transport plan, so that increasing the traffic flow (or, in the case of environmental schemes, reducing it) could be assumed to be a desirable objective in relation to the rest of the transport system.

NOISE, FUMES AND VISUAL INTRUSION

In all this work, the amenity effects of traffic in towns were regarded as unquantifiable, at least in money terms. The main effects usually described are noise, fumes and visual intrusion. These cause annoyance to individuals, who would be prepared to pay something to avoid them; the amount which they would be prepared to pay is an important measure of the value of these costs, although, of course, politicians and planners might wish to attach some different value for paternalistic or other reasons. Several research projects have therefore recently been launched to try to discover what value individuals do attach to a good environment, especially freedom from noise.

As with savings in travel time, there are two ways of approaching this problem: one is to ask people, and the other is to study situations in which they indirectly choose between money and the benefit in question. The first approach is being developed by Social and Community Planning Research.[23] The method used is to give people an imaginary starting position such as a house of stated size and environment, and a limited budget or counters with which they can 'buy' some of a selection of improvements, such as a quieter street, an extra room, a shorter journey to work, or better access to shops or the countryside. From their choices it is possible to derive the relative importance which people, on average, attach to these different amenities. If a money value can be assigned to one of the benefits, values for the others can then be calculated; alternatively a direct saving in money, such as a reduction in fares, can be included among the benefits available. This method has also been used to study the journey to work itself, giving a choice between shorter travelling time, less walking or waiting, fewer interchanges, different modes and degrees of crowding, and so on.

However sophisticated the questionnaire used, there is always a residual doubt as to whether people would in real life make the choices they say they would make. This problem is avoided if actual choices can be studied. The main evidence available on amenities is the way in which house prices vary. A good deal of data is available on this, but it is extremely difficult to interpret because of the many variables which affect house prices and the complexity and imperfections of the housing market.[24] In the long term, it may prove possible to construct a general model of the determinants of house prices; meanwhile various bodies, including the Department of the Environment, the Greater London Council and the Roskill Commission, have undertaken some limited research which attempts to isolate the effect of noise. The Roskill Commission work is described in Chapter 4.

Work has also been done on the cost effectiveness of alternative ways of reducing noise nuisance. For instance, noise from urban motorways can be lessened by constructing baffles on each side, by tunnelling or cut and over, or by diverting the route to avoid residential areas. It is then a matter for political decision how far it is worth resorting to increasingly expensive methods to achieve further reductions in noise.

Relatively little work has been done in this country on fumes from traffic, but the Programmes Analysis Unit has carried out some research for the Department of Trade and Industry on the costs of air pollution generally as an aid to allocating research and development resources[25] (see Figure 5). This study assessed economic costs, such as more expensive construction, damage to crops and cleaning expenditure; the latter did not appear to vary much with pollution (see Chapter 3). Amenity costs were assessed in two ways: as the amount which would have to be spent to achieve the same level of cleanness as in less polluted

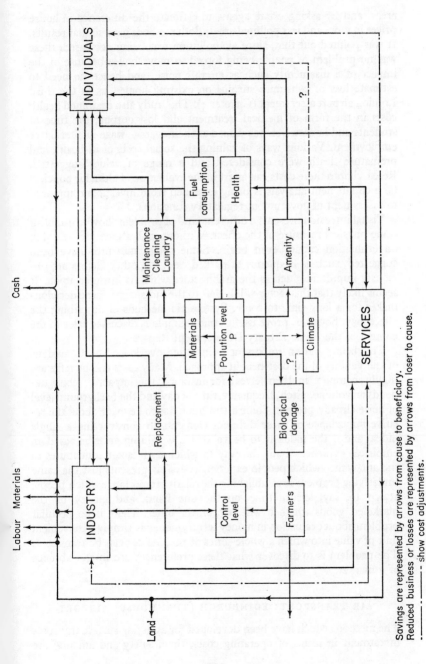

Savings are represented by arrows from cause to beneficiary.
Reduced business or losses are represented by arrows from loser to cause.
– · – · – show cost adjustments.

Transfer model (pollution decreasing).

IOI

areas, and by asking estate agents to estimate the difference in house prices in more and less polluted areas. Both methods gave similar results. It was pointed out that, since air pollution was being decreased, there was no problem of people being forced to move house because of the impact of a disamenity such as aircraft noise, and hence no need to estimate loss of consumer surplus on existing homes, as in the third London airport assessment (Chapter 4). The study also examined health costs in the form of medical treatment and lost output; the time of students and housewives was valued as their average wage in alternative employment. Various ways of valuing the social costs of ill-health and premature death were considered and a range of values suggested. Research into these costs can assist in the evaluation of clean air policies; here cost-benefit analysis is being extended from investment appraisal to assessment of government regulatory functions.

Visual intrusion presents a different kind of problem; how to establish some physical measure of the effect. Without such a measure, research on evaluation cannot even begin. Some rough measures have been suggested, such as frequency of parked cars, but other factors are obviously important, such as the architecture which is intruded upon. It seems likely that this factor will be left to the judgement of the decision-maker for a long time to come. Systematic methods of describing the effect may, however, prove useful; one example is discussed later in the context of the Clyde Estuary Development Report.

This brings out an important point often overlooked in discussions of the validity of the cost-benefit approach. Many costs and benefits are highly complex in themselves; for instance, the impact of noise depends on volume, pitch, frequency, time of day and the background level of noise already present. Some assumption has to be made about the relative importance of these different elements in constructing a single index, and if the index is to be valid this weighting must be based on empirical evidence about the way in which each factor contributes to the annoyance which people experience.[26] This presents just the same underlying problem as establishing the relative importance which people attach to, say, leisure time, on the one hand, and money or the marketed goods which it will buy, on the other. There is no peculiar problem about evaluation in money terms; money is simply a convenient unit of value into which a whole series of preferences can be translated. The problem is to discover what these preferences are in the absence of a market.

AIR TRANSPORT: EDINBURGH (TURNHOUSE) AIRPORT

The methods which have been developed for assessing surface transport investment in terms of operating costs, time, safety and amenity are obviously relevant to air travel as well. The most important study in this field is that of the third London airport, described in Chapter 4. The Department of Trade and Industry has also carried out various studies of airport investment and methods of reducing aircraft noise, and one of these, a study of alternative runway investments at Turnhouse, is described here.[27]

A preliminary study identified three most promising alternatives: (a) to resurface the existing runway, (b) to extend it to the north-west or (c) to build a new 7,700 foot runway; alternative dates were also considered. It was assumed that the airport would remain open and the aim was to discover the least cost way of achieving this. The costs considered were construction and operating costs, the costs of cross-wind diversions for alternatives (a) and (b), the costs of airport closure for alternative (b), and the costs of continuing weight restrictions for alternative (a). Time costs to passengers were valued using Department of the Environment methods, but allowance was made for the greater value of the working time of business travellers. One of the main problems was to forecast the future number of travellers, which depended both on the general growth in air travel and also on technological changes such as the introduction of an advanced passenger train; in addition to the 'best' estimates, maximum and minimum levels were suggested, and the results tested for these. The result of the study was that the extension of the existing runway was best on nearly all assumptions. A separate study was made of the costs and benefits of introducing all weather capability; it seemed doubtful whether this would be worthwhile, but if it was to be introduced the new runway appeared preferable. The study also considered regional benefits, but concluded that development of Turnhouse was unlikely to benefit Scotland as a whole. The Department of Trade and Industry will, however, continue to study regional development effects.

Despite the results, a decision was made to go ahead with a new runway. This did not mean, however, that the study was wasted. One advantage was that the cost of this decision, in terms of the quantified factors, was known and taken into account. Another advantage was that the study opened up the question of the role of Turnhouse in relation to other Scottish airports, and also the issue of the financial loss on the airport, who should pay for the improvements, and future pricing policy.

REFERENCES

[1] Beesley, M. E., Reynolds, D. J. and Coburn, T. M., *The London/Birmingham Motorway: Traffic and Economics*, Road Research Laboratory Technical Paper No. 46 (HMSO, 1960).

[2] Foster, C. D. and Beesley, M. E., 'Estimating the Social Benefit of Constructing an Underground Railway in London', *Journal of the Royal Statistical Society*, Vol. 26 (1963), Part I.

[3] Foster, C. D. and Beesley, M. E., 'The Victoria Line: Social Benefit and Finances', *Journal of the Royal Statistical Society* (1965).

[4] Thompson, J. M., et al., *Motorways in London* (London, Duckworth, 1969).

[5] Ministry of Transport, *Roads for the Future* (HMSO, 1969).

[6] Ministry of Transport, *Proposals for a Fixed Channel Link*, Cmnd. 2137 (HMSO, 1963).

[7] Watson, A. H., 'The Channel Tunnel: Investment Appraisal', *Public Administration* (Spring 1967).

[8] Gillhespy, N. R., 'The Tay Road Bridge: a Case Study', *Scottish Journal of Political Economy* (June 1968).

[9] Quarmby, D. A., 'Transport Planning in a Multi-Resource Context: The Morecambe Bay Barrage', *Regional Studies* (November 1970).

[10] Dawson, R. F. F., *The Cost of Road Accidents in Great Britain*, Road Research Laboratory Report LR 79 (HMSO, 1967).

[11] *Nationalized Industries: a Review of Economic and Financial Objectives*, Cmnd. 3437 (HMSO, 1967).

[12] Clayton, G. and Rees, J. H., *The Economic Problems of Rural Transport in Wales* (Cardiff, University of Wales Press, 1967).

[13] Scottish Development Department, *The Central Borders: a Plan for Expansion*, Vol. 2 (HMSO, 1968).

[14] Ministry of Transport, *The Cambrian Coast Line* (HMSO, 1969).

[15] Ministry of Transport, *Rail Links with Heathrow Airport* (HMSO, 1970).

[16] City of Coventry, *Coventry Transportation Study: Report on Phase I* (1968).

[17] Lichfield, N. and Associates, *Stevenage Public Transport: a Cost-Benefit Analysis* (Stevenage Development Corporation, 1969).

[18] *Transport in London*, Cmnd. 3686, Appendix J (HMSO, 1968).

[19] Ministry of Transport, *Road Pricing: the Economic and Technical Possibilities*. Smeed Report (HMSO, 1964).

[20] Thomson, J. M., 'An Evaluation of Two Proposals for Traffic Restraint in Central London', *Journal of the Royal Statistical Society* (1967).

[21] National Board for Prices and Incomes, *Proposals for the LTB and BRB for Fare Increases in the London Area*, Report No. 56, Cmnd. 3561 (HMSO, 1968).

[22] Weald, D. E., 'A Cost-Benefit Analysis for a Traffic Management Scheme', *Cost-Benefit Analysis in the Public Sector* (London, IMTA, 1971).

[23] Noinville, G., 'Evaluating Community Preferences', *Cost-Benefit Analysis in the Public Sector* (London, IMTA, 1970).

[24] *Land, Infrastructure and Amenity in Cost-Benefit Studies*, unpublished but available from the Management Accounting Unit, H.M. Treasury (September 1969).

[25] Jones, P. M. S., 'The Use of Cost-Benefit Analysis as an Aid to Allocating Resources for Research and Development', Paper to a Seminar on Cost-Benefit Analysis, Edinburgh University, 1970; reprinted in *Cost-Benefit and Cost Effectiveness* (London, George Allen and Unwin, 1972).

[26] Waller, R. A., 'Environmental Quality: its Measurement and Control', *Regional Studies*, Vol. 4 (1970).

[27] Heath, J. B. and Oulton, W. N., *A Cost-Benefit Study of Alternative Runway Investments at Edinburgh (Turnhouse) Airport*, Paper to a Seminar on Cost-Benefit Analysis, Edinburgh University, 1970; reprinted in Cost-Benefit and Cost Effectiveness (London, George Allen and Unwin, 1972).

CHAPTER 6

URBAN AND RURAL PLANNING, LOCATION AND REGIONAL EMPLOYMENT

This chapter describes some applications of cost-benefit analysis to public investment other than transport. It starts with various decisions by central government as to how or where to carry out some activity; the choice may have important side effects, particularly on regional employment and on the cost of housing and other social capital. The chapter then goes on to various problems of urban and rural investment such as town expansion and renewal, rural infrastructure and water resource development.

UNEMPLOYMENT AND THE SEATON CAREW POWER STATION

Outside the transport field, unemployment is perhaps the most important social consideration which is relevant to nationalized industries' investment. The basic hypothesis used in cost-benefit studies is that the cost in real resources, or 'opportunity cost', of employing someone who would otherwise be unemployed is zero. It is generally assumed that nationalized industry investment and other 'micro-economic' planning decisions will only have a direct effect on the level of employment in areas of high regional or local unemployment. To apply the theory to investment in these areas, it is necessary to estimate how many of those employed in new or retained jobs would otherwise have been out of work and for how long. This depends on skill, age, effects on migration and how long high unemployment will continue in the area. There may be chain reactions through which those who move into new jobs from other employment in turn create vacancies filled by the unemployed. Some of those brought into employment might otherwise have been 'inactive', that is out of work but not registered as unemployed. A further complication is that an increase in local incomes may generate further employment, especially in secondary industries, and this 'regional multiplier' must be taken into account. Finally, where jobs are transferred from areas of high employment, this may make it possible to increase the national level of economic activity; this is, however, highly controversial, and the empirical evidence is inconclusive. From about 1967 considerable research has been done on these various effects, and methods of forecasting the consequences of creating jobs in high unemployment areas have gradually been refined, although they are still open to considerable uncertainty.

An early application of the theory was the assessment of the Seaton Carew Power Station in 1968. This study was described briefly in the Treasury evidence to the Select Committee on Nationalized Industries.[1] It was assumed that a power station of specified capacity at Seaton Carew would be commissioned in 1968, and the problem was to assess the relative merits of a nuclear or coal-fired station, the latter either carrying a base load or operated in merit order. The study started with the normal investment appraisal of the alternatives from the point of view of the CEGB. An attempt was then made to adjust the costs so as to reflect the opportunity costs of the resources used in both power stations. The main weight of the adjustments fell on the coal alternative. The price of coal was adjusted to equal the avoidable cost of production at pits which would otherwise close. Freight charges were reduced to exclude the cost of railway track which would have to be kept open anyway. Finally, wage costs were adjusted to exclude the cost of those who would otherwise be unemployed, on alternative assumptions about the average length of unemployment. Because the two types of power station were assumed to have different lives, costs were in each case annuitized over the relevant period, and a comparison made between these annual costs. The results were tested for sensitivity to different assumptions about the life of the nuclear plant, the discount rate and various other estimates about which there was uncertainty. Among the unquantified factors discussed were the side effects on the coal and nuclear power industries and the social benefit of maintaining jobs in areas of high unemployment.

The Seaton Carew study shows how cost-benefit analysis can be useful in an economic context; all the 'quantified factors' were real resources which, unlike leisure time and amenity, are reflected in Gross National Product; the resources all had market prices, but these did not measure the true opportunity cost.

The social cost of unemployment is obviously also important, but can only be valued subjectively. As in the case of accidents, analysis can help by showing the true economic cost of a programme to save lives or create jobs, taking account of the economic cost of accidents or unemployment as well as the direct cost of the programme. In some cases there may be a net economic gain in addition to the social benefit. If not, the analysis can further assist by showing the value which would have to be attached to a particular social benefit to justify the programme, and by comparing the cost of different programmes, but the final decision whether to proceed must depend on political judgement.

LOCATION STUDIES: PORT INVESTMENT

The Seaton Carew study was in a sense not a cost-benefit study at all, since the decision to build a power station had already been taken, and the study was concerned with alternative ways of doing this; strictly, it was cost-effectiveness analysis. A great many cost-benefit studies come into this category, but it is useful to include them in a discussion of cost-benefit methods because secondary costs and benefits are analysed and quantified, even though the main benefit which justifies the project is not. One type of decision which can be, and is increasingly analysed in this way, is where to carry out an investment or activity. The third London airport study is the outstanding example of this, but some others are described to show the range of application and the type of problem which arises.

Port location presents similar problems to that of airports. A cost-benefit method was first developed by the Ministry of Transport in their assessment of the proposed new dock at Portbury,[2] although this study did not itself consider alternative locations; a gravity model was constructed to predict the extent to which traffic would divert to the dock, and savings in transport costs were valued in the usual way. More recently a study was made of alternative sites for industrial development taking advantage of deep water access in the Clyde Estuary.[3] The Metra Consulting Group ranked sites on the basis of economic criteria, and Weddle applied a points system to other social criteria, including atmospheric and water pollution, housing, communications, the journey to work, farming and forestry, conservation, green belt and the value of landscape. This evaluation involved first the collection of physical data, such as the type of landscape and the number of people affected in different ways; then the construction of a single index for each effect; and finally the combination of the different indices into a single ranking system. Advantages of this approach are that it provides a framework for the collection of data and a systematic way of describing such intangibles as landscape quality and capacity to absorb intrusion. On the other hand, the construction of indices and the final ranking depend on a subjective assessment of the relative importance of different factors, and some effects which could be objectively valued, for instance damage to farming, are instead weighted subjectively. The method is probably useful to the decision-maker provided the weights are made explicit and subject to scrutiny. The results can also be tested for alternative weights; it may turn out that some solutions are preferable to others with almost any plausible weighting system. This approach was used in the Clyde Estuary study. In this case a final judgement had also to be made between the economic and social ranking where these conflicted; the study made it possible to say what the economic cost was likely to be if less economic sites were preferred on amenity grounds.

The National Ports Council in 1969 commissioned Peston and Rees to consider how far cost-benefit methods could be used to assess alternative sites for maritime industrial development areas – areas of industrial activity associated with deep-water berths. Their report[4] emphasized the problems of forecasting what the demand would be for such facilities, both from primary industries directly attracted by the port and from secondary industries which might wish to locate near the primary ones. The authors made the point that, with the aid of a computable model, it should be easy and cheap to test the sensitivity of the assessment to alternative forecasts.

The report also discussed the problem of defining and short-listing alternatives, which must include development and improved use of existing ports. Efficient use of existing capacity would in turn depend on pricing policy. The number of possible variations was in principle infinite, and the method of short-listing these for detailed examination would greatly influence the results. This is a widespread problem; it also arose, for instance, in short-listing sites for the third London airport. One danger is that the short-list will reflect the subjective view of planners on what is the right kind of solution, and the alternatives studied will be so similar in their effect that it is not worth undertaking expensive research to choose between them. One remedy sometimes advocated is deliberately to include some 'wild' alternatives, at least for a preliminary calculation of costs and benefits to see if they are starters. In fact, the short-listing process itself is a rough form of cost-benefit analysis, and the best strategy may be to keep in at least one example of each type of solution for later, more detailed consideration.

This brings up another point: that cost-benefit studies frequently are not single stage evaluations but a series of assessments, of increasing refinement, the results of which may in turn change the alternatives which are to be considered. It may happen that the results become obvious at an early stage or that the analysis turns out to be so difficult as to be useless. For these reasons Peston and Rees suggested that the actual study, if carried out, should be phased.

On the question of evaluation, they proposed that economic costs and benefits should be assessed on lines familiar from transport studies: capital and operating costs, including land, housing and infrastructure, and benefits to diverted, non-diverted and generated users. Various social effects were discussed, including employment and amenity, and it was suggested that the latter might be valued through examination of the housing market.

OFFICES AND PUBLIC BUILDINGS: LOCATION AND EFFICIENCY

Government offices and research establishments can also be located in different places, and some work has recently been done on applying cost-benefit methods to this choice. Typically, the points which have to be considered are the efficiency of the organization, the possibility of taking jobs to a development area, and the lower costs of land, office accommodation, housing and other social capital outside London and the South East. Many of these effects can be at least partially valued in money, although the data available is often inadequate, especially on factors which may vary with the precise location, such as empty housing and spare capacity in schools and other services. Loss of efficiency in communications with other parts of government and outside bodies is particularly difficult to quantify or value. Another problem is the valuation of land. The valuation of agricultural and recreational land is discussed later on, but frequently land in and near London is only retained in these uses because of planning restrictions. In this case it has to be assumed that society values the land in these uses at least as much as in the alternative use which would command the highest price on the market, such as commercial or residential development. In these circumstances, land is therefore priced at its estimated market value if planning restrictions were lifted.

A study is in progress on how to improve the selection of blocks of work for dispersal and the choice of new locations, using a computer.[5] Research is being carried out into the communications links between units of government and also between them and outside bodies, which will assist in grouping units for dispersal and will also indicate the degree of communications damage which different alternatives may impose. The model evaluates solutions with respect to multiple criteria: communications loss, effects on public expenditure and on resources, and transfer of jobs to development areas (where applicable). These criteria are used to produce a short-list of good solutions; other factors affecting particular locations can then be taken into account in the final selection.

There are several advantages in using a computer. First, this makes it possible to consider a fairly large system of blocks, where there will be a very large number of initial configurations to evaluate. Secondly, sensitivity analysis is easier, and this not only helps to assess particular solutions but also shows which problems are most worth further research. Thirdly, it is possible to derive the 'efficient' set of solutions, i.e. those which could not be improved with respect to one criterion without being worsened with respect to at least one other. Figure 6 shows an example of this in two dimensions (i.e. with two criteria). Solution S is dominated by solution C in the sense that its communications and exchequer effects are both worse than those of C. Solutions B, C, D, etc., are not dominated by any other solution and are termed 'efficient'. The computer can also be used to explore which initial moves are most robust in the sense that they leave open a fair degree of flexibility in choosing different future moves which may become desirable because of changing circumstances.

Another study which deals with office accomodation and efficiency (though not with location) can conveniently be mentioned at this point. The Ministry of Public Building and Works in 1968 carried out an analysis of the choice between planned open offices with air conditioning and cellular offices without, on sites without serious external noise.[6] Two

Figure 6

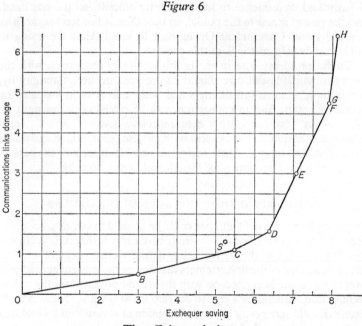

The efficient solutions.

other options were ruled out: planned open offices without air conditioning were not considered physically acceptable, whilst cellular offices with air conditioning had already been shown to be more expensive than open plan (this question was considered further in an appendix). The analysis showed that open plan was more expensive per head than cellular offices without air conditioning, but against this it was thought that there were certain benefits arising from open plan and also from air conditioning, such as better communications, improved productivity because of better working conditions, and the greater flexibility of the building.

Unfortunately, little empirical evidence was available on these benefits, but estimates were made of the possible order of magnitude, using some evidence from the United States and Germany. This showed that benefits might be sufficient to justify the higher costs, and research is now in progress to get further information about the effect of open plan in British conditions.

Local government does not have a choice between different parts of the country, but it often does have a choice in locating various services to the public, such as clinics, libraries and swimming baths; there is also an option between having fewer and more centralized services or more and more dispersed services. Here there may be a conflict between the cost and convenience to local authority officials, on the one hand, and the ease of access to the public, on the other. A few local authorities and the Local Government Operational Research Unit are trying to apply cost-benefit methods to this choice.

Similar problems arise in the health service in connection with the extent to which health care should be provided in the community by, for example, general practitioners and home nurses or in hospitals by specialized staff. Also in connection with hospitals, decisions must be taken about how many large comprehensive district hospitals, small community hospitals, convalescent hospitals, etc., are required and where these should be located. These and similar problems are now the subject of study by the Department of Health and Social Security.

URBAN EXPANSION AND AGRICULTURAL LAND

In principle, cost-benefit analysis could be applied to two distinct problems of urban expansion: which site is best and whether it is worth expanding at all, the alternative being denser development of existing urban land. One of the first attempts to measure the value of agricultural output was made in connection with the second problem, for the public inquiry into Manchester's case to develop a new town at Lymm in 1958. Stone also did some early work on the option of saving land by building higher; he calculated that at 1959 prices, raising buildings from two storeys to three gave a cost of £72,000 an acre, and further increases in height were even more expensive.[7] There are, however, great difficulties in predicting and valuing the effects of greater density compared to expansion, and in the sixties work concentrated on the problem of assessing alternative sites for urban expansion on the assumption that it would take place somewhere. In some cases, such as the study of alternative sites for development at Ipswich,[8] the major problem to be resolved was whether to preserve good agricultural land at the cost of a more expensive or less convenient town development. In other cases, such as the Merseyside study,[9] the differing quality of agricultural land was only one of many differences in cost and benefit. Recreational land may also be at stake, and agricultural land may have amenity as well as food producing value; amenity is very difficult to quantify, but methods of valuing recreational facilities are being developed and are described later in this chapter.

So far as agricultural output is concerned, the fundamental hypothesis is simple: that the value of agricultural land is equal to its future output of food (net of inputs), which in turn is valued at the cost of obtaining the food from the cheapest alternative source. According to the criterion originally proposed by Ward and Wibberley,[10] the difference in value between higher and lower quality agricultural land should be compared with the additional urban costs of using the less valuable agricultural site. There are, however, various issues which have to be considered in applying this criterion, such as the rate at which productivity and the relative price of agricultural products may increase in the future, whether outputs would be replaced from UK or imported sources, and the national security and balance of payments aspects of food supplies. Many economists consider that the price of additional imported rather than home produced food should be taken as the current value of food. This would mean that the market price would be used as a starting-point. On the other hand, it has been suggested that government subsidies represent the value which the community attaches (for balance of payments, security and/or amenity reasons) to home produced food in preference to imports: if this is so, food should be valued at the price to the farmer. The proponents of using market prices suggest that it is better to take explicit account of these external factors; in some cases amenity may even favour preserving the less good or non-agricultural land. A further problem is obtaining adequate data on which to base valuation once a theoretical position has been adopted. This subject is discussed further in Chapter 4 in the context of the third London airport; the whole field has recently been reviewed in an article by Peters.[11] Some evaluation of the agricultural costs of alternative urban development sites has also been attempted in regional studies such as that of Humberside.[12]

The valuation of urban costs and benefits is also difficult, since these include not only the capital and maintenance costs of housing, roads, sewage and so on, but also the convenience and pleasantness of a town for the inhabitants. Some aspects of this, such as the journey to work, can be valued. Costs and benefits vary not only with the site, but also with the form of urban development. Stone has done considerable general research on the choice between expanding existing towns and creating new ones, and on alternatives to onion ring development, such as linear expansion and the development of separate towns or villages, of different shapes and arranged in different patterns.[13]

More recently, the Local Government Operational Research Unit and Cheshire County Council Planning Department have explored the possibility of designing a computer program to evaluate urban land-use plans.[14] The first stage in this project identified six types of cost or benefit which were significant at the level of planning considered: construction and demolition costs, intrinsic benefit (of a land use irrespective of location), site benefit (of a land use in a particular location), neighbour costs (of conflicting land uses adjacent to each other), transport costs (including travel, i.e. user benefits and congestion costs), and sewerage costs. An attempt was made to use linear programming to generate least cost plans in terms of these costs and benefits. This, however, failed because the representation of the way in which people chose where to live (i.e. to balance site benefit against transport costs) had to be simplified to a point where it was not close enough to real life to give a realistic trip distribution pattern. The team concluded that it would only be possible to allocate land use and trips simultaneously by this method if either a more accurate linear representation of transport allocation was produced or non-linear programming techniques became practical on the computer. Instead, the team therefore devised a computer program for evaluating given land use plans; this is being applied to real problems and further work on costs and benefits is in progress. This project is interesting as a pioneering study in evaluating plans for urban expansion as a whole, but to achieve this the evaluation of costs and benefits has had to be greatly simplified.

THE REDEVELOPMENT OF TOWNS

There are two other applications of cost-benefit methods to urban planning which should be mentioned. A town or city is far too complex to be considered as a whole by existing methods, and the consequences of different courses of action cannot be forecast. It may, however, be possible to analyse detailed options within a general planning framework. Transport is one example of this; another is the choice between alternative sites for town centre redevelopment. Part of the benefits of redevelopment can be measured by returns to the developers in increased land values or rents, but there may be important external effects, for instance on traffic congestion, public services and property values in other parts of the town. Lichfield has carried out several studies of this type[15] using his 'planning balance sheet' approach which is discussed briefly in Chapter 9. Some authorities such as the GLC have directly valued the effects on transport of alternative shopping centre redevelopments,[16] and have also used cost-benefit methods to assess schemes for converting industrial or commercial areas to residential use, thus reducing traffic congestion at the expense of lowering the direct return on the land.[17]

Local authorities may have an especially difficult problem in deciding what community they should consider in reaching decisions; they may only wish to consider local residents, but if all local authorities take a narrow view this may lead to losses to everybody, and the central government clearly has to consider the national interest when approving grants. This problem has implications for the choice of discount rate; many authorities use their long-term borrowing rate, but a case could be made out for using the public sector discount rate, at least in the assessment of national costs and benefits, in order to optimize the use of resources within the public sector.

The other application in urban redevelopment is the choice between new building and rehabilitation of sub-standard housing. The basic theoretical position on this has been stated by Needleman.[18] One measure of benefit from alternative schemes is the subsequent increase in the market or rental value of the property, but this may be misleading because of the many imperfections in the housing market. Another difficulty is that such schemes may have social objectives such as eliminating slum conditions, helping the worse off and lessening symptoms such as crime, delinquency, fire and the number of children taken into care. An attempt to construct indices of social stress and housing need is described in Chapter 9; such indices, if the implicit weightings are acceptable, could aid the development of cost effectiveness work. The Institute of Municipal Treasurers and Accountants are also sponsoring studies of the problem by a number of local authorities, following their group of experimental studies published in 1969.[19] A slightly different but related problem is the selection of areas for improvement within a limited budget; here again there may be a conflict between economic criteria, which favour housing with a longer life, and social criteria, which may point to housing which will soon have to be replaced anyway. Several local authorities have examined this problem, and the Department of the Environment has also done considerable work on it.[20]

RURAL WATER SUPPLIES

Relatively little work has been done on rural housing and infrastructure. However, in 1968 the Ministry of Housing commissioned Warford to undertake a study of investment in piped water supplies in rural areas, taking as an example a proposed scheme for the South Atcham district in Shropshire.[21] It had to be assumed that, because of the health hazard, provision of piped supplies was essential, and no attempt was therefore made to assess or value health benefits or to look at other methods of safeguarding the supply, such as local water and sewage treatment.

Instead, the report examined the alternatives of taking piped supplies to scattered dwellings or rehousing some at least of the inhabitants in selected villages; it thus became yet another example of a location study.

Several alternative combinations of relocation and piped supplies were considered, along with no relocation. The study for the first time drew together all the costs of rural dwellings, including costs of sewage, telephones, electricity, postal services, schools, health services, mobile libraries and refuse collection (Tables 11a and 11b). The cost of travel for farmers and their families, to work, shops and entertainment, was also assessed. The three most important factors were, however, found to be the costs of water supply, the costs of rehousing, and side-effects on agriculture. These last two factors raise points of method which are of more general interest.

The problem about housing was that if people were rehoused, the new houses would be of different, probably higher standard than the old abandoned ones. It was assumed that the value of future benefits of living in the new houses, discounted to the present, would equal their costs, and that the benefits of living in the old houses would equal their market value. The cost of relocation would be the cost of the new houses minus the additional benefit of living in them, which on these assumptions would equal the market value of the abandoned housing. Market values were estimated directly for a sample of all affected houses, and an average value calculated. Care had to be taken that benefits of reduced travel were not counted twice, directly and as part of the benefit of the new housing.

So far as agriculture was concerned, the effect of relocation would be to force some farmers to switch from dairy farming, which needed nearby residence, to other forms of agriculture. The change in food output was valued at its market price, i.e. exclusive of subsidy. Milk was valued in its marginal use, where the price is below that of milk sold direct to the consumer. Allowance was made for the possibility that some agricultural workers might not find other employment immediately, and for the initial costs of converting to a different form of agriculture. On these assumptions, the change in agriculture owing to relocation showed a large reduction in the net cost of maintaining agriculture in the area.

The overall result suggested that on most alternative sets of assumptions about housing values, unemployment, the value of travel time and the discount rate, maximum relocation was the least costly solution. As the author stressed, however, this could not be taken in itself as the basis for decision. The political implications and the possibility of alternative local treatment also needed considering. One approach could be to compare the cost effectiveness of this type of health expenditure with others. The report also discussed the future use of cost-benefit methods for other schemes. Clearly it would not be worth undertaking a full study every time, but it was suggested that if a few more pilot studies could be completed in rather different areas, it might turn out that a few of the factors were always of dominant importance. In this case a streamlined method of assessment could be devised, as had been done for inter-urban roads.

WATER RESOURCES, RECREATION AND POLLUTION

Water is a commodity which cannot be valued at a money price because there are, as yet, no reliable techniques which can properly measure the benefit of a water supply against the benefits of investments for other purposes. In addition, the Water Resources Board considers that although the cost of new sources of supply will generally exceed the cost of existing sources, given the comparative abundance and cheapness of water in this country they do not expect the rate of increase in cost to be such that if it could be brought to bear on the consumer it would noticeably affect his demands. Demand is, therefore, forecast on the basis of existing pricing policy, and the objective is to meet this demand at minimum cost, bearing in mind the less tangible and unquantifiable effects on landscape and amenity. In any water conservation scheme, there are important side-effects on agriculture, conservation and amenity; reservoirs may both destroy and create major recreational facilities. Estuarial barrages may also bring transport benefits if used to carry a road, and may affect land use, employment and regional development.

The most comprehensive cost-benefit assessment of such effects so far is the Morecambe Bay study, not yet published. This considered three alternative methods of storing water in the bay: a barrage across the bay, a higher barrage across the Kent and/or Leven estuaries with one pumped storage reservoir in the bay, or several such reservoirs with no barrage. In addition to the direct costs, the factors valued in money terms were transport and recreation benefits and agriculture. The method used to value transport costs and benefits, other than recreation traffic, is described in the preceding chapter.

To value recreation benefits,[22] Mansfield first assessed the demand for recreation in the Lake District, using data from a 1966 traffic and recreation study of the area. Full day and half-day trips and holidays were considered separately, but the data did not make it possible to differentiate types of recreation activity. Consumer surplus in the Lake District was then calculated using the Clawson method described in Chapter 8. Time spent travelling to a recreation facility was valued on the basis of direct evidence, giving a figure slightly below the 25 per cent of income figure for commuting journeys. The lake which would be created by a barrage was regarded as an extension to the Lake District, the facilities offered for motoring and boating being somewhat similar.

Table 11a
Present Worth of Costs at 10 per cent (£) $(R_1T_1H_1)$

Item	Table	None	B	C	D	B+C	B+D	C+D	B+C+D
					Area Relocated				
Water supply	6.8	806,104	615,641	760,102	714,199	569,639	523,736	668,197	477,734
Agriculture (R_1)	7.27(A)	1,275,884	980,433	1,192,273	1,062,046	896,822	766,595	978,435	682,984
Sewage disposal	8.3	322,515	294,807	308,324	302,978	281,616	275,813	288,787	264,708
G P O telephones	9.5	11,430	7,673	10,286	9,366	6,529	5,609	8,222	4,465
Electricity supply	10.7	29,435	31,566	29,539	31,141	27,494	29,537	31,245	25,464
G P O mail	11.5	110,463	89,380	100,891	98,274	79,891	74,281	86,700	67,139
Schools	12.5	271,075	245,491	271,075	272,299	245,491	245,491	272,299	245,491
Travel to work etc. (R_1T_1)	13.23(A)	—	77,375	4,942	74,716	82,317	110,185	79,658	115,127
Miscellaneous transport	14.6	—	−6,079	−3,191	−699	−9,270	−12,575	−3,890	−15,766
Housing (T_1H_1)	15.10(A)	—	462,356	154,142	284,671	616,498	747,027	438,813	901,169
Total		2,826,906	2,798,643	2,828,383	2,848,991	2,797,027	2,765,699	2,848,466	2,768,515

Table 11b

Net Benefits of Relocation: All Sectors (£). Present Worth at 10 per cent

Assumptions	Area Relocated						
	B	C	D	$B+C$	$B+D$	$C+D$	$B+C+D$
$R_1T_1H_1$	28,263	-1,477	-22,085	29,879	61,207	-21,560	58,391
$R_1T_2H_1$	76,876	1,015	25,799	80,985	128,862	28,816	128,538
$R_1T_1H_2$	127,551	31,675	60,859	162,319	243,439	94,536	273,775
$R_1T_2H_2$	176,164	34,167	108,743	213,425	311,094	144,912	343,922
$R_2T_1H_1$	52,830	1,482	2,617	57,405	110,476	6,101	110,619
$R_2T_2H_1$	103,005	4,244	52,094	110,342	181,286	58,340	184,191
$R_2T_1H_2$	152,118	34,634	85,561	189,845	292,708	122,197	326,003
$R_2T_2H_2$	202,293	37,396	135,038	242,782	363,518	174,436	399,575

R_1 = 2-year re-employment lag
R_2 = zero re-employment lag
T_1 = value of NWT taken as $\frac{1}{3}$ WT
T_2 = value of NWT taken as zero
H_1 = maximum estimate of value of abandoned domestic properties
H_2 = minimum estimate of value of abandoned domestic properties

Source: Warford, J. J., *The South Atcham Scheme: An Economic Appraisal* (HMSO, 1969), Tables 16.17 and 16.35. Reprinted with permission of the Controller, H.M. Stationery Office.

An estimate was then made of how this new facility would divert users from the Lake District and generate new use; travel savings to diverted users and consumer surplus on generated use were calculated in the usual way to give a value in the first year. Finally this had to be projected forward, allowing for increasing population, income and car ownership, and the resulting values discounted back to the base year. This complex calculation rested on many assumptions that might be questioned, and the results were tested for sensitivity to variations in some of these. It was, however, the best estimate which could be made in the present stage of knowledge, and was useful as an indication of the order of magnitude of recreation benefits.

For agriculture, the main effect was that a barrage would in any case necessitate expenditure on drainage; for very little extra expenditure, standards of drainage could be greatly improved. The increase in future output, net of extra inputs and capital expenditure, was estimated and discounted to the base year. An estimate was also made of gains and losses to commercial fishing. Other factors which were discussed but not evaluated included effects on wildlife and landscape, and broader economic effects, for instance on employment, migration and the journey to work. It was pointed out that a full barrage with a road would make it possible to commute from the Furness area to central Lancashire, thus linking two labour markets which were to some extent complementary in their demands for male and female labour.

The various secondary effects of the alternative schemes could influence the choice between them, since transport, recreation and other benefits would be greatest with the various barrage schemes, but these would also cause the greatest changes in the tidal régime of the Bay with consequential siltation problems and dredging costs. The best of the Morecambe Bay schemes will also have to be compared with other estuarial schemes and inland reservoirs in planning overall water resource development in Northern England. Here again secondary benefits could influence the choice. Work is also in progress on the transport, recreation and other effects of a road crossing combined with water storage in the Dee Estuary, and Volume I of the phase IIA report on this, which includes a cost-benefit assessment of alternative scheme, has just been published.[23]

Inland reservoirs, like towns, are important users of land, and there is often a similar conflict between less costly provision of water and preservation of agricultural land. This is an area where the interests of agriculture and recreation may conflict, if for instance the alternative to agricultural land is open moorland. Inland reservoirs may also bring recreation benefits from fishing and sailing. As methods of valuing alternative land uses improve, cost-benefit methods may become increasingly useful; other applications to rural policy may open up, such as forestry (which also has employment repercussions), mineral extraction, the restoration of derelict land and the creation of country parks. Another important problem facing the Water Resources Board is how water may be used and reused within a river system where abstractions are made from the river and effluents discharged into it. The more a river is polluted the more expensive it becomes to purify water for some uses, but the treatment of sewage and industrial waste before discharge into the river is also costly. The Board, the Trent River Authority and the Water Pollution Research Laboratory are at present carrying out a study of the River Trent to discover the optimum way of using the resources of the river system, including the groundwater resources and the possibility of dual supply systems. The study also takes account of amenity and recreation, and Kavanagh, Gibson and Smith are making an evaluation of the potential benefits from fishing, again using the Clawson method. The Local Government Operational Research Unit has developed an economic model which is central to the study. Indirectly, this will produce shadow prices for the different levels of water pollution in the Trent in terms of the costs it creates.

REFERENCES

1 *Cost-Benefit Analysis as Applied to the Nationalized Industries*, Treasury Memorandum, Appendix 8, Vol. III of the First Report of the Select Committee on Nationalized Industries (HMSO, 1968).

2 Ministry of Transport, *Reasons for the Minister's Decision Not to Authorize the Construction of a New Dock at Portbury, Bristol* (HMSO, 1966).

3 Clyde Estuary Development Group, *Report on Possible Industrial Developments in the Clyde Estuary* (1969).

4 Preston, M. H. and Rees, R., *Feasibility Study of a Cost-Benefit Assessment of Maritime Industrial Development Areas* (National Ports Council, 1970).

5 Elton, M. C. J., *et al.*, *An Approach to the Location of Government*, Paper to the TIMS Conference (London, 1970).

6 Department of the Environment, *Planned Open Offices: Cost-Benefit Analysis* (Whitehall Development Group, 1971).

7 Stone, P. A., 'Housing, Town Development, Land and Costs', *Estates Gazette* (1963).

8 Shankland Cox and Associates, *Expansion of Ipswich: Consultants Supplementary Report* (HMSO, 1968).

9 Traffic Research Corporation, *The Selection of a Land-Use Plan* Technical Report No. 12, Merseyside Area Land Use/Transportation Study (Liverpool, 1969).

10 Wibberley, G. P., *Agriculture and Urban Growth* (London, Michael Joseph, 1959).

11 Peters, G. H., 'Land Use Studies in Britain: a Review of the Literature with Special Reference to Applications of Cost-Benefit Analysis', *Journal of Agricultural Economics* (May 1970).

12 *Humberside: Feasibility Study* (HMSO, 1969).

13 Stone, P. A., op. cit.

14 Local Government O.R. Unit, *Systems Design Project: Macclesfield and District*, Series of Reports, 1969-70.

15 Lichfield, N., *Cost-Benefit, Analysis in Town Planning: A Case Study of Cambridge* (Cambridge and Isle of Ely County Council, 1966). See also his 'Cost-Benefit Analysis in Town Planning: a Case Study – Swanley', *Urban Studies* (November 1967).

16 Saalmans, P. D., *Evaluation of Town Centre Redevelopment Schemes*, Proceedings of the Planning and Transportation Research and Computation Company Seminar on Urban Renewal (November 1967).

17 Flowerdew, A. D. J. and Stannard, R. B., *Cost-Benefit in Central London Redevelopment*, Paper to the Urban Studies Conference (September 1967).

18 Needleman, L., 'The Comparative Economics of Improvement and New Building', *Urban Studies*, Vol. 6 (1969).

19 Institute of Municipal Treasurers and Accountants, *Cost-Benefit Analysis in Local Government* (London, IMTA, 1969).

[20] *Old Houses into New Homes,* Cmnd. 3502 (HMSO, 1968).
[21] Warford, J. J., *The South Atcham Scheme: an Economic Appraisal* (HMSO. 1969).
[22] Mansfield, N. W., 'The Estimation of Benefits from Recreation and the Creation of a New Facility', *Regional Studies,* Vol. 5 (1971), No. 2.
[23] Binnie and Partners, *The Dee Estuary Scheme – Phase IIA* (HMSO, 1971).

CHAPTER 7

RESEARCH, EDUCATION AND TRAINING

This chapter is concerned with various aspects of acquiring and using knowledge, including research and development, information services, education, industrial training and health screening. In many of these cases, government expenditure is of direct or indirect assistance to industry, and the problem is to discover the national benefit, especially in increased output and gains to the balance of payments.

RESEARCH AND DEVELOPMENT: THE NRDC AND PAU

One of the first attempts to value research was made by Heath and Grossfield for the Board of Trade in 1965.[1] In order to see whether it was possible to assess public benefits, they studied a National Research Development Corporation project to develop a potato harvester which had already been successfully completed. The costs which were assessed included initial research and development, assistance to the firms which produced and sold models, patenting costs and also the costs of supporting earlier unsuccessful harvesters. To estimate benefits, it was assumed that the successful harvester might otherwise have been put on the market in 1962 instead of 1960 or else not at all, and that a proportion of those who had purchased it, rising to 95 per cent by 1965, would otherwise have bought another roughly equivalent machine. Consumer surplus was estimated separately for each group of purchasers; those who would not have bought an equivalent machine would have continued to use a simpler machine requiring more labour. In addition to consumer surplus, there were benefits to the producer reflected in royalty payments made. The report concluded that, whilst royalties were unlikely to cover research and development costs of successful and unsuccessful ventures, these costs were jointly justified if public benefit in the form of consumer surplus was taken into account.

In 1967, the Ministry of Technology and the Atomic Energy Authority set up a Programmes Analysis Unit specifically to test and develop methods for the appraisal of research and development programmes, and to undertake practical evaluation.[2] About seventy evaluations were made in the first 2 years, including assessments of specific projects, the selection of portfolios of projects, and exploration of general areas of research such as marine technology to discover what benefits might stem from initially unspecified research.[3]

Some of the problems which arise in this field are illustrated from a study of research programmes into hydrostatic extrusion carried out in 1968. First, products which could usefully be produced by hydrostatic extrusion techniques had to be identified and the costs of this method compared with the costs of competing processes such as rolling mills and continuous casting, which varied greatly with the particular products and might also be improved over time. A mathematical model was used to examine the sensitivity of the estimated cost of hydrostatic extrusion to uncertain factors. A study was then made of how far industry was likely to adopt the new process. This would depend not only on cost comparisons but also on the need to replace existing equipment and the rate of growth in the market; if new equipment was not needed anyway, the full costs of hydrostatic extrusion would be compared to the marginal costs of existing methods. Investment grants and tax relief would also affect decisions. Potential overseas sales were assessed as well as the home market. Since much of the benefit from using hydrostatic extrusion could be derived from using imported equipment, the net benefits of UK research were seen to be the earlier exploitation of the technique in this country, exports of machinery, avoidance of imports, receipt of royalties from abroad and avoidance of royalities to other countries. Overseas technology was therefore considered, and it was estimated that UK research would reduce delay very considerably because the UK was in the lead in this field. Finally, the benefits were compared with the costs, both in present value terms, and expressed as a benefit/ cost ratio. Results were tested for sensitivity to various estimates such as different costs, utilization factors and delays in development and implementation. Levels of benefit associated with different forms of hydrostatic extrusion were also studied to compare possible lines of research and to assist in the division of effort between the various facets of the programme.

Obviously the worst problem in this kind of assessment is the forecasting; there may be great uncertainty about the costs and success of the programme, other technical innovation at home and overseas, and general economic and social developments which will affect the size of the potential market. There are various sophisticated mathematical tools for analysing risk, but in this case a very simple approach was adopted, that of estimating highest and lowest values for uncertain factors and combining the most and least favourable values to get maximum and minimum estimates of total costs and benefits. It may happen, as in this case, that even the minimum estimated benefit justifies going ahead with the programme. Analysis also helps to compare the probable return on different programmes and different aspects of a single programme; it shows the development and marketing expenditure which must be incurred if the potential benefits of successful research are to be realized, and draws attention to the option of buying results from overseas. As programmes are completed, it will be possible to compare actual results with earlier assessments, and bring this experience to bear on future forecasting.

Although by far the greatest work on evaluating R & D has been done by the Programmes Analysis Unit, other government departments are increasingly concerned to develop criteria for the selection of research projects. One example is a paper by the Building Research Station,[4] which examined the factors influencing the success of projects, and emphasized that benefits are highly dependent on the degree of application.

CURIOSITY-ORIENTED RESEARCH

So far only 'mission oriented' research with a specific objective has been considered. Some work has however been done by the Department of Education and Science and the Council for Scientific Policy on basic research motivated by curiosity. This work started with a theoretical paper by Byatt and Cohen on how benefits might be estimated in this field.[5] It was suggested that changes in government support for research might delay or accelerate discoveries, which in turn might delay or accelerate the birth of science-based industries. If so, changes in the net present value of the industry could be compared with costs of research, using the same base year. World-wide and national benefits would have to be distinguished. Economic benefits would include profits of firms directly involved and consumer surplus; there might be effects on profits of other firms and externalities such as regional unemployment or atmospheric pollution. The paper considered some empirical evidence on the number of major world discoveries in the twentieth century and the time-lags before these gave rise to new industries. It was pointed out that a discovery might not give rise to a new industry for a very long time, if other necessary discoveries or appropriate technologies were lacking or if society was not in a position to invest appropriately; substantial economic benefits only arose from discoveries made at about the right time. From the UK point of view, there was the option of buying knowledge from abroad; net economic benefit would depend on the extra costs and delays in applying discoveries made elsewhere.

The paper suggested that, as a first step, the proposed method should be applied to some existing science-based industries to test various relationships and establish some of the parameters. If this was successful, an attempt might then be made to apply the method *ex ante*; this would involve great uncertainty, and allowance would have to be made for the fact that only some discoveries would show an economic pay-off. Following this recommendation, the Department of Education and Science commissioned some feasibility studies to test the method in relation to specific industrial processes such as the Pilkington process for glass manufacture. The initial studies suggested that the notion of delay might be difficult to apply in practice, but work is still in progress at Manchester University and the Manchester Business School.

PARTICIPATION IN EUROPEAN PROJECTS

Special problems arise in deciding on research and development policy when there is a further option of participating in an international programme. In 1967 Wolfe and Youngson carried out an analysis on the costs and benefits to the UK of participation in the 300 GeV accelerator project if this was sited in the UK, compared to participation with siting elsewhere or no participation.[6] This study was not concerned with the worthwhileness of the project, but only with the economic costs to the UK if the project was sited here, and benefits in the form of foreign exchange receipts. Alternative assumptions were made about whether resources used in the UK would otherwise be unemployed. Foreign exchange was discounted at a higher rate than resources, on the assumption that the preference for foreign exchange would fall over time (the study was made before devaluation). The final calculation was of the premium which would have to be attached to foreign exchange to justify participation with siting in the UK in preference to participation with siting elsewhere and in preference to no participation.

Similar problems arise in considering the development of satellites for civil purposes such as communications, television and weather forecasting. For instance, the Ministry of Technology did some exploratory work on the costs and benefits of extending reliable weather forecasts from the present 24 hours to a period of up to a week, using alternative systems of data collection such as balloons interrogated by satellites. This study identified various weather-sensitive decisions which have to be taken 2 to 7 days in advance, such as routing ships, regulating dams and planning building construction, agricultural operations and the production of electricity and gas. The advantages and disadvantages of national, European and global satellite programmes were discussed, but in this study it was not possible to make a full assessment of costs and benefits.

INFORMATION

Another way in which the Government can assist industry is through advisory services to increase the use of existing knowledge. One example is the Production Engineering Advisory Service, which seeks to get firms to adopt more efficient methods, such as using throw-away tips for machine tools and undertaking value engineering exercises. In 1969 the Ministry of Technology estimated the costs and benefits of two activities of this service, visits by mobile demonstration units and production advisory assignments. In both cases the study was based on a sample of reports on firms where the initial activities had been followed by an assessment visit and the assessor had been able to estimate savings arising from the improvement. On the basis of this sample, an estimate was made of average net first-year savings. Total benefits from all visits and assignments were then calculated and compared with the total costs of these activities. The study suggested that even first-year savings exceeded the costs involved, but there were various qualifications, and the report suggested ways in which information about economic returns might be improved.

Two other examples are worth a brief mention. The first is a study by Wolfe and others at Edinburgh University of the costs and benefits of scientific and technical information systems.[7] This study was limited to the supply of reference material (bibliographies, abstracts, etc.) to those working on applied research and development in certain selected industries, including chemicals, textiles and agriculture. A random selection of firms was examined in each industry. Various measures of effectiveness were devised, including the time saved by the research worker as a result of using the information service. The information systems were costed, distinguishing different services where possible, and cost effectiveness comparisons were made between different services, different types of service and different characteristics of a particular service.

The second is a pilot study of Durham University Library commissioned by the Department of Education and Science.[8] This study analysed the cost of different inputs such as senior and junior staff time, new stock, seating and shelving. It considered the criteria implicit in the decisions of librarians, for instance in deciding between acquiring a book or arranging an inter-library loan, and suggested how these implied weights might be applied to future activity and inputs.

ECONOMIC RETURNS ON EDUCATION

Most of the work on the costs and benefits of education in the UK has been done outside government, but this chapter would not be complete without a mention of it. Analysis has mainly been concerned with economic returns in the form of increased productivity; other benefits, such as non-economic satisfactions to the individual and spillover effects, have not been possible to measure. The underlying theory, the problems of measurement, and some evidence on returns on particular levels of education in the UK were discussed in a book by Blaug, Peston and Ziderman,[9] and in two papers by Blaug.[10] The most recently published study is a paper by Maglen and Layard on engineering education;[11] this example is described here to illustrate the method. Further work on higher education is now in progress in the Department of Education and Science, and some first results are now available.[12]

The study of engineering education used information on the electrical engineering industry for 1966/7 collected by the Industrial Manpower Project at the London School of Economics. It was assumed that the labour market was sufficiently competitive for gross earnings to equal marginal product, and for people with similar ability and qualifications in other employment to be similarly paid. Five routes from compulsory schooling to various levels of scientific and engineering qualification were identified (Figure 7). For each route, the earnings at different ages of those reaching each level of qualification along that route were then calculated. The additional life output associated with each additional qualification was thus identified. Some of the difference in income might, however, be due to the different ability, drive and so on of those acquiring additional qualifications; evidence from the USA suggested that about one-third of income differentials might be due to these other factors. There was no evidence on this point for the UK, and the study made alternative assumptions of none, one-third and one-half. It was assumed that earnings differentials would all increase at about 2 per cent a year in real terms. A calculation was also made of private returns to the individual, taking account of direct taxation and of the risk that extra income might fall below the average differential.

The social costs of education were calculated as the costs of tuition plus the value of output which the students would otherwise have produced. Costs of tuition were difficult to assess; average rather than marginal costs had to be used, university costs allocated between teaching and research, and capital costs of buildings annuitized. Output foregone on full-time courses could be assessed as earnings at the preceding level of qualification, but part-time courses presented problems, and leisure time was not valued in this study. No information was available on benefits to drop-outs; these benefits were ignored, and returns to successful students averaged first over all successful students and then over all students including drop-outs. Finally, private costs were also calculated; these were lower than social costs because of tax on earnings foregone, free or subsidized tuition and maintenance grants.

Finally, a calculation was made of the internal rate of return on education expenditure, i.e. that discount rate at which the present values of costs and benefits were equal. The results in general confirmed those of earlier studies, and suggested that social returns on higher education did not compare all that favourably with the 10 per cent minimum return on nationalized industries' investment. Rates varied with different qualifications, and sixth-form science showed a surprisingly low rate. Part-time education compared very favourably with full-time. Private returns on many qualifications greatly exceeded the rate at which individuals could borrow money, and the report discussed why people did not borrow more to finance further education.

Figure 7

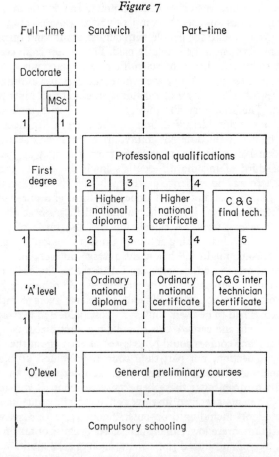

Transitions for which rates of return are calculated.

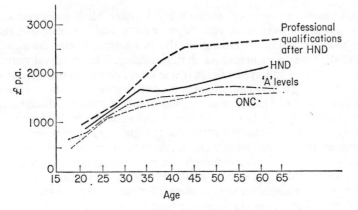

Mean salaries by age and education – Routes 2 and 3.

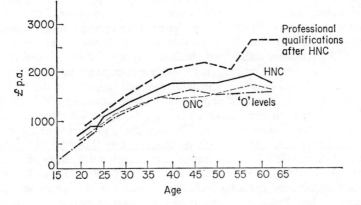

Mean salaries by age and education – Route 4.

INDUSTRIAL TRAINING AND THE EMPLOYMENT SERVICES

The Department of Employment have commissioned some work on the economic returns of specific training schemes. The first of these, by Thomas, Moxham and Jones, was a pilot study to test whether cost-benefit methods could be applied to industrial training carried out by private firms, and was concerned only with benefits to the firm.[13] The study concentrated on training for operatives at a particular factory which had adopted an improved training scheme in 1965 and gone back to previous less expensive methods 2 years later. High quality records of personnel, wage costs and output were available throughout this period. The costs of training by the two methods were compared, including wages of operatives during training. The increased output resulting from improved training (net of increased wages) was calculated by comparing the output profiles of the groups trained in different ways, taking account of labour turnover and length of training. Discounting increased output at 10 per cent, the results showed a benefit/cost ratio of 6:5; a quarter of the benefit was due to higher performance and three-quarters to reduced labour turnover. An immediate result of the study was that the firm decided to revert to the new training system. The report also concluded that cost-benefit methods could be successfully applied, but only if reliable data were available; further research on training for different types of activity is now in progress.

The Department of Employment also commissioned a report by Hughes on the use of cost-benefit analysis to evaluate retraining programmes at government training centres.[14] This report considered the theoretical approach to estimating benefits to the individual, to society and to the Government. It was suggested that benefits to individuals who completed a course could be estimated by comparing their future income with that of a carefully designed control group; the probability of dropping out must be taken into account. Gains to the economy would arise where individuals obtained employment or increased their output as a result of training; a net increase in employment would occur where there was structural unemployment and training was directed to filling shortages of skilled manpower. Various secondary effects would have to be taken into account, including the multiplier effect and any effect on inflationary pressure. There might also be important distributional effects, particularly in reducing poverty. The report surveyed empirical results of various studies elsewhere, but did not include any analysis of actual UK retraining programmes. Meanwhile Crossley and Ziderman carried out some preliminary analysis of the economic costs and benefits of adult retraining at government training centres,[15] which suggested that returns might be of the order of 30 per cent. A full-scale study has now been commissioned by the Department of Employment.

The Department has itself carried out some analysis of manpower policies, including the employment services (these could also be regarded as an information service). Thirlwall referred to this work in an article in 1969.[16] In this he identified three types of economic benefit: bringing employers and workers together more quickly so that the economy could operate with a smaller pool of unemployed, helping job seekers to find more productive jobs than they would otherwise have done, and reducing occupational, industrial and geographical imbalances in the labour market. It was suggested that in these ways the services would make possible a higher level of employment and growth without increased inflation or balance of payments disequilibrium.

The article referred to the problems of estimating these benefits numerically, and gave calculations of various break-even points at which benefits would equal costs. The first of these was concerned with the effect of the employment service as a whole; it was estimated that, to cover its costs in resource terms, the service would have to reduce the national pool of unemployed by 7,100. The other calculations were concerned with the marginal effect of additional placings. These were estimated to cost £6, and this cost would be covered (on certain assumptions) provided a man's productivity was increased by 0.4 per cent compared to what it would otherwise have been, or provided his re-employment was speeded up by 15 days. Although no evidence was given as to whether benefits did exceed these break-even points, the author commented that it seemed very probable that this was so, and that benefits could perhaps be increased more by improving the quality of placings than by speeding them up.

The Civil Service also has large training programmes for its own staff and needs to evaluate alternative methods. The Department of Health and Social Security is at present carrying out a cost-benefit study of the use of programmed learning instead of a conventional training course for executive and clerical staff assessing sickness, injury and maternity benefits. This study is considering the total costs of the alternative methods, including staff time, and any difference in working speeds and quality of performance after training.

HEALTH SCREENING

There has been some work in this country (and far more in the United States) on the cost-effectiveness of health services, but most of this has been concerned with cost minimization, for instance with how costs per case vary with throughput in hospitals. A few studies have, however, looked at differences in benefits, particularly economic benefits in the form of increased output and reduced medical costs as a result of prevention or improved treatment. For instance, the Office of Health Economics has done some studies of the economic costs and benefits of new forms of treatment for tuberculosis and pneumonia, and of immunization against poliomyelitis.[17] In the last case, the purely economic savings would only exceed costs if the number of cases would otherwise have remained at an unusually high level.

In 1967 the Nuffield Provincial Hospitals Trust carried out a study of various screening tests in this country,[18] including two types of cancer, deafness in children and pulmonary tuberculosis. The study estimated the costs of initial screening, further investigation of possible cases and treatment, including loss of output by those attending. Benefits included reduced cost of treatment owing to earlier diagnosis, and the prevention of premature death and disability. No attempt was made to put a money value on the social benefits of life and good health.

The study included a discussion of various ways in which the results could be related to policy options. Social and economic returns would vary with the way in which the population for screening was selected, the type of test used and the level of reaction taken as significant, so that analysis could improve the choice of methods of screening. It could also make possible comparisons between the cost effectiveness of screening for different diseases, and between screening and other health expenditure designed to achieve similar benefits, so that a better selection of projects could be made within a specified health programme. The report showed that the cost effectiveness of screening depends very much on the possibility of identifying high risk groups for screening, the reliability of the test (false positives mean additional expenditure on diagnosis), and the effectiveness of available treatment.

More recently Pole published an assessment of mass radiography. This suggested a method of assessing benefits from preventing future cases of disease, using changes in incidence over time as a way of measuring the rate of infection.[19]

The Department of Health and Social Security have also explored this method of evaluating screening in their study of the multiple health screening clinic at Rotherham.[20] In this case it was only possible to calculate costs to the health service, and the comparison was made between the costs per true positive case detected and the unquantified benefits of earlier detection for each of the tests performed. The report discussed the problems of evaluating economic benefits and costs to clients of attending, and also suggested that the financial costs to the National Health Service might understate the opportunity cost of the resources used.

Some of the studies described in this chapter, particularly in the health and education fields, mark a new departure in cost-benefit analysis into areas of social policy where many of the benefits, perhaps the most important ones, cannot at present be valued or even measured. There is clearly a danger that those effects which can be valued, for instance the impact on GNP of more education or reduced sickness, may be given undue weight. This is not an argument for refusing to quantify important effects which can be valued, but it does make it even more important that analysts should set out and draw attention to unquantifiable effects as well, and that decision-makers should recognize that the analysis is to assist and not to pre-empt their judgement. There may be many good reasons for selecting an alternative inferior to others on those items valued in money terms, including unquantified factors, distributional effects, uncertainty and the political costs and benefits; such a selection does not imply rejection of the cost-benefit approach. If there is any general conclusion to be drawn from this survey, it is perhaps that a good analysis always helps in reaching a decision, but rarely produces an obvious best choice.

REFERENCES

1 Heath, J. B. and Grossfield, K., 'The Benefit and Cost of Government Support for Research and Development: A Case Study', *Economic Journal* (September 1966).
2 Jones, P. M. S., 'The Evaluation of Government R & D Programmes', *R & D Management*, Vol. 2 (1971), No. 2.
3 Projects listed in written reply to Mr L. Reed, House of Commons Debate, November 20, 1970.
4 Dick, J. B., *Effectiveness of Some Recent Research at the Building Research Station U.K*, Building Research Station Paper CP 87/68 (HMSO, 1968).
5 Byatt, I. C. R. and Cohen, A. V., 'An Attempt to Quantify the Economic Benefits of Scientific Research', *Science Policy Studies*, No. 4 (HMSO, 1969).
6 Wolfe, J. N. and Youngson, A. J., *The Proposed 300 GeV Accelerator*, Cmnd. 3503 (HMSO, 1968).
7 Wolfe, J. N., *et al.*, 'Cost-Effectiveness in Secondary Information', Paper to a Seminar on Cost-Benefit Analysis, Edinburgh University, September 1970; reprinted in *Cost-Benefit and Cost Effectiveness* (London, George Allen and Unwin, 1972).
8 Hawgood J. and Morley R., *Project for Evaluating the Benefits from University Libraries* (University of Durham, 1969).
9 Blaug, M., Peston, M. and Ziderman, A., *The Utilization of Educated Manpower in Industry* (London, Oliver and Boyd, 1967).
10 Blaug, M., 'The Rate of Return on Investment in Education in Great Britain', *Manchester School* (September 1965); 'The Private and Social Returns on Investment in Education: Some Results for Great Britain', *Journal of Human Resources* (Summer 1967).
11 Maglen, L. and Layard, R., 'How Profitable is Engineering Education?', *Higher Education Review* (Spring 1970).
12 Morris, V. and Ziderman, A., 'The Economic Return on Investment in Higher Education in England and Wales', *Economic Trends* (May 1971).
13 Thomas, B., Moxham, J. and Jones J. A. G., 'A Cost-Benefit Analysis of Industrial Training', *British Journal of Industrial Relations* (July 1969).
14 Hughes, J. J., *Cost-Benefit Aspects of Manpower Retraining*, DEP Manpower Paper No. 2 (HMSO, 1970).
15 Ziderman, A., 'Costs and Benefits of Adult Retraining in the United Kingdom', *Economica* (November 1969).
16 Thirlwall, A. P., 'On the Costs and Benefits of Manpower Policies', *Employment and Productivity Gazette* (November 1969).
17 Office of Health Economics, *Progress Against Tuberculosis* (1962); *Pneumonia in Decline* (1963) *The Price of Poliomyelitis* (1963).
18 McKeowen, T., *et al.*, *Screening in Medical Care*, Nuffield Provincial Hospitals Trust (London, Oxford University Press, 1968).

[19] Pole, J. D., 'Mass Radiography: a Cost-Benefit Approach', *Problems and Progress in Medical Care*, Vol. 5 (1971).

[20] *Multiple Health Screening Clinic, Rotherham 1966: Social and Economic Assessment*, DHSS Reports on Public Health and Medical Subjects, No. 121.

PART IV

ORIGINAL CASE STUDIES

CHAPTER 8

THE BENEFITS OF RECREATION:
A SURVEY AND CASE STUDY

INTRODUCTION

Recreation is a growth industry. Those to whom it is essentially a private thing, meaning solitude or sport, prefer not to think of it like this, just as those who travel for pleasure prefer not to think of themselves as consumers of the product of one of the world's greatest industries. Nevertheless, the facts are clear. In the United Kingdom the total expenditure on entertainment and recreational services, other than the cinema, rose from £153m. in 1956 to £332m. in 1966 (1958 prices), an increase of 117 per cent, while real personal disposable income rose less than 50 per cent between 1950 and 1966. If population, prosperity and leisure continue to grow, much that was once free and unrestricted – such as access to the more popular places of recreation – may have to be regulated, and planned recreational opportunities will have to grow, either for their own sake or as a by-product of other kinds of development. Both trends have, of course, already begun.

One of the most powerful magnets has always been water, for sailing, fishing, swimming – and now for water ski-ing. Although we have lost a great deal through the pollution of rivers and of the coast, we are gaining from the growth of inland reservoirs. This study concerns the economics of fishing in a reservoir, and we may well preface it by some general remarks about the sport of angling* and the use of public water resources.

Everyone is familiar with those who sit day-long by the banks of rivers and canals, but few realize the numbers involved or the scale of the supporting activities, in terms of travel, equipment and publications. There are now some 2.5m. adult male anglers in Great Britain, 39 per cent of whom belong to angling clubs, and not only is the number steadily growing but the age level is steadily falling. It is in fact the most popular of all *participant* sports, being enjoyed by 14 per cent of the adult male population, as compared with 11 per cent for soccer, 8 per cent for golf, 6 per cent for cricket and 5 per cent for tennis. Over 50 per cent go fishing once a week, nearly 20 per cent once a fortnight and

* The terminology is confusing for the amateur. 'Angling' is a compendious term which includes hook and line fishing for coarse fish and fly-fishing for trout and salmon. The distinction is made between 'coarse angling' and 'game angling'.

about 15 per cent once a month. The average coarse angler now travels over 40 miles for his day's sport and the game angler over 60, both predominantly by private car; one very remarkable figure, showing the car's influence, is that in 1969 no fewer than 21 per cent of all anglers travelled over 200 miles, compared with 3 per cent in 1961.*

These, then are the 'customers'. Among the potential suppliers are the water authorities, to whom Water Resources Act of 1963 gave specific powers to provide recreational activities at reservoirs and on inland waterways and, most significantly for the purposes of this study, to charge for their use. More recently the Countryside Act of 1968 gave powers to statutory water undertakings 'to take steps to facilitate the use of their reservoirs and other waters for recreation'.

In studying the economics of fishing in a reservoir, we are not dealing, therefore, with one of the remoter by-ways of recreation, but with one of its major manifestations, and one in which public authorities can play an important part.

THE BENEFITS OF RECREATION

Why is it necessary to measure the benefits of recreational enjoyment in economic terms? Simply because the provision of recreational facilitates involves an economic cost in the sense that scarce resources of the community have to be devoted to making the enjoyment possible. Such costs may take the form of physical investment (e.g. fishing lodges, buildings for sailing clubs) or of administrative costs. A considerable part of the cost may be in the form of a necessarily more thorough treatment of water to make it ultimately drinkable. There are also likely to be conflicts between different potential recreation users of water resources – for example between anglers and week-end sailors. Because of the costs and the conflicts involved in recreation, it becomes necessary to estimate the benefits which different users derive from the recreation in order to decide which types of facilities will result in the greatest benefit and whether the total benefits exceed the cost of investment.

How then can we obtain an objective measure of the benefits of recreation? In a free market, consumers make their tastes felt through the prices they are willing to pay and the choices they make. Consumers have limited incomes, and they have to choose one good rather than another; prices reflect these choices. The fact that people are willing to pay more to fish at A rather than B is a piece of information to be used in determining how these consumers value the relative benefits of the two fisheries.

Objections have been voiced against the use of 'willingness to pay' as

* The source of this information is a survey undertaken in 1969 by Associated Industrial Consultants for the *Angling Times*.

a measure of the value of recreation. It has been claimed that recreation provides a subjective experience and that therefore any monetary valuation is inappropriate if not irrelevant; the view has been expressed in such words as

'Inspiration such as this cannot be measured in dollars and cents.'[1]

'Primary benefits from recreation are personal and varied and therefore not readily measurable in dollar terms.'[2]

But the benefits received from any good are personal, varied and subjective, though in most cases no objection is raised to the use of a price as an indicator of value. Although benefits are always subjective, the economist is able to make some objective assessment of a good's relative value in the market because consumers are constantly comparing one good with another and making their choices known by prices.

It will be noticed that the quotations just employed were transatlantic in origin, and since American economists have been experimenting since 1945 with ways of attaching monetary values to the benefits of recreation, something ought briefly to be said about their work. It will be seen from the examples which follow that a great deal of research has been done, by a variety of agencies, into a field of activity largely neglected until recently by British economists.

Some of the early methods were crude and unsatisfactory, for example the 'gross expenditure approach', which counted as benefits the total amount spent by those using water for recreation, including travelling, food and drink, accommodation and parking, as well as actual admission fees. For whether or not these sums are spent with the use of the recreation site as the ultimate objective, some of them would have been incurred in any case, and the services they bought had utility in their own right. The *reductio ad absurdam* of this method would be that recreation areas should be planned as far away as possible from centres of population so as to maximize benefits! Equally unsatisfactory was a method employed by the American National Park Service in 1950[3] which assumed benefits to be equal to some multiple of the cost of providing the facilities, so that all recreational projects appeared profitable, and moreover equally profitable, and there was no objective way of choosing between them. The *reductio ad absurdam* here is that to maximize benefits one should maximize costs.

A third method has been used by the Corps of Engineers in their analysis of the recreational use of beaches. They have made use of the fact that some beaches are privately owned and charged for, measuring the benefit of a public beach by what people are willing to pay for an equivalent private beach. The main difficulty here is that private recreation facilities tend to offer a different service, namely exclusiveness, and another bias arises by virtue of the fact that public facilities are provided free of charge and this tends to force downwards the price of private facilities.

According to the Outdoor Recreation Resources Review Commission,[4] the United States Forest Service has customarily made its decisions about recreational facilities on the basis of qualitative judgements, and many of the other agencies have at times used figures based at least partly on value judgements. The 1964 supplement to the US Senate Document 97[5] states that in Federal projects, the value of a 'general outdoor recreation day' (swimming, picnicking, boating, etc.) should lie in the range $0.5 to $1.5, while the value of a 'specialized outdoor recreation day' (hunting, etc., where large expenditures are involved on the part of the user and where intensity of use is low) should be between $2 and $6. These prices are intended to

'Measure the amount that users should be willing to pay if such payment were required to avail themselves of the project recreation resources.'

However, these values are essentially based on subjective judgement, not on objective evidence, and although they represent a consensus of opinion of experienced people they must still be considered arbitrary. They can only lead to uniformity of treatment in planning, but not to an economically correct treatment.

Ultimately, if he is to measure benefits, the economist must be able to determine what admission charges the public would be willing to pay, for this will help him to know what they are willing to sacrifice for the sake of the recreation itself. It will also give some guidance about the level of charges which will maximize a water undertaking's revenue from this source. A methodology which aimed to give this information was developed in the United States in 1958 by an American economist, Marion Clawson,[6] and since it has been adapted for the purposes of this study some account of it must be given.

Its purpose was to produce a demand curve which would show recreational benefits to be measured by reference to the criterion of 'willingness to pay'. Demand curves are commonly used to show a visual relationship between supply and demand in terms of price: they commonly indicate that as more goods are offered (or in this instance as more visits take place) the lower will be the price that will be charged for them. The shape of the curve indicates the nature of the demand. If it declines gradually, it indicates that new purchasers are readily available and that the decline in price will be slow; in which case the demand is said to be elastic. If it declines sharply, it indicates that utility diminishes rapidly and that the decline in price with increasing supply will be abrupt; in which case the demand is said to be inelastic (see Figure 8).

Clawson draws the distinction between the demand curve for the whole recreation experience (which is taken to include the planning, the journey, the visit to the site itself, any food and accommodation purchased, and the recollection of the day) and the demand curve for the recreation site *per se*. Then he proceeds to show how the latter can be derived from the former, which only requires data on the numbers of people participating in recreation and their geographical origin. The area surrounding a recreation site is divided into distance zones, by drawing concentric circles of different radii around the recreation site, and then it is necessary to discover how many visits are made from each zone. So as to eliminate the effect of differences in population, the number of visits from each zone is divided by the zone's population. The

Figure 8

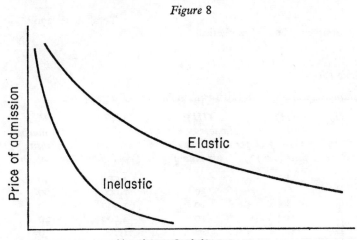

resulting visitation rates, together with estimates of the total monetary cost of a visit (including expenditure on food, drink, accommodation, etc.) from each zone form the cross-section data for the derivation of a demand curve for the whole recreation experience, for in effect they provide information on price (that is total cost) and quantity purchased (number of visits). The next task is the derivation of the demand curve for the recreation area *per se*.

The basic features of Clawson's methodology can be explained by a simple arithmetic example. The data shown in Table 12a are hypothetical and represent the initial situation at which no admission charge is made. If no admission charge is made initially, we have one point on the demand curve for the recreation site *per se*, namely the point where the admission charge is zero and the number of visits is 270. Now assume

Table 12a

Relationship of Visits to Costs

(I)	(II)	(III)	(IV)	(V)
	Cost of	Number of visits per 1,000 population		Total number of visits
Zone	visit (n.p.)	per season	Population	per season
A	20	50	1,000	50
B	40	40	2,000	80
C	60	30	3,000	90
D	80	20	2,000	40
E	100	10	1,000	10

Total visits: 270

Source of data: Hypothetical.

Table 12b

Relationship of Visits to Costs with Admission Charge of 20p

(I)	(II)	(III)	(IV)	(V)
	Cost of	Number of visits per 1,000 population		Total number of visits
Zone	visit (n.p.)	per season	Population	per season
A	40	40	2,000	40
B	60	30	2,000	60
C	80	20	3,000	60
D	100	10	2,000	20
E	120	0	1,000	0

Total visits: 180

Table 12c

Final Clawson Demand Schedule

(I)	(II)	(III)
Admission charge (n.p.)	Total visits	Total revenue (£)
0	270	0
20	180	36
40	100	40
60	40	24
80	10	8

an admission charge of 20p is made, meaning that costs are now raised to the levels shown in Table 12b. To discover the number of visits per 1,000 population at the new levels of cost, we must look back to Table 12a; at a cost of 40p (zone B) the visitation rate is 40, therefore as the cost from zone A is now 40p the visitation rate from that zone will now be 40 per 1,000 population. Similarly the new visitation rate from zone B will be equal to the old rate from zone C. At an admission charge of 20p then the visits will be as shown in Table 12b. The same procedure is repeated for further simulated increases in the level of the admission charge, and in this way we obtain the demand schedule for the recreation site itself as shown in Table 12c. This is the final Clawson demand schedule, which illustrates the impact of various levels of admission charges on the number of visits and therefore provides us with possible measures of the benefit of recreation. The total recreation benefits may be taken as either the maximum revenue obtainable at any one price (that is £800) or as the area under the demand curve (i.e. including the consumers' surplus).

This technique provides the basic methodology for the case study described below. Obviously it could be improved. Other factors than price affect the number of visits, for example income, leisure time available, age, and alternative opportunities for recreation. There is also the important factor of time, which could be as important as income. The visitation rate from zone A at a price of 20p will only be equal to the visitation rate from zone B at zero admission charge if the time costs, as well as the money costs, are equal. The failure to take account of this time constraint means that the visitation rate from zone A with a 20p admission charge is underestimated; similarly the number of visits from each zone for each simulated increase in price will be underestimated and therefore the final demand curve will be biased to the left of the true curve, hence resulting in an underestimate of benefits. However, despite these limitations, the resulting demand curve has the characteristics of a typical demand curve of economic theory.

THE GRAFHAM WATER STUDY

The aim of the case study was to apply the methods described above to measure the recreational demand for trout fishing at a reservoir. The reservoir selected is known as Grafham Water, and is situated about 2 miles west of the A1 road at Buckden in Huntingdonshire. It provides storage for the water abstracted from the Great Ouse, the total area of the land being 2,400 acres and of the reservoir itself 1,570 acres at top water level. Even before the passing of the Water Resources Act the Great Ouse Act of 1961 had given the Great Ouse Water Authority power to provide facilities for public recreation.

The nearest towns are Huntingdon (5 miles, 15,000 population), Bedford (15 miles, 68,000), Wellingborough (20 miles, 34,000), Peterborough (22 miles, 66,000), Northampton (30 miles, 124,000) and Leicester (50 miles, 267,000). North London is 50 to 60 miles away. The total population within a 60-mile radius of the reservoir is about 11 million.

The fishing is administered by the Water Authority, who have stocked the reservoir with brown and rainbow trout and have provided a fishing lodge for the use of anglers. Fishing was first permitted in 1966, and the data used in the present study relate to the 1967 season. Although there are a few season ticket holders, most of the anglers purchase day tickets at a price of £1 for bank fishing. Pulling boats and motor boats are available at additional charges of £2 and £5 respectively, and during 1967 the twenty boats were fully booked throughout the season. Altogether nearly 23,000 permits were issued.

The quality of the fishing has been reputedly good. In 1967 a total of over 32,000 fish were caught, the average weight of brown trout being 2 lb. 6 oz. and of rainbow trout 1 lb. 13 oz.; the largest fish caught was a rainbow weighing 7 lb. 6 oz. Every angler must sign his name and address in the anglers' register at the fishing lodge, and therefore there is an accurate record for each day of the number of fishermen and of their geographical origin. In addition all anglers are requested to fill in a record of their catch, and in 1967, 79 per cent actually did so.

The first task is to identify the factors which influence demand. The basic factor is *distance*. Clearly, the longer the journey, the fewer will undertake it; but this generalization needs to be tested and its implications more precisely determined. Anglers were therefore 'zoned' according to the addresses given on the daily fishing permits, and a mean distance calculated for each zone. As a preliminary test, thirteen towns were selected, the results being shown in Table 13. Unfortunately, these selective figures do not at first sight indicate a clear-cut relationship, because of the distortions in the cases of Northampton, Hertford, Oxford and Coventry. Such distortions could be caused, for example, by above average income levels or the existence of particularly well-organized angling clubs. Nevertheless, regression analysis showed a relatively high degree of correlation between distance and visitation rates, which could be interpreted to indicate that almost 70 per cent of the variation in visitation rates can be statistically ascribed to variations in distance. On the whole, the statistical results provided encouraging evidence to support the Clawson approach.

A more sophisticated exercise was then undertaken which had the effect of 'ironing out' some of the predominantly urban variations encountered above. In this case the total attendance at Grafham Water from all points of origin was analysed. The 23,000 issued licences were distributed in eight distance zones as shown in Table 14. Once again, regression analysis showed a high degree of correlation between distance and visitation rates: in this case distance accounts statistically for over 90 per cent of the variation in visitation rates. This higher degree of correlation than that obtained from the data in Table 13 is undoubtedly due to the fact that in large zones, individual differences in factors such as income are likely to cancel out to a large extent.

Table 13

Town	Distance (miles)	Visits per 10,000 of population
Bedford	13	56
Kettering	18	54
Cambridge	20	40
Northampton	25	128
Luton	30	13
Hertford	36	52
Leicester	42	8
London (North)	52	6
Oxford	55	12
Nottingham	60	6
Coventry	62	14
London (South)	65	3
Birmingham	70	3

Table 14

Zone	Mean distance from Grafham Water	Total visits 1967	Zone population	Visits per 100,000 of population
A (0–20)	10	4,005	680,510	589
B (20–40)	30	6,076	1,692,910	359
C (40–60)	50	7,206	8,863,505	81
D (60–80)	70	3,698	10,682,455	35
E (80–120)	100	1,237	13,246,460	9
F (120–160)	140	235	8,520,080	2.8
G (160–200)	180	39	3,208,910	1.2
H (over 200)	220	75	6,371,920	1.2

If we ask ourselves *why* distance seems to have an effect on whether we go fishing at a particular reservoir, the answer is that distance *itself* is not important, the important factor is the level of *cost* which distance implies. The data on distance therefore need to be converted to travel costs if a measure of benefits in monetary terms is to be obtained. However, certain difficulties arise as to what measure of costs to use.

First, in the present study, we have assumed that all visits to Grafham Water take place by car, although it is clear that a minority of anglers still use motor cycles and bicycles. However, in the absence of data on this point, we must make this assumption. (If data on other travel modes were available the results could be adjusted.) Which figure of costs is it which determines how many visits are made? Is it just the cost of petrol, the cost of petrol and servicing, or the average cost per vehicle-mile including depreciation? Economic theory tells us that the appropriate measure is the marginal cost of a visit, that is the extra cost which is attributable to the journey under consideration. Strictly speaking, this should be confined to the cost of petrol alone, which is a figure of 0.83p per mile. If, on the other hand, people attributed a full share of depreciation to their fishing trip, the cost would be nearer 4.17p per mile. The most sensible idea would seem to be to include all those costs which are normally termed 'running costs' which, on the definition of the Automobile Association, include petrol, oil, tyres, servicing and repairs and replacements; this cost, for a car with an engine capacity of 1001 to 1500 c.c. was estimated at 1.575p per mile. This figure was applied to the distances in column two of Table 15 for the return journey, a correction factor of 115/100 being applied to the straight line distances so as to make them more accurate estimates of true road distance.

One other assumption which was made regarding travel costs relates to vehicle occupancy rates. Clearly, several anglers may travel together in one car, and where this is the case, individual travel costs will be reduced. However, in the absence of information on this point and in view of the fact that angling is a 'solitary' sport, we feel that the assumption of a 1:1 car occupancy rate is not grossly unreasonable.

In addition to travel costs, certain other factors need to be considered in order to assess the total cost of a recreational experience. Some allowance needs to be made for the cost of food and drink. But people have to eat and drink anyway and a pilot survey of anglers showed that the differential cost was neither systematic nor significant. Accommodation, which is an element in Clawson's figures, is also insignificant, as very few anglers stayed away overnight.

Table 15 below tabulates the results obtained from the travel cost conversion. The 'total cost' column includes the cost of a day's fishing permit (100p). From this data, an equation of slightly different form from those previously used was calculated by using regression analysis. By referring to this equation, we can calculate the visitation rates expected from each zone at increasing fishing permit charges, then, by multiplying by population we obtain the number of visits expected. When this calculation is carried out for a number of increases in the fishing permit charge we derive a simulated demand schedule showing

Table 15

Zone	Length of return journey (miles)	Travel cost (n.p.)	Total cost (n.p.)	Visits per 100,000 population
A	23	36	136	589
B	69	110	210	359
C	115	181	281	81
D	161	253	353	35
E	230	362	462	9
F	322	507	607	2.8
G	414	652	752	1.2
H	506	797	897	1.2

the number of visits expected at different charges. The results of these calculations are shown in Table 16. From this data, the demand curve shown in Figure 9 can be drawn.

From this demand curve it is possible to estimate the total recreational benefits. The financial benefit to the Great Ouse Water Authority is simply the product of the number of visits expected and the admission charge (area BCDO) at a charge of 100p; the financial benefits are £21,143 per season. However, the consumers' surplus accruing to the

Table 16

Final Clawson Demand Schedule for the Recreation Site, 1967

Change in fishing charge from present level of 100p (n.p.)	Actual charge (n.p.)	Visits
0	100	21,143
20	120	15,837
40	140	12,270
60	160	9,734
80	180	7,865
100	200	6,447
120	220	5,347
140	240	4,477
160	260	3,755
180	280	3,194
200	300	2,737
220	320	2,345
240	340	2,014
260	360	1,736
280	380	1,499
300	400	1,295

Figure 9

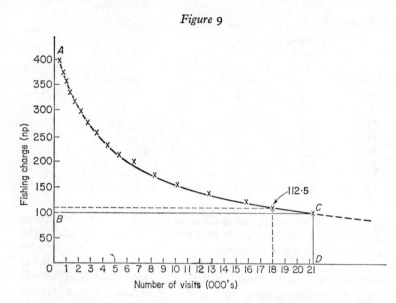

anglers, £18,801 (i.e. the amount they would have been willing to pay over and above 100p per visit, represented by area ABC), can be added to the financial benefit to arrive at an estimate of social benefit of £39,944 for the season.

Theoretically, it is possible to estimate the number of visits to be expected if the fishing charge is reduced, but this involves extrapolating the demand curve into an area where there are no observations, and this could be misleading since factors other than price may become more important in determining visitation rates as admission charges are reduced. However, in this case, the curve was extrapolated and it shows that the optimal charge for admission from the point of view of the Water Authority is 112.5p, which would produce revenue of about £22,700 per season.

Finally, it should be noted that measures of recreational benefits derived from the Clawson method described above are almost certainly underestimates because they fail to take account of the value of travel time. Without information about the values which anglers place on their travel time it was decided that the model should be recalculated to assess its sensitivity to different time values, namely 10p, 20p and 27.5p per hour (time costs for each zone being based on an average travelling speed of 40 m.p.h.) The demand schedules for each assumption about travel time cost are shown in Table 17. The gross recreational benefits (including consumers' surplus) in each case are:

(1) Time costs – 10p per hour: Benefits = £42,500.
(2) Time costs – 20p per hour: Benefits = £45,630.
(3) Time costs – 27.5p per hour: Benefits = £48,283.

Table 17

Final Clawson Demand Schedules for Different Time Valuations 1967

Change in fishing charge (n.p.)	Actual charge (n.p.)	Visits for time cost = 10p hour	Visits for time cost = 20p hour	Visits for time cost = 27.5p hour
0	100	21,032	20,945	20,952
20	120	16,211	16,515	16,739
40	140	12,871	13,374	13,722
60	160	10,448	11,056	11,463
80	180	8,621	9,779	9,718
100	200	7,209	7,883	8,332
120	220	6,092	6,761	7,211
140	240	5,195	5,849	6,293
160	260	4,459	5,093	5,521
180	280	3,856	4,461	4,871
200	300	3,349	3,923	4,321
220	320	2,921	3,473	3,854
240	340	2,468	3,079	3,442
260	360	2,244	2,741	3,087
280	380	1,975	2,445	2,777
300	400	1,739	2,187	2,501

These figures compare with benefits of £39,940 when the costs are assumed to be zero. Clearly, the system is not highly sensitive to different assumptions about time values, but the bias could be significant in a number of cases, especially where the decision to invest or not to invest in a recreation project is a marginal one.

This exploratory study of Grafham Water has shown how the Clawson methodology can be applied in practice, and the results, which appear to be intuitively reasonable, indicate that the approach offers some hope for the future development of recreation analysis. Clearly, many assumptions have had to be made, but many of these could be obviated by the existence of relevant data. Work is now going on to collect more data on anglers and to introduce more variables into the demand function. This seems to be one area of cost-benefit analysis where local authorities could make real progress. The technique need not be confined to water-based recreation – golf courses, multi-purpose sports centres and large swimming pools are examples of local authority developments which seem to be susceptible to this kind of approach.

REFERENCES

1 Outdoor Recreation Resources Review Commission (ORRRC), Study Report No. 3.
2 Trice and Wood, 'Measurement of Recreational Benefits', *Land Economics* (August 1958).
3 U.S. National Park Service, *A Method of Evaluating Recreational Benefits for Water Control Projects* (1950).
4 ORRRC, Study Report No. 24.
5 *Policies, Standards, and Procedures in the Formulation, Evaluation, and Review of Plans for Use and Development of Water and Related Land Sources*, 87th Congress, 2nd Session, Senate Document No. 97 (Washington, DC, 1962). See also *Evaluation Standards for Primary Outdoor Recreation Benefits*, Supplement No. 1 to Senate Document No. 97.
6 Clawson, M., *Methods of Measuring the Demand for and Value of Outdoor Recreation*, Reprint No. 10 (Washington, DC, Resources for the Future, 1959).

FURTHER READING

Mack, R. P. and Myers, S., 'Outdoor Recreation', in Dorfman, R. (ed.), *Measuring Benefits of Government Investments* (Washington, DC, Brookings Institution, 1965; London, Allen and Unwin, 1968).
Mansfield, N. W., 'The Estimation of Benefits from Recreation and the Creation of a New Facility', *Regional Studies*, Vol. 5 (1971), No. 2.
'The Estimation of Benefits Accruing from the Construction of a Major Recreational Facility', *Cost-Benefit Analysis in the Public Sector* (London, IMTA, 1971).
'Recreational Trip Generation', *Journal of Transport Economics and Policy* Vol. III, No. 2. (May 1969).
Smith, R. J. and Kavanagh, N. J., 'The Measurements of Benefits of Trout Fishing', *Journal of Leisure Research*, No. 4 (1969).

CHAPTER 9

URBAN REDEVELOPMENT AND THE SOCIAL COST OF SLUMS: A SURVEY AND CASE STUDY

INTRODUCTION

The common thread running through the previous chapters has been that a narrow economic criterion based on financial profitability is often irrelevant as a basis for decision-making in the public sector. This chapter continues the argument and is written in four distinct parts. First, it describes an established theoretical framework for the evaluation of urban redevelopment schemes, using the narrow profitability criterion. Secondly, it introduces a specific cost-benefit approach to the analysis of town centre redevelopment projects in Britain. Thirdly, it discusses the view that certain urban conditions (popularly described as 'slum' housing) involve the community in tangible social costs. And fourthly, it describes a recent attempt to devise a methodology aimed at measuring these social costs.

THE ECONOMICS OF URBAN RENEWAL: A NARROW VIEW

The objectives of urban renewal are many and varied. Each type of urban redevelopment process will therefore involve distinct sets of costs and benefits. This chapter is concerned with two types of urban renewal which are significant so far as local and central government in the United Kingdom are concerned, namely, town centre redevelopment, and programmes of slum clearance and rehousing. Generally, their economic problems have the same basic cause, the phenomenon of 'blight'.

The centres of many English towns and cities suffered heavily from bombing during the Second World War. The devastation of shopping and commercial centres provided a stimulus to large-scale redevelopment in the late fifties and early sixties. Added to this is the fact that most town centres were just not built to accommodate the huge influx of motor vehicles experienced in the sixties. This and other changes in social behaviour led many planners to believe that the outworn fabric of our town centres had to be replaced to cater for new demands. One interesting fact has, however, emerged from personal observation of the process of town centre redevelopment; this is that really large-scale and comprehensive redevelopment has not been an activity which the private market has been eager to promote (with certain notable exceptions, e.g. in London and one or two other large cities). It has been left to the local authorities to secure 'integrated' redevelopment of town centres, often at a financial cost to themselves as a result of subsidizing private enterprise.

Part of the explanation of this phenomenon may lie in an analysis of the causes of blight – especially housing blight. The problems of areas of old housing are, on the surface, similar in many respects to the problems of obsolescent town centres. The impact of industry and motor vehicles added to the factors of age and condition of the housing stock have had the result of turning many areas of housing (usually those areas in or near city centres) into 'slums'. The terms 'blight' and 'slum' are often used synonymously. However, this is based on a confusion of the *ethical* and the *economic*. The word 'slum' has ethical and emotional connotations which in many respects defy objective analysis. The word 'blight'* refers to a market situation which can be explained in economic terms. Whinston and Davis in their study 'The Economics of Urban Renewal',[1] attempted to define the nature of and explain the existence and persistence of blighted areas. Their objective in doing so was to provide a cost-benefit criterion to be used in evaluating urban renewal programmes.

Blight stems essentially from a situation where individual property owners, *acting rationally*, fail to keep their property in a state of adequate repair. Continuance of this kind of behaviour results in blighted property, and if neighbouring owners pursue such a course of action a whole neighbourhood may become blighted. Whinston and Davis stated three conditions by which blighted property could be identified. These are where:

(1) strictly individual action does not result in redevelopment;
(2) the co-ordination of decision-making via some means could result in redevelopment;
(3) the sum of benefits from renewal could exceed the sum of costs.

Why these conditions are important is now examined.

The slum clearance and re-housing programme of a local authority is a response to a number of pressures. In economic terms, it is a response to a peculiarity of the urban property market. The value of a piece of property, like a house, depends not only on its structural condition but also on attributes of the neighbourhood in which it is located. That part of the value which is due to its *location* is called the 'neighbourhood

* The concept of blight used here refers to a market phenomenon and is not to be confused with so-called 'planning blight' which can arise in an area because of local authority planning procedures.

effect value'. To maintain or increase the neighbourhood effect value requires the co-ordination of decisions of property owners as to repairs and improvement of their properties. Where such co-ordination is not possible, an individual property owner may reason that the benefits of repairs and improvement to his property may not exceed the costs of such repairs and improvements and so refrain from keeping his property in an acceptable state of repair.

The decisive factor in the mind of the property owner in reaching his decision is the state of repair and the improvements needed in surrounding properties. These may be such that the individual considers that they depress the neighbourhood effect value of his property so much that he has nothing to gain by committing his own resources to repairs and improvement. The paradox of this decision is that other property owners in the neighbourhood reason along the same lines and come to a similar conclusion about their own properties. The net effect of *all* their decisions is to lead to underestimation of the benefits to be gained from repairs and improvements. If, by chance, all had simultaneously engaged in repairs and improvements, the effect would be an increase in the neighbourhood effect value of each property. A like result could be produced if some means of co-ordination of individual decision-making had been visible. An important consequence of an individualistic calculation about the allocation of resources to repairs and improvements to properties in a neighbourhood is that it can result in a vicious circle of deteriorating structures changing the image of the neighbourhood, thereby reducing further the neighbourhood effect value of properties. This, in turn, may lead to further underestimation of the benefits of repairs and improvements needed, and so the vicious circle continues. The key feature of a blighted area is that co-ordination of decisions may result in the benefits of repairs and improvements exceeding the cost of such repairs and improvements. In the absence of co-ordination, the benefits are likely to be less than costs. Finding a means of co-operation is the key problem. Voluntary co-operation may or may not be too difficult where there are a few properties concerned. However, where there are a large number of properties, such co-operation is most improbable as some property owners may reason correctly that by opting out of a repair and development scheme they can realize some of the benefits of the decisions of other property owners without incurring any of the costs.

With voluntary co-operation unlikely to succeed, the next seemingly obvious solution is for a private developer to buy out all the properties and profitably undertake repairs and improvements. Such private development is likely to be frustrated by price gouging and stubborn tenants. Price gouging is particularly important where assembling tracts of land is an essential condition for redevelopment.

Voluntary co-ordination has, therefore, practical difficulties which would not exist if there were only one property owner, but a single property owner's attempts to develop may be frustrated. Unless these difficulties can be eliminated, a blighted area will persist. In these circumstances there is a role for the public sector. In some cases, the extreme position can be avoided by the application by local authorities of codes as to minimum standards of repair and upkeep of property, although such codes are extremely difficult to apply in practice. However, areas which are already severely blighted cannot be treated by preventive policies and the more usual action is for a local authority to use its powers of compulsory purchase in order to gain ownership of the whole area and engage in comprehensive demolition and redevelopment.

The whole point of cost-benefit analysis is to provide local authorities with a criterion with which they can make choices about priorities for redevelopment. Clearly, some areas are more blighted than others and the benefits of redevelopment may therefore be correspondingly higher. The criterion suggested by Whinston and Davis is one which considers solely the revenues and expenditures of a redevelopment project as the relevant benefits and costs. Their cost-benefit framework is a simple 'profit and loss account' (see Table 18), counting only the financial costs and benefits accruing to the local authority.

Table 18

Benefits	Costs
1. Receipts from sale of land to private developers.	1. Acquisition of land, demolition and site improvement.
2. Net additions to local authority tax revenues.	2. Cost of relocating (and compensating) displaced tenants.
3. Income from public amenities.	

There are two major criticisms to be made of this cost-benefit framework. The first derives from the distinction made earlier between the terms 'blight' and 'slum'. 'Blight' is defined by Whinston and Davis in terms of a misallocation of resources in a neighbourhood, whilst the term 'slum' is used to convey an ethical judgement about the physical conditions of a neighbourhood in which people live. The solution to the problem of blight is by means of a redevelopment programme, whilst the solution to slums may well be achieved by means of an income redistribution policy. However, it can usually be shown empirically that a blighted area contains a preponderance of defective, unsafe, insanitary and overcrowded dwellings – conditions usually associated with the popular conception of a slum. The cost-benefit framework in Table 18 does not identify the wider social effects arising from these conditions. It may well be the case that the spillover effects of physically poor housing may impose costs on a community. Clearly, these factors should be considered in any cost-benefit analysis of housing redevelopment proposals in order to make the 'best' set of choices. This argument is developed further later in this chapter.

The other criticism made of the 'profit and loss criterion' is that it only takes account of the financial benefits and costs accruing to the *local authority*. It makes little attempt to identify the impacts of redevelopment schemes on the many sectors of the community affected, and this sort of information is vital to decision-makers concerned with the complex issues of large-scale redevelopment. One approach to this particular problem is described below.

TOWN CENTRE REDEVELOPMENT: A SPECIAL CASE OF COST-BENEFIT ANALYSIS

The methodology developed by Professor Nathaniel Lichfield is not primarily concerned with *measurement* of benefits and costs, although some progress has been made in this respect. The main emphasis has rather been on the issue of the *incidence* of benefits and costs, i.e. who receives the benefits and who bears the costs of public investment decisions concerned with large-scale redevelopment. This is merely a recognition of the fact that no matter what economists might like to think, decisions on the allocation of public resources are not usually taken on economic grounds alone. In a democratic society, these complex decisions must, in the final analysis, be taken by politicians who are swayed more by *people* than by economic analysis. It is not enough to be told that the discounted net present value of scheme A exceeds that of scheme B. 'Value to the community' is not a meaningful criterion to the politician – he is often more concerned with the effects of public decisions on groups of people *within* it.

Town centre redevelopment is a perfect example of a complex decision situation which responds to this sort of analysis. A town centre scheme affects many different (and overlapping) sectors of the community: shoppers, shopkeepers, pedestrians, car drivers, house owners, office workers and many others. Apart from considering how any redevelopment scheme is likely to affect these groups of people, the decision-maker will have to weigh other factors, some of which are tangible (e.g. the effect on the finances of the local authority), and some of which are rather more imponderable (e.g. the 'prestige' value of any scheme). The rest of this section describes briefly how Lichfield treats some of these complex issues and how the decision-making process can be assisted by the drawing up of a 'planning balance sheet' which attempts to present the choice to be made in terms of the effects of a decision on different groups and organizations within the local community.

As stated earlier, the essence of Lichfield's methodology is to identify the impacts of a redevelopment scheme on various homogeneous groups within the community, and wherever possible to make a comparative assessment of these impacts in quantitative terms. The corollary to this, of course, is that the decision-maker, faced with this information, is able to make a choice in the light of the weight or significance he attaches to each of the various sectors of the community identified in the analysis.

The first stage in the analysis is to enumerate the various groups affected by the project. These are classified as either 'producers' (groups who produce or operate the project) or 'consumers' (groups who consume the services produced by the project). So far as is possible, each producer is linked directly to a consumer; for instance, in the case of a town centre redevelopment project, current property owners who are to be displaced are classed as producers and the new occupiers are classed as the corresponding consumers. Each pair of producers and consumers may be considered as engaging in a 'transaction', as a result of which each side incurs costs and receives benefits. These costs and benefits can be valued in many cases at market prices, especially so far as producers (e.g. local authorities) are concerned. However, some categories of costs and benefits to consumers have no market price. In these cases, Lichfield advocates that they should be included in the planning balance sheet as dimensions of utility or welfare (usually a crude ranking or preference system). It is recognized that failure to measure these costs and benefits in monetary terms places a limitation on the planning balance sheet as a basis for decision-making. However, there is no doubt that this approach highlights the number and the kind of value judgements which the decision-maker has to make in coming to a final decision. The balance sheet presents for his information all the groups involved in a public decision, and the differences in all their respective costs and benefits (where possible in absolute monetary terms, or otherwise in relative terms). With this information, he is in a position to make a decision in accordance with some concept of 'equity', and he is able to discern the cost (if any) of the decision in terms of 'efficiency'.

THE SOCIAL COST OF SLUMS: A SURVEY

In addition to identifying the impact of redevelopment proposals on various groups in the community, it is obviously important to make some attempt to measure the spillover costs and benefits involved in the decision, many of which are usually considered as 'intangible'. The narrow profit and loss criterion does not take account of these wider social effects and little research has been undertaken to *measure* the spillover effects of slum housing redevelopment.

The association of certain social effects and slum housing conditions has fascinated researchers for many years. Many empirical studies have shown (especially in the USA) that slum areas exhibit rates of illegitimacy juvenile delinquency, violent crime, mental illness, residential fires, tuberculosis and other communicable diseases far in excess of the average for major cities. The data shown in Table 19 relating to Los Angeles in 1944 are typical. Ignoring for the moment the issue of *causality* (i.e. do slum housing conditions create these social pathologies?), the association of housing conditions and social pathology clearly has implications for local authorities, concerned as they are with the provision of public services to alleviate ill-health and to combat crime and fire.

Table 19

Incidence Per 10,000 Persons

	Blighted Area	'Good' Area
Tuberculosis	705	91
Communicable diseases	69	14
Venereal diseases	13	1
Health service visits	356	54
Fire alarms	256	142
Police arrests	350	100
Juvenile delinquency cases	69	10

Source: Rumney, J., 'The Social Cost of Slums', *Journal of Social Issues*, Vol. VII (1951), Nos 1–2.

Rothenberg was one of the earliest writers to consider this question in cost-benefit terms.[2] He saw two types of social costs arising from slums: costs to the slum dwellers themselves and costs to the community at large. His view is summarized as follows:

'Given overcrowding, filth and inadequate sanitary facilities, slums are a health menace, increasing the frequency and severity of illness for both inhabitants and outsiders through contagion. Through subsidized medical care for some slum dwellers, the costs are borne in part by the tax payer. Other costs are borne at large through the effect of illness on the welfare of individual citizens and on the overall productivity of the economy.

'Slums breed crime: overcrowding and lack of privacy tends to undermine respect for the individual and for property, create frustration over the constant obtrusion of others, and promote opportunities for crime and recruitment into criminal sub-cultures.

'Personality difficulties result from poverty, despair and bitterness, and hinder many in their attempts later in life to join the dominant culture of society.'

Such a generalized statement is, however, of only limited assistance in practical terms. The real crux of the problem, is, of course, as always in cost-benefit analysis, the *measurement* of social cost. If we enumerate the social costs of slums as (a) increased fire hazards, (b) increased menace to health and social welfare of inhabitants of the slums and the city or town in which they are treated, (c) increased crime rate, and (d) personality difficulties, then we must attempt to include meaningful assessments of these factors in any analysis of alternative slum clearance/redevelopment programmes. The next section describes some of the difficulties of quantification which were encountered in our own research exercise. The remainder of this section reviews some earlier empirical studies which provided valuable insights into some of the problems.

Although Rothenberg was one of the first to see the relevance of social costs to the selection of housing redevelopment projects, he was not notably successful in providing quantitative estimates of such costs for use in analysis. Table 20 shows the cost-benefit framework used in his appraisal of five housing redevelopment projects. Clearly, the part of the analysis which was capable of evaluation is very similar to the narrow profitability criterion of Whinston and Davis. Item 2(b), the spillover effect on neighbouring land, is included in the analysis on the argument that the value of the housing services provided by a dwelling unit is a function not only of the unit itself, but also of the character of the surrounding neighbourhood (this is what Whinston and Davis call the neighbourhood effect value). A redevelopment project will therefore lead to an improvement in quality of *surrounding* dwelling units, and this improvement should be included as a social benefit in the analysis. The twin problems of determining the extent of the 'impact neighbourhood' (the cut-off point) and measuring the improvement benefit were found by Rothenberg to be extremely complex and, although methods of solving the problems were suggested, no numerical results were obtained for inclusion in the table. So far as item 2(c) is concerned, Rothenberg was content simply to acknowledge that the quantification problem requires a treatment that goes far beyond the scope of his study. However, although no measurements appear in Table 20, he did sketch out the nature of some of the social costs identified earlier (fire risk, health hazard, crime and personality difficulties).

An estimate of the benefit of reduced fire risks may be obtained by comparing the total value of fire damage and the value of fire protection services in slum areas with that in non-slum areas. Property damage data may be available in many cases and the value of human life lost and damaged can be estimated, although some controversy surrounds the issue. Differential fire protection costs can be roughly approximated to actual fire department expenditures, although actual service levels might in any case be inadequate in slum areas as opposed to non-slum areas. The slum health hazard can be measured in two ways: (a) the value of medical goods and services, and (b) the value of human life and costs imposed by illness. Both methods have disadvantages. The level of

Table 20

Benefit/Cost Summary of Five Redevelopment Projects in Chicago ($000)

Benefit and cost categories	Blue Island	Hyde Park 'B'	Hyde Park 'A'	Michael Rees	Lake Meadows
1. Resource cost of project					
(a) Gross project costs	396	638	10,534	6,235	16,761
(b) Less initial value of land	46	49	6,449	1,596	8,777
(c) Total resource costs	350	589	4,085	4,639	7,984
2. Benefits produced by the project					
(a) Increased productivity of site land	29	30	5,016	1,719	12,711
(b) Increased productivity of neighbouring real estate (spillover)	+	+	+	+	+
(c) Decreased social costs associated with slums	+	+	+	+	+
3. Total costs not offset by site land benefit (1c–2a)	321	559	−931 (gain)	2,920	−4,727 (gain)

police protection will probably bear a closer relationship to the amount the public is willing to pay to avoid losses due to crime than the level of services in the two previous categories. However, in practice it would seem reasonable to assume some correlation between the police budget and the cost of crime. The costs of personality and social adjustment difficulties pose very special measurement problems. The influence of housing conditions on family and social relationships cannot be described in terms of black and white, and it is probably wise to be realistic and accept that quantified assessments of these effects are not likely to be forthcoming in the near future.

Another illustration of cost-benefit analysis in redevelopment projects is provided by a study undertaken by Mao[3] in relation to a housing project in East Stockton, California. Table 21 sets out measured benefits and costs of the project.

Table 21

Summary of Tangible Social Benefits and Costs of the East Stockton Urban Renewal Project ($000)

Benefit	Amount ($)	Cost	Amount ($)
1. Increase in the value of project area land	228	1. Survey and planning	113
2 Increase in the value of neighbourhood properties	416	2. Project execution expenditures (a) Administrative, travel and office furniture	202
3. Value of public improvements: schools and parks*	823	(b) Legal services (c) Acquisition expenses, salaries of relocation staff and other related	114
4. Reductions in costs of municipal services (a) Savings in fire protection cost	700	items (d) Site clearance	387 93
(b) Savings in health protection costs	425	(e) Disposal, lease, retention costs (f) Project inspection	59 33
(c) Savings in police protection cost	1,167	(g) Value of improvements demolished	2,342
		3. Site improvements	701
		4. Public and supporting facilities	552
		5. Relocation payments	85
	3,759		4,681

* It is assumed that these public investments have social values equal to their costs. On the right side of the table, these costs are included under 3 and 4 (dates of reckoning have been omitted).

It will be noted that the Mao table refers to *tangible* benefits and costs of the project. This is a reminder that only items capable of measurement have been included in the cost-benefit framework. It would seem that Mao has gone somewhat further than Rothenberg in providing monetary estimates of benefits and costs. But many of his measures are not wholly satisfactory from a conceptual point of view. Some figures in Table 21 may therefore be but a crude monetary measure of the appropriate concept.

The Rothenberg and Mao studies relate to renewal or replacement housing projects. Under the provisions of a recent Housing Act greater emphasis is now being placed on rehabilitation instead of renewal. The background to this shift is discussed in *Old Houses into New Homes*.[4] With the passing of this Act there should be greater scope for the use of code-enforcement procedures to improve housing conditions. Some of the difficulties of code-enforcement have been mentioned earlier. On the positive side, code-enforcement is usually assumed to be the least costly and most convenient method for both the city and its property owners to achieve better quality housing, whilst lessening the threats

Table 22

Estimated Tangible Costs and Benefits of a 10-Year Code Enforcement, Neighbourhood Rehabilitation, and Property Conservation Programme, Beacon Light District, 1965

Estimated Costs	$000
1. Costs of administering the programme	2,100
2. Public expenditures to provide improved public services and facilities	11,500
3. Private expenditures	
(a) Repairs and rehabilitation of properties	8,100
(b) Demolitions	900
Total estimated costs	22,600
Estimated Benefits	
1. Reduction in city service costs	6,900
2. Increases in private property values	31,900
3. Increases in property tax revenues	6,400
Total estimated benefits	45,200

to public health and safety posed by decayed housing. The merits and demerits of code-enforcement have long been argued, but in the end the advantages one way or the other can only be resolved by examining a code-enforcement project against a renewal project for the neighbourhood in question.

The main problem then is to decide a cost-benefit framework for a code-enforcement renewal programme. Case[5] suggests a possible framework and provides estimates of tangible costs and benefits for a project relating to the Beacon Light District in California. The results are summarized in Table 22.

Before leaving Case's results, it is of interest to reproduce some other results from his paper. The Beacon Light District, he notes, conforms to the pattern of a blighted area. Public expenditures are much greater and tax revenues much lower than in other areas of the City of Los Angeles, as can be seen from the data in Table 23. The collection of this type of information is a prerequisite to the use of cost-benefit analysis in housing project selection, but as anyone with a cursory knowledge of local government finance will know, requests for information of this type are likely to be met with a blank stare by treasurers and accountants in many local authorities in Britain.

Table 23

Direct Per Capita *Expenditures in the Beacon Light Study Area, 1965*

| | Per capita *cost* | | |
| | Beacon Light | | |
Type of expenditure	Dollar totals ($)	As percentage of Los Angeles expense (%)	City of Los Angeles ($)
Police	36.87	180	20.49
Refuge and sewage disposal	4.34	100	4.34
Public assistance	34.58	864	4.00
Fire service	14.04	105	13.33
Parks and recreation	3.90	84	4.52
Street maintenance	7.16	100	7.16
Education	5,020.86	153	3,280.97
Health	4.48	188	2.38
Other items	24.60	100	24.60

The role of cost-benefit analysis as reviewed here places emphasis on the spillover or external effects associated with unsatisfactory housing conditions. These effects are reflected in *real* costs, not only to the individuals living in them and the local community, but also to the wider community of which they are a part. Which categories of externalities are important in British housing conditions is difficult to say. The subjective evidence of social workers in the field varies, whilst quantitative evidence is scanty and results can usually be queried on methodological grounds. This raises the whole question of causality which has been neglected until now. The causal relationship between slum living and external social costs is complicated and interrelated with other causal factors. For example, standards of health are influenced by such factors as income, occupation, ethnic background, age and environment, factors which *themselves* are interrelated. Fire risk is not only a function of housing conditions, it depends also on human behaviour. A redevelopment project may demolish buildings, but it only *redistributes* the human population. Furthermore, information about these factors, whether qualitive or quantitative, is often imprecise and the probabilistic element in the relationships makes it difficult to distinguish between pure chance and significant variations. Most of the empirical studies which have been carried out have found that shifting social factors tend to obscure the statistical relationships found between classes of housing conditions and health. What *is* certain is that an enormous research effort will be needed to make any impact on these problems.

THE HARINGEY CASE STUDY

The Haringey study was an attempt to examine the problems of measuring the social cost of slums. It is necessary, however, to make one initial qualification to what follows – no serious investigation of the causality issue was attempted. Such an investigation would have required a far more ambitious investment in interdisciplinary research effort than was available to the RIPA research team.

The study started from an investigation of a so-called 'twilight area' in the London Borough of Haringey. The houses in the area were 70–90 years old and generally too large for single family use. The area was experiencing a great deal of multiple occupation, in the sense that, although houses became occupied by several households, they were not physically adapted to maintain acceptable standards. The *structural* condition of most of the houses was reasonably good and many of them had a remaining life of 25–30 years. From a policy point of view, three alternative solutions were possible:

(1) undertake early comprehensive rehabilitation of the area;
(2) undertake early demolition and renewal;
(3) postpone demolition and undertake renewal at a future date when constraints on (2) are not operative.

Using a purely financial investment criterion, the choice between (1) and (2) could be determined along lines suggested by formulae developed by Needleman.[6] Such formulae were subsequently incorporated into MHLG Circular 65/69 under the 1969 Housing Act which followed up *Old Houses into New Homes*. However, because of constraints, only (1) and (3) could be considered as feasible policy alternatives. Under a postponed renewal policy, the council would merely have been required to maintain minimum code-enforcement standards (with regard to health, sanitation, fire regulations, multiple occupation, etc.). The question therefore arose as to whether this kind of policy would result in significant *social* costs to the community which might be avoided if *immediate* comprehensive rehabilitation were undertaken. It is this question to which our study was addressed.

There were two distinct parts to the problem. First, it was necessary to assess the externalities of bad housing conditions in *physical* terms. Secondly, it was thought desirable to evaluate these externalities in terms of money in order to assess the scale of social cost incurred. We saw earlier that previous American research into these questions had not gone very far, so any attempt to identify even the existence of these externalities in British conditions clearly had to start in unexplored territory. Our first objective, therefore, was to determine by empirical investigation whether the general statements about bad housing conditions and their alleged externalities could be supported. The original intention was to undertake an exercise similar to that illustrated in Table 19, i.e. some kind of cross-sectional analysis to determine whether areas of 'bad' housing exhibited different social characteristics from areas of 'good' housing. The first major difficulty presented itself immediately. The problems involved in delineating 'bad' and 'good' housing areas proved to be a major obstacle and so the scope of our inquiry had to be widened to attempt to provide a measure of housing quality against which to compare measures of the physical incidence of externalities.

The objective of the case study was therefore an extremely limited one in terms of cost-benefit analysis. In a nutshell, it was to explore the feasibility of estimating statistically significant relationships between quantitative measures of housing quality and various aspects of social behaviour which could be described as spillover effects of housing conditions. Our feeling was that if a link could be established between housing quality and such factors as crime rates, fire incidence and other social pathologies, then knowledge of the impact of public investments designed to improve housing standards would have taken a step forward, paving the way for more ambitious attempts at cost-benefit analysis in this field.

In the light of the novelty of the study, to us at least, a pragmatic approach seemed to offer a fruitful source of investigation. This took the form of contacting departments of the local authority and other community services as seemed appropriate (police, probation and fire services). It became apparent from discussions with many of the officers of the services concerned that there was no clear answer to the causality aspect of the study. Experiences of different officers varied; however, it became clear that any investigation in depth would require the examination of a wide range of data. This was not always possible because of confidentiality requirements, the type of data kept by the service departments and the length of time records were kept, as well as the form in which they were kept. The striking feature that emerged was the absence of comprehensive information systems likely to be of use in cost-benefit studies. The data collected are summarized in Appendixes 1 and 2. It is important to emphasize that these data represent what it was possible to collect over a period of 9 months with the co-operation of several local authority departments and the police, probation and fire services.

From the outset it was clear that it was not operationally useful to talk about 'slums' and 'twilight areas'. Instead, it was decided to think in terms of an index of housing quality, and therefore the first task was to find criteria for measuring housing quality. An examination of previous attempts to do this revealed a broad measure of agreement on the principal factors to be considered, namely, the level of amenities offered by a housing structure, its physical condition, and the intensity at which it is used, i.e. the level of occupation. However, the *relative* contribution of each of these factors to the *overall* assessment of housing quality is a matter which has to be agreed. In the construction of an index of housing quality, a system based upon penalty scores for deficiencies is often favoured, and this was the approach we adopted. In the absence of a universally agreed weighting system, we decided to allot a penalty weight to each deficiency in accordance with our own value judgements (these weights are shown in Appendix 1). It was felt that factors associated with the *level of occupation* were of greater significance in the assessment of housing quality than the physical condition of the dwelling structure (i.e. state of internal and external repair), which in turn was considered to be more important than the lack of any single amenity such as a bath or shower. (It is a matter of simple arithmetic to recalculate the index with different penalty weights.)

The index shown at Appendix 1 is based on *weighted* housing penalty scores for the *electoral wards* of the London Borough of Haringey. The use of such large areas was an unfortunate necessity, governed more by considerations of data availability and compatibility than by the research objectives. Data from two secondary sources (the 1966 Census and the Housing Age and Condition Survey of the GLC) were used to obtain measures of the percentage of the housing stock in each ward which was 'deficient' in any of the indicators of housing quality covered by the index. This percentage was then multiplied by the penalty weight assigned to that deficiency to produce a penalty score. Consider as an example hot water facilities: 8.2 per cent of the dwellings in ward A were shown to have no hot water facility; the penalty weight assigned to this deficiency was 6, and the penalty score for the deficiency was calculated as 49.2 (8.2 × 6). Individual penalty scores were aggregated first to give penalty scores for amenities, condition and occupancy, which together made up the total penalty score on which wards were ranked. The lowest penalty score (ward A) indicates the highest level of housing quality (ranked 1) and vice versa.

The index revealed a number of interesting features. The ward rankings produced bore a close resemblance, at least at the two extremes of the scale, to subjective assessments of comparative housing conditions made by the council's officers. This fact encourages the opinion that the factors included in the index and the penalty weights assigned to each are reasonable as a basis for quantitative assessment. It is also clear that there is no consistent relationship between existence of amenities, the condition of dwellings, and the level of overcrowding. The area designated as a twilight area has a high penalty score, and the ward of which it forms a part is ranked eighteenth in terms of overall housing quality. However, its major deficiency is shown to be the high percentage of above-average occupancy levels and shared accommodation; in this respect, it is by far the worst area in the Borough. In terms of amenities and physical condition, however, it is by no means abnormal.

Having established a basis for a quantitative inter-ward comparison of housing quality, the next stage in the exercise was to obtain measures of various social activities which may give rise to external effects. If it could be shown that wards with 'poor' housing quality produced a high incidence of certain social pathologies, a *prima facie* case could ultimately be put forward for the measurement of housing externalities in so far as they involve resource costs to the community.

We were able to obtain data for only five types of social pathology. Appendix 2 ranks wards in terms of these five characteristics, which are discussed individually below. It is important to emphasize that there was nothing definitive about selecting these particular types of social stress; it merely happened that we were able to collect and process data relating to them.

Several studies undertaken in the United States have indicated the existence of a significant statistical relationship between slum housing conditions and high crime rates. For this reason, considerable effort was put into analysing crime in Haringey by ward areas in the hope that the pattern which emerged would bear some resemblance to comparative housing quality. The results clearly disappointed our hopes for they do not support a consistent relationship between our measures of housing conditions and crime rates experienced in the electoral wards of Haringey. For instance, the area with the best housing conditions, ward A, is almost the worst area in terms of crimes committed per thousand population, and the worst housing area ranks only midway in the crime table. However, these rather confused results may in large part be explained by the type of data available. The available data related to the physical incidence of indictable crime in Haringey in 1966. This information was then analysed by ward and the result gives a picture of the location and incidence of crime in the borough. It is not, therefore, surprising that the figures show that the area offering the richest pickings attracts a lot of crime. Ideally, the measure of crime which should have been used is not one based upon the geographical location of the offence, but one based on the neighbourhood of origin of the *criminal*. It was unfortunately not possible to obtain such information for two reasons: (a) it would require a 100 per cent detection rate for all types of crime – for obvious reasons such a detection rate is not practicable, and (b) it is police policy not to disclose the addresses of criminals in research exercises of this nature. In fact, therefore, our statistics relate only to the neighbourhood origin of reported crime and the use of this measure in UK conditions may well have blurred the statistical evidence. A more detailed analysis of the data did reveal some evidence of a link between bad housing conditions and certain types of crime, notably some categories of petty larceny (stealing milk bottles and robbing gas meters!). However, factors such as police 'purges' on certain offences (e.g. shoplifting) tended to further distort the figures. One final point to be made is that parallels with American experience in this field are rather dangerous. Compared with crime rates in the USA, the situation in Britain, especially in the area of *violent* larceny and physical assault which might reasonably be considered as 'slum-oriented', is nothing like so bad. In these circumstances it is not altogether surprising that our results did not tend to confirm the results of similar investigations in the United States.

Data on juvenile delinquency in the Borough were also collected. The data made available related to the *stock* of cases on the books of the Probation Service at the end of 1968. Once again, the data were not ideal – it is clear that the Probation Service does not deal with *all* delinquents but only with those who are apprehended and assigned to probation officers by the courts. However, this time we were at least able to obtain information on the location of the delinquent rather than the location of the offence. However, once again the results are not consistent with our initial hypothesis. It was clear from talking to probation officers at the outset that the major problem areas for juvenile delinquency were not the areas with the worst physical housing conditions. They considered that post-war housing estates with their relative lack of social and community facilities for young people had the worst record of juvenile delinquency. Our investigation confirmed this. Wards C, I and L all include substantial areas of local authority housing and exhibit relatively low levels of housing stress. Yet the delinquency problems in these areas are more serious than in many areas with poorer housing conditions.

The data and results relating to the incidence of fires were more encouraging. It is possible to detect a positive relationship between housing quality and fire incidence by examining the respective ward rankings in Appendix 2, e.g. ward A is the best housing ward and ranks second so far as fire incidence is concerned. (A rank correlation exercise produced a coefficient of rank correlation of 0.62.) However, it was not possible to analyse the fire data by cause of fire, i.e. chimney fires and fires caused by cooking were included along with types of fire which could be caused by bad housing conditions, e.g. fires caused by oil heating appliances and faulty electrical wiring. If it had been possible to isolate these occurrences, it seems probable that a more detailed analysis would have improved the results.

The other broad area for which we were able to collect data was the local authority social services, i.e. the welfare of the aged and the care of deprived children. The results in Appendix 2 do not show a consistent positive relationship between the incidence of children or old people taken into local authority care and the quality of housing. Yet again, there are obviously many causal factors involved and housing condition is likely to be only one of them, especially in regard to the incidence of children taken into care through the influence of bad housing on parental relationships and personality difficulties.

In considering other possible areas of social behaviour in which housing might be considered a factor, discussions were held with officers of several departments of the local authority. Data problems became a serious constraint at this stage. The impact of housing conditions on health, both physical and mental, was clearly a strong contender for investigation. However, it proved impossible to collect the necessary data during the course of the study. Certain diseases, notably tuberculosis, are nurtured in conditions of dark and damp housing, and improvements in domestic sanitation have of course played an important part in reducing the incidence of other diseases in this country. In the absence of empirical investigation, it is only possible to speculate that a significant link between housing and physical health would not be substantiated, except possibly in very small and localized areas of appallingly low housing quality. Fortunately, areas of this type are relatively few and far between in our cities today.

The case of *mental* health is rather different. It seems likely that housing conditions play an important part in many kinds of mental illness. However, it is not necessarily the *quality*, as measured by our index, which is the key factor – modern blocks of high-rise apartments would clearly score a low mark for housing deficiency as defined here. There is increasing evidence that the breakdown of traditional community relationships (often seen at their best in so-called 'slum' areas) is the basic causal factor in many cases of mental illness. This should serve as a salutary reminder to the planners that merely to improve the quality of the *physical* environment does not by itself guarantee an improvement in the 'quality of life'.

One final area which we hoped would produce numerical results is concerned with the educational development of children. However, in the event, it was not possible to obtain data. In any case we found considerable difficulty in establishing which sort of data available to us could be used as a surrogate for educational achievement. Many educational experts now believe that poor housing conditions, especially overcrowding, have a major influence on a child's educational standards. The causal element involved here is intuitively more obvious than in most of the other social characteristics considered in this study and, with hindsight, it is clear that the research should have concentrated more heavily on this aspect.

Appendix 3 is an attempt to summarize all the results in order to compare an index of social stress with the index of housing stress. The indices are different from those in Appendixes 1 and 2 in that each ward

Figure 10

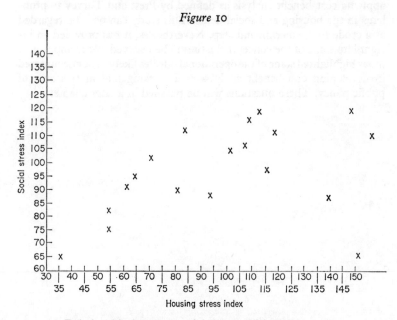

Relationship between social stress and housing stress.

is expressed as a percentage of the whole borough average. In spite of the fact that no positive relationship between the two indices can be claimed in terms of *statistical* significance, it is clear from Figure 10 that social stress generally does increase with housing stress. This is not a particularly world shattering conclusion, yet it does give some basis for encouragement of further work in this field. Such research will need to overcome two major difficulties (a) the problems of establishing purely *quantitative* measures of social pathologies, and (b) the shortcomings of much of the available data. Both types of problem were experienced during this exercise. However, the statistical validity of the results would probably have been much improved if data relating to smaller geographical areas than electoral wards could have been used. Most of the wards contained a mixture of different types of housing, exhibiting fairly wide-ranging conditions. It is possible that analysis of data by enumeration district might have produced more positive correlations of housing quality with some of the social pathologies identified. It is certainly probable that analysis on these lines would provide local authorities with a useful guide to establishing priorities in policies for housing renewal and rehabilitation.

Nevertheless, the final conclusion must be that we are a long way from applying cost-benefit analysis as defined by Prest and Turvey to problems in the housing and social fields. This study can only be regarded as a crude first experimental step. Nevertheless, it has provided an insight into some of the conceptual issues to be resolved. More important, it has highlighted some of the operational hurdles likely to be encountered in developing cost-benefit analysis as a working tool in this area of public policy. These questions will be pursued in a later chapter.

REFERENCES

[1] Davis, O. A. and Whinston, A. B., 'The Economics of Urban Renewal', *Law and Contemporary Problems* (Winter 1961).
[2] Rothenberg, J., *Economic Evaluation of Urban Renewal* (Washington, DC, Brookings Institution, 1967).
[3] Mao, J. C. T., 'Efficiency in Public Urban Renewal Expenditures through Benefit-Cost Analysis', *Journal of the American Institute of Planners* (March 1966).
[4] *Old Houses into New Homes*, Cmnd. 3602 (HMSO, 1968).
[5] Case, F. E., 'Code Enforcement in Urban Renewal', *Urban Studies*, Vol. 5 (November 1968), No. 3.
[6] Needleman, L., 'Comparative Economics of Improvement and New Building', *Urban Studies*, Vol. 6 (June 1969), No. 2.

FURTHER READING

Lichfield, N., *Cost-Benefit Analysis in Urban Redevelopment*, Research Report of the Real Estate Research Programme (Berkeley, Calif., Institute of Business and Economic Research, University of California, 1962).
'Cost-Benefit Analysis in City Planning', *Journal of the American Institute of Planners*, Vol. XXVI (November 1960).
'Cost-Benefit Analysis in Plan Evaluation', *Town Planning Review*, Vol. XXXV (1964–5).
Cost-Benefit Analysis in Town Planning: a Case Study of Cambridge (Cambridge and Isle of Ely Council, 1966).
'Cost-Benefit Analysis in Town Planning. A Case Study: Swanely', *Urban Studies* (November 1967).
Lichfield, N. and McKean, R., 'Costs and Benefits from Different Viewpoints' in Schaller, H. G. (ed.), *Public Expenditure Decisions in the Urban Community* (Washington, DC, Resources for the Future, 1963).
Lichfield, N. and Margolis, J., 'Benefit-Cost Analysis as a Tool in Urban Government Decision-Making', in Schaller, op. cit.

APPENDIX I

Housing Quality Index: Haringey Wards

Penalty Scores Based on Weighted Percentage Deficiencies in Housing Amenities, Condition and Occupancy Levels

								Penalty weight						
	4		4		10		3		10		3		6	
						Housing deficiencies								
Ward	No stove/sink		Share inside w.c.		No inside w.c.		Share bath/shower		No bath/shower		Share hot water		No hot water		TOTAL penalty score (Amenities)
	%	Score	%	Score	%	Score	%	Score	%	Score	%	Score	%	Score	
A	1.3	5.2	13.1	52.4	4.1	41.0	14.4	43.2	5.9	59.0	8.2	24.6	8.2	49.2	274.6
B	3.7	14.8	27.1	108.4	2.6	26.0	31.1	93.3	2.0	20.0	11.2	33.6	8.1	48.6	344.7
C	4.6	18.4	35.4	141.6	3.4	34.0	42.0	126.0	1.1	11.0	14.1	42.3	11.8	70.8	444.1
D	6.6	26.4	28.9	115.6	13.4	134.0	30.0	90.0	15.9	159.0	16.5	49.5	18.7	112.2	686.7
E	4.3	17.2	28.1	112.4	13.6	136.0	46.0	138.0	8.6	86.0	20.9	62.7	19.9	119.4	671.7
F	3.8	15.2	21.5	86.0	2.5	25.0	26.0	78.0	1.6	16.0	10.1	30.3	4.0	24.0	274.5
G	4.7	18.8	43.7	174.8	6.5	65.0	55.5	166.5	2.6	26.0	16.3	48.9	16.1	96.6	596.6
H	9.5	38.0	53.5	214.0	5.6	56.0	65.6	196.8	9.7	97.0	29.6	88.8	23.7	142.2	832.8
I	3.6	14.4	3.8	15.2	21.8	218.0	5.9	17.7	19.1	191.0	5.2	15.6	18.5	111.0	582.9
J	1.3	5.2	11.6	46.4	30.4	304.0	11.0	33.0	30.0	300.0	7.1	21.3	28.9	173.4	883.3
K	2.0	8.0	13.4	53.6	11.2	112.0	32.6	97.8	8.2	82.0	13.9	41.7	12.4	74.4	469.5
L	2.3	9.2	13.6	54.4	24.2	242.0	25.8	77.4	23.3	233.0	11.3	33.9	23.5	141.0	790.9
M	1.2	4.8	8.0	32.0	39.2	392.0	6.8	20.4	43.0	430.0	4.2	12.6	40.7	244.2	1,136.0
N	4.6	18.4	32.2	128.8	18.3	183.0	35.6	106.8	23.6	236.0	14.5	43.5	29.1	174.6	891.1
O	4.6	18.4	12.9	51.6	46.6	466.0	12.9	38.7	48.4	484.0	6.1	18.3	37.7	226.2	1,303.2
P	3.9	15.6	16.0	64.0	30.4	304.0	14.1	42.3	37.8	378.0	4.1	12.3	35.6	213.6	1,029.8
Q	5.0	20.0	15.7	62.8	27.4	274.0	23.6	70.8	25.2	252.0	11.6	34.8	22.0	132.0	846.4
R	1.6	6.4	20.2	80.8	5.0	50.0	27.3	81.9	3.4	34.0	8.1	24.3	9.4	56.4	333.8
S	1.0	4.0	19.5	78.0	10.3	103.0	22.6	67.8	10.8	108.0	6.4	19.2	18.5	111.0	491.0
T	1.9	7.6	9.5	38.0	31.1	311.0	14.5	43.5	24.7	247.0	6.5	19.5	26.9	161.4	828.0
Twilight Area (part of Ward H)	12.6	50.4	59.1	236.4	3.6	36.0	66.4	199.2	11.7	117.0	35.6	106.8	21.1	126.6	872.4

	Penalty weight													
	5	20				5		20		10				
	'Fair' Condition		'Poor' Condition		TOTAL penalty score (Condition)	Housing deficiencies						TOTAL penalty score (Occupancy)	TOTAL PEN-ALTY SCORE	Rank
						Persons per room 1.0-1.5		Persons per room > 1.5		Net dwelling shortage				
Ward	%	Score	%	Score		%	Score	%	Score	%	Score			
A	14.4	72.0	1.2	24.0	96.0	5.2	26.0	2.0	40.0	4.4	44.0	110.0	481	1
B	23.2	116.0	0.7	14.0	130.0	6.8	34.0	2.3	46.0	30.6	306.0	386.0	861	5
C	29.3	146.5	2.9	58.0	204.5	4.9	24.5	5.7	114.0	30.6	306.0	444.5	1093	7
D	27.6	138.0	7.5	150.0	288.0	12.8	64.0	7.3	146.0	27.8	278.0	488.0	1463	12
E	29.2	146.0	2.5	50.0	196.0	18.9	94.5	5.6	112.0	34.8	348.0	554.5	1422	11
F	29.0	145.0	0	0	145.0	7.2	36.0	2.2	44.0	22.9	229.0	309.0	729	3
G	31.2	156.0	1.8	36.0	192.0	12.5	62.5	8.3	166.0	47.6	476.0	704.5	1493	13
H	41.5	207.5	4.9	98.0	305.5	15.2	76.0	11.3	226.0	50.2	502.0	804.0	1942	18
I	29.3	146.5	10.4	208.0	354.5	12.4	62.0	4.0	80.0	2.5	25.0	167.0	1104	8
J	37.7	188.5	11.9	238.0	426.5	9.2	46.0	4.1	82.0	10.7	107.0	235.0	1545	14
K	4.6	23.0	0	0	23.0	11.0	55.0	4.0	80.0	19.4	194.0	329.0	822	4
L	11.1	55.5	0.7	14.0	69.0	10.5	52.5	5.7	114.0	22.6	226.0	392.5	1252	9
M	31.4	157.0	13.3	266.0	423.0	8.8	44.0	5.4	108.0	12.9	129.0	281.0	1840	17
N	24.4	122.0	3.9	78.0	200.0	11.7	58.5	5.8	116.0	28.6	286.0	460.5	1552	15
O	41.1	205.5	13.6	272.0	477.5	11.4	57.0	3.7	74.0	15.7	157.0	288.0	2069	20
P	27.9	139.5	21.7	434.0	573.5	12.6	63.0	9.8	196.0	15.5	155.0	414.0	2017	19
Q	24.1	120.5	21.8	436.0	556.5	6.7	33.5	6.5	130.0	19.5	195.0	358.5	1761	16
R	23.8	119.0	1.5	30.0	149.0	8.2	41.0	2.1	42.0	14.6	146.0	229.0	712	2
S	21.8	109.0	4.1	82.0	191.0	6.1	30.5	4.7	94.0	13.1	131.0	255.0	938	6
T	46.7	233.5	5.0	100.0	333.5	8.3	41.5	2.2	44.0	10.5	105.0	190.5	1352	10
Twilight area (part of ward H)	41.5	207.5	4.9	98.0	305.5*	14.9	74.5	13.1	262.0	50.2	502.0	838.5	2016	18

* No breakdown of ward H figures was available from the GLC survey.

Notes

1. Penalty scores are calculated by multiplying the ward percentage of each deficiency by the penalty weight. Highest penalty score indicates lowest housing quality.

2. Data on amenities and occupancy are from the 1966 Census.

3. Data of physical condition are from the GLC Housing Age and Conditions Survey, 1967.

APPENDIX 2

Incidence in Haringey of Various Social Phenomena by Ward

Ward	Housing deficiency (i.e. penalty score) total		Indictable offences per 1,000 population		Fires per 1,000 dwellings		Juvenile probation cases per 1,000 children		Children taken into care per 1,000 children < 16 yrs		Admissions, etc., to welfare homes per 1,000 population > 65 yrs	
	Score	Rank	No.	Rank	No.	Rank	No.	Rank	No.	Rank	No.	Rank
A	481	1	48.0	19	4.85	2	2.34	2	1.13	1	5.08	3
B	861	5	50.4	20	9.52	16	6.78	7	2.67	2	5.37	4
C	1,093	7	45.8	18	5.75	7	10.77	16	4.12	4	3.40	2
D	1,463	12	29.7	9	12.80	18	4.76	4	12.84	17	7.66	14
E	1,422	11	27.9	7	5.5	5	7.56	10	10.24	15	11.19	19
F	729	3	23.5	3	7.2	12	8.74	11	2.90	3	6.97	9
G	1,493	13	36.6	13	6.98	11	7.41	9	11.97	16	11.52	20
H	1,942	18	32.2	12	9.92	17	11.33	17	9.30	12	9.46	17
I	1,104	8	21.2	2	6.70	8	15.23	20	10.10	14	7.04	11
J	1,545	14	36.7	15	12.96	19	8.80	12	8.36	10	5.42	6
K	822	4	17.9	1	7.41	13	6.95	8	9.52	13	8.12	16
L	1,252	9	25.1	4	4.39	1	12.16	19	4.53	5	7.36	13
M	1,840	17	37.8	16	7.99	14	4.88	5	5.11	6	6.98	10
N	1,522	15	30.3	10	6.78	9	9.68	15	7.76	9	6.72	8
O	2,069	20	31.8	11	9.01	15	8.87	13	13.27	18	7.05	12
P	2,017	19	29.5	8	6.86	10	0	1	8.91	11	2.38	1
Q	1,761	16	36.6	13	13.28	20	11.54	18	14.12	19	7.83	15
R	712	2	25.6	5	5.71	6	4.74	3	7.33	8	5.38	5
S	938	6	26.3	6	5.33	3	5.97	6	17.84	20	5.96	7
T	1,352	10	42.6	17	5.51	4	8.94	14	5.52	7	9.95	18
Twilight Area (part of Ward H)	2,016	18	30.7	10/11	9.76	16/17	13.04	19	N.A.	—	8.40	16/17

Notes

1. Crime figures are for 1966 and relate to indictable offences occurring in each ward.
2. Fire figures are for 1966 and relate only to fires in inhabited dwellings.
3. Juvenile delinquency figures relate to the *stock* of cases at the end of 1968, i.e. to the location of *offenders* rather than offences.
4. Children in care figures relate to 1967.

178

Indices of Social and Housing Stress in Haringey

	Social stress							Housing stress	
Ward	Indictable offences	Fires	Juvenile probation cases	Children taken into care	Admissions to welfare homes 60 yrs and over	Total	Rank	Housing deficiency score	Rank
	(100.0)	(100.0)	(100.0)	(100.0)	(100.0)	(100.0)		(100.0)	
A	147.2	63.8	29.2	12.9	72.6	65.2	2	36.4	1
B	154.6	125.3	84.5	30.6	76.7	94.4	9	65.2	5
C	140.5	75.7	134.3	47.2	48.6	89.2	7	82.7	7
D	91.1	168.4	59.4	147.1	109.4	115.0	17	110.7	12
E	85.6	73.4	94.3	117.3	159.9	106.0	13	107.6	11
F	72.1	95.7	109.1	33.2	99.6	82.0	4	55.2	3
G	112.3	91.9	92.4	137.1	164.6	119.6	18	113.0	13
H	98.8	130.5	141.3	106.5	135.1	122.4	19	147.0	18
I	65.0	88.2	189.9	115.7	100.6	111.8	14	83.6	8
J	112.6	170.6	109.7	95.8	77.4	113.2	15	117.0	14
K	54.9	97.5	86.7	109.1	116.0	90.8	8	62.2	4
L	77.0	57.8	151.6	51.9	105.1	88.6	6	94.8	9
M	116.0	105.1	60.8	58.5	99.7	88.0	5	139.3	17
N	92.9	89.2	120.7	88.9	96.0	97.6	10	115.2	15
O	97.5	118.6	100.5	152.0	100.7	113.8	16	156.6	20
P	90.5	90.3	8.2	102.1	34.0	65.0	1	152.7	19
Q	112.3	174.8	143.9	161.7	111.9	141.0	20	133.3	16
R	78.5	75.1	59.1	84.0	76.9	74.8	3	53.9	2
S	80.7	70.1	74.4	204.4	85.1	103.0	11	71.0	6
T	130.7	72.5	111.5	63.2	142.1	104.0	12	102.3	10
Twilight area (part of ward H)	94.2	128.4	162.6	106.5	120.0	122.4	(19)	152.6	(18)

Note: Borough = 100

179

CHAPTER 10

CAR PARKING AND SHOPPING:
A CASE STUDY

INTRODUCTION

The Buchanan Report, *Traffic in Towns*, a study of long-term problems of traffic in urban areas, concluded:

'The motor vehicle (or some equivalent machine) is a beneficial invention with an assured future, generally on account of the great advantages it offers for door to door travel and transport. There is an enormous potential demand for its services, and we think a constructive approach to the problem of accommodating it in towns and cities is both required and justified.'

No one would deny that a constructive approach is urgently needed to what has become a major cause of frustration and delay in the ordinary daily lives of hundreds of thousands of people. If analysis should ever reach the point of sophistication when a monetary value could be attached to the economic disbenefit of bad temper, we should see some startling results. It would be more feasible, though laborious, to calculate the cost of productive time lost in looking for somewhere to park. Meanwhile it ought to be practicable, by the use of cost-benefit techniques whose value has been proved in other fields, to assess the role of car parking in terms of its effect on public and private transport, of the provision of land, of construction and maintenance and of its effects on social and commercial life – notably on the lives of commuters and shoppers, employers and shopkeepers. It was accordingly decided to undertake such a study in a city where the problem was acute.

The choice of city was largely determined by the fact that its council had already commissioned a long-term study by an independent group, which included its own chief officers and representatives of government departments, and that an opportunity was made available to the research team to participate. The city itself was reasonably large, and was a natural centre for a populous part of the country, drawing both commuters and shoppers from a wide area. Moreover, the whole area was a prosperous one, with one of the highest levels of car ownership in the country.*

* There can be remarkable differences in car ownership from one place to another, as is shown by the figures taken from the General Registrar Office, *National Sample Census* (HMSO, 1966). (See table at foot of page 181.)

The study group appointed by the city council had been asked to consider the interaction of a number of different factors affecting the total traffic problem of the area, such as the extent and manner in which public and private transport systems were currently operating, the effectiveness of existing road networks and traffic management, and car parking – all, of course, within the wider context of optimum land use within the city's boundaries. Our own particular study deals with car parking; it suggests a benefit/cost framework, and attempts to provide some quantitative analysis of demand, using data collected for the city council's study group.

THE CITY AND ITS SURROUNDINGS

It is first necessary, however, to describe the setting in a little more detail. The city itself is in the 300,000–400,000 population range and occupies about 30 square miles; but the surrounding area for which it is in large measure an employment, shopping and business centre is twice its own population and covers possibly 400 square miles.

It is estimated that at the present time more than 21 per cent of the people working in the city travel from outside its boundaries, but that between now and 1981 72 per cent of all *new* jobs created will have to be taken by people from outside. This could mean that some 64,000 people would then have to be transported daily into the city.

The present trend, here as elsewhere, is for public transport to decline and for private car traffic to increase. On the one hand, there has been a steady decline in both the number of trips per head and the actual number of passenger journeys on the corporation buses since as long ago as 1951. On the other hand, car ownership has risen steadily, and if recent trends were to continue it is estimated that by 1981 only 14 per cent of households would be without a car and that 32 per cent would own *two or more* cars. For these and other reasons, the growth in private car traffic has been estimated to increase by some 160 per cent over the period 1966–81.

City	Population	Cars per 100 households
Bristol	433,920	51
Southampton	208,710	51
Cardiff	260,340	49
Birmingham	1,115,630	46
Sheffield	490,930	40
Edinburgh	473,270	37
Manchester	644,500	31
Newcastle	260,756	31
Glasgow	1,018,580	22

The core of the *parking* problem, however, as distinct from the problem of road networks and traffic flow, is, of course, to be found in the central area, where the estimated 20,000 daily commuters are reinforced by shoppers and other miscellaneous users of offices and places of entertainment, who travel to the city centre from at least as wide an area as the commuters. In this particular city the 'magnet' area can be reckoned as about half a mile square, and a survey carried out in 1967 in a central precinct showed that, on average, 67 per cent had shopping as their main purpose in coming into the city and another 9 per cent were there for 'recreational/social/educational' purposes. Whilst the survey showed that most central area shoppers used *public transport* to make shopping trips, an analysis of *non-resident shoppers*, i.e. shoppers who come into the centre from outside the city boundaries, showed that the *private car* is the more popular mode of transport (see Table 24).

Table 24

Shopping Trips to Central Area, by Mode of Travel (Percentages)

(a) *All central area shoppers*

	Tuesday	Friday	Saturday	All Days
Bus	70	67	59	64
Private car	23	24	34	28

(b) *Non-resident shoppers*

	Tuesday	Friday	Saturday	All Days
Bus	31	59	16	25
Private car	68	39	81	73

THE ROLE OF CAR PARKING

The car parking policy of the council is a significant part of the overall transportation network plan. The special importance of car parking has been described as follows:

'With traffic congestion approaching saturation on the present road system at peak periods, car parking involves not only meeting demands for parking space but *considering its role as a means of controlling the flow of road traffic*. With this aim in view, the city council is currently developing a general policy of prescribing maximum as opposed to minimum parking provisions, so that the amount of parking space available in any one part of the city will be in keeping with the traffic capacity of the road system.'

In the central area, public car parking space is made up of 3,420 paying places and 3,540 free places – in all, 6,960 places (see Table 25). Outside the central area, car parking is virtually free to the user.

There is a differential pricing system which distinguishes between long-stay and short-stay parkers (as shown in Table 26).

It is clear from these tables that both the provision and the price of car parking space in the central area is weighted heavily in favour of the long-stay parker, i.e. essentially, the commuter. Any consideration of the role of car parking as a means of controlling the total flow of road

Table 25

Central Area Parking Availability (Autumn 1967)

Public paying	Number of places
Multi-storey: long stay	1,740
Multi-storey: short stay	140
Surface level	1,540
Total public (paying) parking places	3,420
Free Parking	
Private off-street	2,160
Unofficial off-street	790
Public on-street	590
Total free parking places	3,540
Total Car Parking Provision	6,960

Table 26

Central Area Parking Charges

Type of Stay	Charges up to November 1967 (n.p.)	Charges since November 1967 (n.p.)
Long-stay	7½p per day	12½p per day
Short-stay	Half-hour, 2½p Then each additional hour, 5p Up to a maximum of 50p	Half-hour, 2½p 1 hour, 7½p 1½ hours, 17½p Then each additional half-hour, 5p Up to a maximum of 50p

traffic cannot neglect the problem of the 'commuter peak', but this topic is not pursued here. Within the confines of a short case study, our objective is to suggest a cost-benefit framework useful for policy appraisal and to illustrate some of the problems of estimating relationships from which benefits and costs can be measured or imputed. The illustration used will investigate the spillover effect on shopping of a car parking pricing policy.

CAR PARKING IN THE CENTRAL AREA: A BENEFIT/COST FRAMEWORK

There are basically two alternative ways of approaching the problem of ever-increasing traffic congestion:

(a) *Maximum private transport*
A large-scale investment in an intra-urban motorway network and additional car parking facilities which would meet predicted travel behaviour. Under this arrangement the public transport system would be a residual element. Or,

(b) *Maximum public transport*
Prohibit the use of private cars in and near the city centre and provide a *comprehensive mass transit system* (with a minimum investment in roads) which would meet predicted levels of travel.

In fact, both of these mutually exclusive policies can probably be ruled out for practical reasons. However, they will serve to indicate the nature of the benefits and costs which might be expected to flow from any compromise policy which is adopted.

In order to identify benefits and costs, it is first necessary to decide from whose point of view the analysis is being undertaken. If we are concerned merely with the benefits and costs to the local authority as the operator of the system, we are faced with relatively few problems. Benefits can be measured by the revenue which it receives from users of the facilities it provides, i.e. roads, car parks and public transport services. The costs incurred are the *resource* costs of providing and maintaining the road network, car parks and public transport services. In other words, the benefit/cost statement will be analogous to the profit and loss account of a commercial undertaking, as is shown in Tables 27a and 27b.

However, if as Prest and Turvey state in their survey article, cost-benefit analysis 'implies the enumeration of all the relevant costs and benefits,' we must take account of *external* or *spillover* effects, i.e. the effects which impinge upon a community as a whole, and upon various groups within it. The difficulty lies in deciding what is, or is not, 'relevant'. For instance, a wide-scale prohibition of private cars in or near city centres has long-term implications for the motor vehicle manufacturing industry (and the national economy). However, apart from the *practical* problems of evaluating such effects, they may be of relatively little significance for *local* decision-makers, concerned as they are with the social benefits and costs as these affect their jurisdictional area. From this point of view, the relevant benefit/cost framework relates only to the decisions of the city council and their effects on the inhabitants of the city. Using this approach we can identify two categories of costs/benefits to be included in the overall framework.

First, the council's transport policy has implications for all the inhabitants who travel by car or public transport within the city. The policy will affect journey times, vehicle operating costs, bus fares and car park charges, all of which combine to make travelling more or less costly. Any additional travel costs or cost savings accruing to the inhabitants should therefore be included in the benefit/cost framework.

Table 27a

Statement of Costs and Benefits accruing to the Council under Policy Alternative (a) Maximum Private Transport

Benefits	Costs
1. Revenue from municipal car parks	1. Costs of road construction and maintenance
2. Revenue from residual public transport service	2. Costs of providing car parks and ancillary services
	3. Costs of providing residual public transport service

Table 27b

Statement of Costs and Benefits accruing to the Council under Policy Alternative (b) Maximum Public Transport

Benefits	Costs
1. Alternative use of existing municipal car park land	1. Costs of road construction and maintenance
2. Revenue from public transport service	2. Costs of providing public transport service

The second effect follows on from the first. Assuming that price affects the demand for travel, then a policy which affects the price of travel to the city centre will alter the number of people who visit the area. In the short run, the effect is likely to be confined to shopping and recreation trips, but there may well be a long-term effect on employment and industrial location. An assessment of transport policy alternatives should attempt to include an evaluation of the loss or gain to city centre shops and businesses (and ultimately the loss or gain to the council as landlord and rate collector) resulting from a change in the level and pattern of travel demands. Allowing for these factors, the benefit/cost framework may be set out as shown in Table 28. This type of framework implies that benefits are something more than mere revenues to the council such as those considered in Tables 27a and 27b. The measurements of benefits 1 and 2 in Table 28 imply a consumers' surplus approach. To obtain measures of consumers' surplus would require estimates of the relevant demand curves – this is not an easy matter. In practice, one can envisage revenues being used as surrogates – a quick though not conceptually correct solution to the problem. With regard to the category of 'gains (losses) to trade and commerce in the central area' for the purpose of our study, trade and commerce are held to be synonymous with 'shopping', i.e. it is not proposed to attempt to measure the longer-term effects on *employment* of alternative transport policies. The item on the cost side, 'travel costs to individual users', is spillover costs incurred by *residents of the city*.

Table 28

Benefit/Cost Framework: Central Area Transport System

Benefits	Costs
1. Benefit from public transport service	1. Costs of road construction and maintenance
2. Benefit from municipal car parks	2. Costs of providing car parks and ancillary services
3. Alternative use of existing car park land	3. Costs of providing public transport service
4. Gains (losses) to trade and commerce in the central area	4. Travel costs to individual users of the transport system (including travel time and vehicle operating costs)

Clearly, the alternative policies outlined in Tables 27a and 27b are extreme ones. Alternative (a) may possibly turn out to be unacceptable on the grounds of capital cost alone; the cost of this city's road building programme had already doubled during the 5-year period 1962–7 and the expenditure needed to complete the planned road network has been estimated as £52.5m. Expenditure on this scale is subject to a *political* as well as a *resource constraint*. Further, experience in some urban areas of the United States tends to confirm the view that a policy of additional road building is not in itself a final solution. Alternative (b), as well as overriding trends in consumer preferences, has obvious political implications which render its feasibility open to doubt. The importance of the motor vehicle industry to the national economy, and the strength of the motorists' lobby would seem to ensure that a place will have to be made for the private car in the urban transport system of the foreseeable future. This point was emphasized in *Traffic in Towns* as follows:

'One particular result of the growth of car ownership deserves to be singled out, both because it might be overlooked and also because it has a direct bearing on much that we shall have to say in the paragraphs that follow. Before very long, the majority of the electors in the country will be car owners. What is more, it is reasonable to suppose that they will be very conscious of their interests as car owners and will give them a high priority. It does not need any gift of prophecy to foresee that the Governments of the future will be increasingly preoccupied with the wishes of the car owners.'

Given the political constraints, it is clear that a solution will be sought which lies somewhere between the two extreme policies. From the point of view of the efficiency of resource allocation with which we are concerned, some intermediate solution is also likely. Any attempt to arrive at an efficient solution will require answers to three basic questions.

(1) The major question is how can the demand for travel be influenced by a local authority? An authority has three alternatives – it can either limit capacity, or it can impose a price, or it can combine both. The demand for travel by public transport is already influenced by an authority through the pricing structure of bus fares *and* through the capacity of the service it is willing to provide. Travel by private car may be influenced indirectly by limiting road capacity (thereby imposing congestion costs), or directly, by administrative regulations controlling parking capacity, or again, by using prices to regulate car parking (and thereby travel) demands. (The use of road pricing to allocate road space is considered by many to be the ultimate answer, but does not appear to be a feasible proposition in the near future.) The economist's approach is that *demand* for travel can be determined by the *price* of travel, and this is the assumption we shall work on. Two questions now remain to be answered.

(2) How do changes in prices affect patterns and overall travel demands?

(3) How do alterations in travel patterns and demands affect the categories of benefits and costs in Table 28?

Questions (2) and (3) are of operational significance, and it is the aim of the remainder of this chapter to demonstrate a methodology which may be useful in answering them.

MEASURING THE DEMAND FOR CAR PARKING IN THE CITY CENTRE: SOME PRELIMINARY CONSIDERATIONS

In order to make some assessment of spillover effects on shopping, it is necessary to identify and evaluate a number of factors:

(1) the demand for car parking;
(2) the *modal* substitution effect;
(3) the *locational* substitution effect.

Assuming that the demand relationship is downward sloping, an increase in car parking prices will reduce the number of car trips to the city centre. These 'displaced parkers' will now do one of two things – either (a) divert to *another means of transport* into the city centre (i.e. modal substitution), or (b) cease to use the city centre and divert to suburban centres or to centres *outside* the city (i.e. locational substitution). This *locational* substitution is the source of the spillover effect on shopping and it is this which must ultimately be evaluated. As a starting-point, we need to measure the demand by shoppers for car parking space in the city centre. Once the response of shoppers to variations in parking prices is known, it will be possible to attempt to quantify the implications for 'shopping' in the central area.

In general, there are two operational methods which may be used to predict travel demands. A *trip generation model* would involve isolating the impact of certain variables upon household trip generation rates. Experience has shown that the dominant factors are household size and car ownership. However, other factors have been found to be of varying significance in explaining trip generation rates, e.g. land use, trip distance, population density, income, occupation, etc. This type of analysis could be extended to predict the composition of trips in terms of travel modes and trip purposes which would be necessary to predict parking demands.

The disadvantage of the trip generation method is that it attempts to predict demand *in a vacuum* because it ignores the relationship required, i.e. the relationship between price and quantity demanded. In a paper called *Parking Space for Cars: Assessing the Demand*, Gabriel Roth has stated:

> 'To the economist, "demand" means the number of units of a commodity or service bought in a given period *at a price*; the term is meaningless unless a price is stated or implied because demand varies with it. Yet most of the parking surveys carried out in this country and in the USA attempt to assess the demand for parking space without taking account of the price of parking. In other words they assume that it will be both free and nevertheless available in unlimited amounts. The information obtained from such surveys can hardly be used as a basis for planning parking space in a society where most other commodities have to be paid for because there is not enough of them to satisfy unlimited demand at zero prices. . . .
>
> 'The problem is to assess the likely usage of parking space at *different parking charges*.'

Thus, an economist's approach to the problem is to express the demand for car parking space as a function of price and quantity. This, in practice, as Roth has discovered, is no easy task simply because the market data required are non-existent, although sample surveys may be undertaken to provide them. However, there are basic difficulties inherent in the survey technique when asking people to state their reaction to a hypothetical price increase. These arise because respondents are asked to predict their future behaviour faced with a hypothetical change in the price of car parking, and this may lead consciously, or unconsciously, to biased responses. However, a method developed by Marion Clawson appears to offer a way out of these difficulties.

MEASURING THE DEMAND FOR CAR PARKING IN THE CITY CENTRE:
APPLICATION OF THE CLAWSON METHODOLOGY

Marion Clawson has suggested a methodology aimed at measuring the demand for an outdoor recreational activity† which would seem to have some general characteristics in common with the demand for parking space. The basic features of this methodology can be illustrated by a simple example using the hypothetical data in Table 29a which represents shopping visits by car from residential areas at different distances from the city centre car parks, where parking is free. The relationship between zonal trip rates and trip cost is assumed to be inverse. Using the information in Table 29a, we can obtain the *total* number of trips at zero parking price, and so we have one point on the demand curve for car parking. In this case, with user charge zero, the total

Table 29a

Relationship of Car Trips to Cost of Travel by Car to Central Area Car Parks from Homogeneous Zones surrounding the City Centre

Zone	Cost of trip* (n.p.)	Number of trips per 1,000 population per period	Population	Total number of trips per period
A	10	50	1,000	50
B	20	40	2,000	80
C	30	30	3,000	90
D	40	20	2,000	40
E	50	10	1,000	10

Total trips = 270

* Trip cost is measured in terms of, say, vehicle operating costs plus the cost of car parking (which is set at zero in Table 29a). The role of time has also to be considered.

† See Chapter 8.

189

number of visits is 270 (i.e. the aggregate of trips from zones A to E in the time period).

Interest now centres on obtaining other points to trace out a *demand curve* for car parking space under a price régime. We can proceed as follows: assume a price of 10p is imposed for admission to central area car parks; this increases the trip cost from each zone by 10p. Thus, zone A residents are now faced with a trip cost of 20p (made up of 10p travel cost plus 10p parking charge). Faced with this price, it is assumed that they will adopt the behavioural pattern of zone B residents at zero parking price. On this assumption the number of trips from zone A falls to forty per thousand population. Zone B residents will, in turn, now face a trip cost of 30p (made up of 20p travel cost plus 10p parking

Table 29b

Relationship of Car Trips to Cost of Travel by Car to Central Area Car Parks from Homogeneous Zones surrounding the City Centre: Car Parking Charge 20p

Zone	Cost of trip (n.p.)	Number of trips per 1,000 population per period	Population	Total number of trips per period
A	20	40	1,000	40
B	30	30	2,000	60
C	40	20	3,000	60
D	50	10	2,000	20
E	50	0	1,000	0
				—

Total trips = 180

charge) and we assume that their visitation rate will fall to thirty per thousand population, and so on. (It is assumed that zone E residents faced with a total trip cost of 60p will cease to make the trip by car.) Table 29b shows the effect of a 10p parking price on zonal trip rates to central area car parks.

The same procedure is followed for further *simulated* 10p increases in car parking charges, and in this way we derive a *demand schedule* for car parking shown in Table 29c. Figure 11 is a graphical representation of the demand schedule in Table 29c. The Clawson methodology is a conscious attempt to relate quantity demanded of a unit of a commodity in a given time period to the price per unit, and it relies on data founded on past behaviour. The method may be used to measure the monetary benefits of car parks in a consumers' surplus sense and also to predict the effects of alternative car parking prices on shopping trips. An attempt to illustrate the methodology using data relating to the city will now be described.

Table 29c

Derived Demand Schedule for Car Parking in a City Centre

Car parking charge (n.p.)	Total trips per period
0	270
10	180
20	100
30	40
40	10
50	0

Figure 11

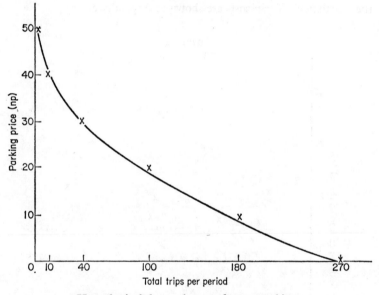

Hypothetical demand curve for car parking.

In order to estimate a demand curve, it is necessary to have data on trips and trip costs for *homogeneous* zones surrounding the central area, but this was not possible. However, data collected as part of a wider study had to be adapted to obtain an estimated demand curve. Relevant features of these data will be described first before proceeding to the calculation of the demand curve for car parking.

Data on trips were taken from a car parking survey carried out on a succession of Tuesdays, Fridays and Saturdays in August and September 1967. These data relate only to two multi-storey car parks in the city centre; 7,817 car drivers were interviewed (a 48 per cent sample), providing information about the purpose and timing of their visit to the city centre, their place of residence, and the number of people in their car, etc. Additional data on various social characteristics (income, etc.) were obtained on a zonal average basis from a home interview survey. The zones themselves were numbered consecutively 1–73 for city zones, and 74–95 for zones in the sub-region surrounding the city.

Having assembled data on zonal population characteristics and travel patterns, the next step was to measure trip distances from each zone to the city centre and to calculate corresponding trip costs. This was undertaken for the sub-region zones *only* by reference to an overall transportation network. However, as this proved to be impractical for the city zones, distances and costs were imputed. The formula used and the calculations of trip costs are shown in Appendix 2.

Figure 12

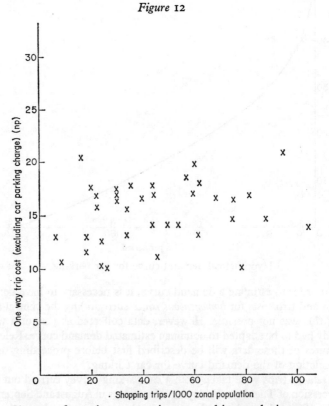

Shoppers from city zones: trip rates and imputed trip costs.

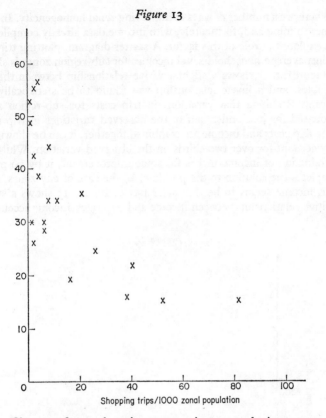

Figure 13

Shoppers from sub-region zones: trip rates and trip costs.

Figures 12, 13, 14 and 15 reveal some of the relationships between the variables, and these will now be discussed. In Figure 12 a scatter diagram of shopping trip rates against imputed trip costs is shown for the city zones, whilst Figure 13 shows the corresponding variables for the sub-region. It is apparent from these diagrams that for city zones, the relationship between the two variables is not systematic whilst there is a systematic inverse relationship between them in the case of sub-region zones. Statistical tests of significance confirm these patterns, and the relationship for the sub-region was found to be statistically significant with trip costs accounting for approximately 49 per cent of the variations in zonal trip rates (assuming a linear equation). The result for the sub-region zones provides encouraging support for a Clawson-style approach and could no doubt be bettered if the sub-region zones were more homogeneously designed.

N   193

There are a number of ways of improving zonal homogeneity. Income comes to mind and, fortunately, with income data already compiled we can explore the role of this factor. A scatter diagram, plotting trip rate against average household zonal incomes for sub-region zones is shown in Figure 14. It shows a slight positive relationship between the two variables, and a linear relationship was found to be statistically significant. Recalling that variations in trip costs for sub-region zones accounted for just under half of the observed variations in trip rates, when trip costs and income are combined together, it can be shown that they account for over two-thirds on the observed variation. Whilst the introduction of income makes for some improvement, it by no means completes the solution to the problem. In the case of city zones, however, income seems to be the major factor. Figure 15 shows a strong positive relationship between income and trip rates, income accounting

Figure 14

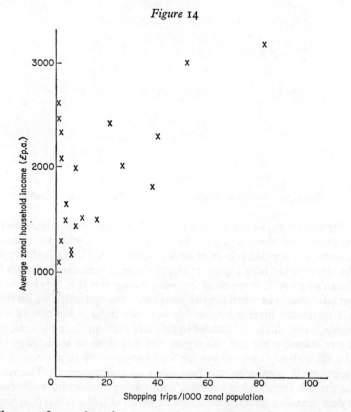

Shoppers from sub-region zones: trip rates and average zonal income.

Figure 15

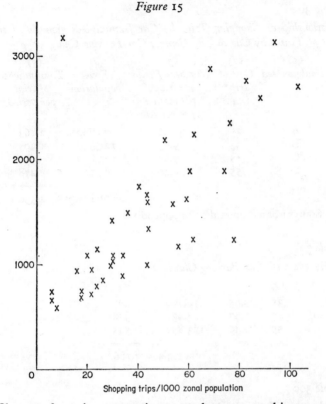

Shopping trips/1000 zonal population

Shoppers from city zones: trip rates and average zonal income.

for 72 per cent of the observed variation in city zone trip rates (assuming a linear equation). Because of the relatively narrow range of trip costs for city zones (the maximum one-way cost was 22p), it was not surprising that trip cost did not seem to be a significant factor in influencing their trip rates. For this reason it was decided that a Clawson-style analysis should be confined to the sub-region zones.

For the sake of pursuing the analysis, it was necessary to adjust the data. Estimates, made from these data, are shown in Table 30a. It will be noted that there has been a reduction in the number of sub-region zones from twenty to four and this has created a number of difficulties. Apart from the problem of measurement errors in the variables, the statistical problems associated with small samples also arise, and for this reason, it was decided not to rely on results obtained by subjecting the data to regression methods. We can now proceed with the Clawson

Table 30a

Relationship of Shopping Trips by Car from Sub-Region Zones to the Cost of Travel by Car to City Centre: Car Parking Charge $7\frac{1}{2}p$

(1) Amalgamated zone	(2) Cost of trip* (n.p.)	(3) Number of trips per 1,000 population per period	(4) Zone population	(5) Total number of trips per period
A	25	30.56	70,790	2,163
B	35	9.65	124,930	1,205
C	45	7.67	123,850	950
D	55	4.40	63,220	278

Total trips = 4,596

* Source: based upon data in appendixes.

Table 30b

Table 30a with Car Parking Charge 17p

(1)	(2)	(3)	(4)	(5)
A	35	9.65	70,790	683
B	45	7.67	124,930	958
C	55	4.40	123,850	545

Total trips = 2,186

Table 30c

Table 30a with Car Parking Charge $27\frac{1}{2}p$

(1)	(2)	(3)	(4)	(5)
A	45	7.67	70,790	543
B	55	4.40	124,930	550
C	65			
D	75			

Total trips = 1,093

Table 30d

Table 30a with Car Parking Charge $37\frac{1}{2}p$

(1)	(2)	(3)	(4)	(5)
A	55	4.40	70,790	311
B	65			
C	75			
D	85			

Total trips = 311

Table 30e

Demand Schedule for Car Parking in the City Centre: Shopping Trips from Sub-Region

Car parking charge (n.p.)	Total number of trips per period
$7\frac{1}{2}$	4,596
$17\frac{1}{2}$	2,186
$27\frac{1}{2}$	1,093
$37\frac{1}{2}$	311

method of simulating parking price increases. Tables 30b, 30c and 30d show the results obtained using car parking prices of $17\frac{1}{2}$p, $27\frac{1}{2}$p and $37\frac{1}{2}$p respectively.

The demand schedule for car parking by sub-region shoppers derived from the method outlined above is shown in Table 30e. The schedule, plotted in Figure 16, shows an inverse relationship between

Figure 16

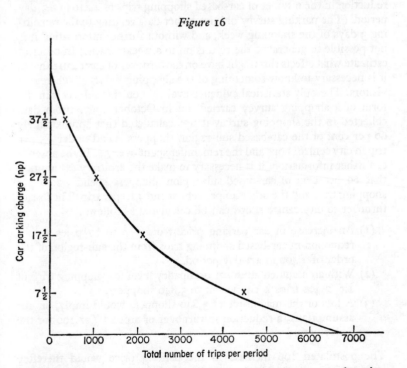

Clawson-style demand curve for car parking in the city centre: shopping trips from sub-region.

simulated car parking prices and trips per period, i.e. it has the form of the typical downward sloping demand curve economic theory. By simulating a negative price of 2½p, it is possible to show that the curve cuts the horizontal axis at approximately 6,600 (i.e. zero price will mean 6,600 car-based shopping trips per period). Through the four points, a freehand curve has been drawn. Such a curve may be used in two ways: (a) to provide a measure of benefits (consumers' surplus), or (b) to predict total trips in response to changes in car parking prices. As we are interested in predicting the number of trips made by car for shopping, we concentrate on the latter.

Once the effect of changes in parking price on car-based shopping trips is known, it is possible to make some assessment of the wider effect on city centre shops. However, because of the lack of appropriate data, much of what follows must be regarded as speculative and consequently has only expository value.

From the demand curve in Figure 16, it can be seen that an increase in city centre parking prices from 7½p to 17½p per day will result in a reduction in the number of car-based shopping trips of 2,410 in a 3-day period. (The parking survey did not gather data relating to the remaining 3 days of the shopping week, and without further information it is not possible to generalize the results on to a weekly basis.) In order to estimate what effects this might have on the turnover of city centre shops, it is necessary to know something of the shopping habits of sub-region visitors. The only statistical evidence available on this subject is in the form of a shopping survey carried out in October 1967. From data collected in the shopping survey it was calculated that approximately 60 per cent of the car-based sub-region shoppers spend under £5 per trip in city centre shops and the remainder spent over £5. In the absence of further information, it is necessary to make the arbitrary assumption that 60 per cent of car-based sub-region shoppers spend £2.50 per shopping trip, and the other 40 per cent spend £10 per trip. The loss of turnover to city centre shops can be calculated as follows:

(1) An increase in car parking price from 7½p to 17½p leads to a reduction in car-based shopping trips from the sub-region of the order of 2,400 in a 3-day period.

(2) With an assumed adult car occupancy level for shopping trips of 1.6, 2,400 trips is equivalent to 3,840 shoppers.

(3) A loss of the magnitude of 3,840 shoppers would imply, on our assumptions, a reduction in turnover of around £21,100 for the 3-day period.

The postulated 10p increase in the parking price would therefore involve city centre shopowners in losses of £21,100 per period. However, this result is based upon only *one* possible hypothesis about the behaviour of shoppers and there are a number of alternative hypotheses to be considered.

Our results imply that a rise in car parking charges will lead to a reduction in car-based shopping trips from sub-region zones. However, whether there is a reduction in the number of sub-region shopping trips *in toto* depends first on the degree of substitution of other modes of transport for the private car. For people living in the sub-region, the only practicable wide-scale alternative mode of travel to the city centre is the bus, and it is considered unlikely that large-scale substitution of bus for car would occur because the sub-region zones are not comprehensively covered by a city-oriented bus service.

If modal substitution is unlikely, then there are two possible courses of action open to car-based sub-region shoppers faced with an increase in city parking prices:

(1) They may divert to competing shopping centres. This will occur when a car trip to another shopping centre becomes relatively cheaper than the customary trip at the increased parking price. If this happens, there is a loss of turnover in the city centre shops as described above.

(2) They will continue to shop in the same city but will make fewer car-based shopping trips while increasing the value of purchases per trip. This pattern of behaviour is consistent with the simplest kind of inventory model, i.e. the increase in parking charges can be regarded as a rise in the reorder cost of goods, and there will be a tendency for people to hold bigger stocks and make fewer trips. However, this pattern of behaviour assumes that there is no increased cost involved in holding larger stocks.

A further point to consider is that the reduction in car trips may also affect congestion costs in the city centre. A reduction of 2,400 vehicles per period in the city centre (much of the reduction falling on Saturday – the worst day for non-commuter congestion) will have repercussions on traffic flows and some reduction in congestion may result. However, no data is available for this hypothesis to be tested in the present study.

Although no quantitative assessment can be made at this time about the significance of modal and locational substitution, the 'inventory model effect', and congestion costs, it is clear that any attempt to measure the effect on city centre shops of changes in central area parking charges involves much more than merely predicting the number of car-based shopping trips as the Clawson methodology does. The value of even this exercise could be increased if the methodology were incorporated into a wider model of sub-region shopping behaviour. However, this would require data on trips and trip costs from all sub-region residential zones to all sub-region shopping centres, and such data were not available for the present study. For this reason, the figure of £21,000 for the possible loss in turnover to the city centre shops should be regarded as merely speculative. Nevertheless, it seems likely that further research along the lines indicated in this study might make progress towards solving some of the problems outlined above, and this type of problem must be solved if cost-benefit analysis is ever to be a useful tool for local decision-makers.

APPENDIX I

Basic Data

(1) City zone number	(2) Zone population	(3) Total trips per period	(4) Trip rate	(5) Average household income ($£$)	(6) Average number of cars per household	(7) Trip cost (n.p.)
1	296	12	40.54	783	0.340	—
2	126	14	111.12	717	0.309	—
3	568	—	—	670	0.286	—
4	22	—	—	115	0.050	—
5 Central	104	—	—	1,067	0.462	—
6 area	327	28	85.63	708	0.304	—
7	261	18	68.97	764	0.331	—
8	143	2		909	0.397	—
9	27	—		465	0.179	—
10	222	—		438	0.165	9
11	—	—		—	—	9
12	200	—		536	0.217	9
13	80	—		637	0.269	8
14	7,344	176	23.97	791	0.344	10
15	10,415	81	7.78	597	0.249	11
16	7,407	49	6.62	676	0.289	13
17	7,486	136	18.17	713	0.307	12
18	8,396	62	7.38	769	0.334	14
19	6,416	140	21.82	729	0.315	16
20	—	—	—	—	—	13
21	—	—	—	—	—	15
22	6,560	407	62.04	2,252	0.807	18
23	—	—	—	—	—	19
24	—	—	—	—	—	15
25	7,698	135	17.54	762	0.331	13
26	10,885	370	33.99	906	0.395	15
27	8,442	379	44.90	1,673	0.662	17
28	12,485	508	40.69	1,759	0.685	17
29	7,640	229	29,28	1,431	0.589	17
30	6,217	274	44.08	1,346	0.562	17
31	13,827	220	15.92	949	0.414	20
32	6,791	408	60.08	1,910	0.725	20
33	—	—	—	—	—	22
34	14,925	329	22.04	950	0.414	17
35	9,731	290	29.80	1.023	0.444	17
36	—	—	—	—	—	21
37	7,382	192	26.01	855	0.373	10
38	7,057	378	53.56	1,509	0.614	14
39	—	—	—	—	—	21
40	8,230	486	59.05	1,386	0.575	17
41	8,423	480	56.99	1,172	0.501	18
42	11,626	1,096	94.27	3,135	0.974	21
43	—	—	—	—	—	15
44	8,790	666	75.76	2,345	0.827	16
45	—	—	—	—	—	18
46	5,110	348	68.10	2,874	0.930	17
47	—	—	—	—	—	10
48	8,836	211	23.88	1,160	0.497	13

(1) City zone number	(2) Zone population	(3) Total trips per period	(4) Trip rate	(5) Average household income (£)	(6) Average number of cars per household	(7) Trip cost (n.p.)
49	4,891	245	50.10	2,206	0.796	14
50	—	—	—	—	—	12
51	14,224	475	33.40	1,118	0.481	13
52	10,638	475	44.65	1,000	0.435	14
53	—	—	—	—	—	15
54	9,159	335	36.57	1,519	0.617	17
55	7,549	150	19.87	1,109	0.478	17
56	—	—	—	—	—	14
57	40	—	—	115	0.050	19
58	—	—	—	—	—	20
59	7,539	589	78.12	1,234	0.524	10
60	4,101	361	88.03	2,606	0.880	14
61	3,919	293	74.76	1,988	0.745	15
62	6,789	202	29.76	1,114	0.480	17
63	1,200	1	—	309	0.100	19
64	—	—	—	—	—	15
65	—	—	—	—	—	19
66	8,879	262	29.51	1,053	0.456	16
67	7,653	473	61.81	1,249	0.529	13
68	—	4	—	—	—	13
69	10,053	452	44.97	1,616	0.645	11
70	6.543	684	104.54	2,705	0.899	14
71	7,699	626	81.31	2,755	0.909	17
72	—	—	—	—	—	17
73	5,590	6	10.17	3,175	0.980	17
74	36,350	588	16.18	1,482	0.605	20
75	60,550	395	6.52	1,193	0.509	28
76	20,860	537	25.74	2,035	0.756	25
77	1,600	60	37.50	1,830	0.705	13
78	55,140	438	7.94	1,456	0.599	34
79*	—	—	—	—	—	—
80	1,790	147	82.12	3,175	0.980	15
81	43,520	273	6.27	1,233	0.523	30
82	6,570	140	21.31	2,429	0.845	35
83	17,180	145	8.44	2,007	0.750	44
84	19,760	786	39.78	2,316	0.821	22
85	18,570	201	10.82	1,516	0.616	34
86	17,870	83	4.64	1,642	0.653	56
87	27,130	45	1.66	2,333	0.825	55
88	11,290	582	51.55	2,991	0.950	15
89	99,190	89	0.90	2,621	0.883	30
90/91	1,064,220	235	0.22	1,105	0.441	49
92	78,050	52	0.67	2,470	0.853	53
93	42,190	90	2.13	2,107	0.774	26
94	28,170	50	1.77	1,314	0.551	43
95	43,590	171	3.92	1,503	0.612	38

Notes:
Col. 2 From 1966 Census.
Col. 3 Extracted from Parking Survey tabulations. Figures relate to a 3-day period (Tuesday, Friday, Saturday).
Col. 4 Calculated as total trips per 1,000 zone population.
Col. 5 From home interview survey.
Col. 6 From home interview survey.
Col. 7 Calculated according to formula in Appendix 2.
  * Included in city zones.

Calculation of Trip Costs

(a) *Sub-region zones*

Distances and journey times by car were obtained from data used in a wider study for trips from sub-region zones to the city centre, and these were applied to the cost figures shown in Table 1.

Table 1

*Costs for Private Vehicle Operation**

Speed (m.p.h.)	Time costs (n.p. per mile)	Vehicle operating costs (n.p. per mile)	Total costs (n.p. per mile)
1	26.8	9.7	36.5
5	5.4	4.0	8.4
10	2.7	2.2	4.9
15	1.8	1.9	3.7
20	1.3	1.8	3.1
25	1.1	1.7	2.8
30	0.9	1.6	2.5

* Table 1 was calculated from a cost formula devised by the Ministry of Transport. Time elements were incorporated into the formula at a value of 15p per hour for non-working time, and 70p per hour for working time. Cost per miles =

$$\frac{a+b+c}{v}$$

a = a proportion of running costs (not varying with speed)
b = fixed costs per hour
c = running costs varying with speed
v = average journey speed on link

Table 2

Travel Costs* from Sub-Region Zones to City Centre

Zone	Distance (miles)	Time (min.)	Average speed (m.p.h.)	Cost/mile (n.p.)	Total costs† (n.p.)
74	5.3	21	15.1	3.7	19.61
75	7.7	30	15.4	3.7	28.49
76	8.8	21	25.1	2.8	24.64
77	4.5	11	24.5	2.8	12.60
78	13.6	26	31.4	2.5	34.0
80	4.6	15	18.4	3.3	15.18
81	9.7	29	20.1	3.1	30.07
82	11.4	33	20.7	3.1	35.34
83	17.6	35	30.2	2.5	44.0
84	7.0	22	19.1	3.1	21.70
85	11.0	31	21.3	3.1	34.10
86	20.1	47	25.7	2.8	56.28
87	19.7	47	25.1	2.8	55.16
88	4.9	15	19.6	3.1	15.19
89	11.5	24	28.8	2.6	29.90
90/91	16.8	42	24.0	2.9	48.72
92	19.5	44	26.6	2.7	52.65
93	10.5	20	31.5	2.5	26.25
94	15.2	37	24.6	2.8	42.56
95	13.7	34	24.2	2.8	38.36

* Travel costs excluding car parking charges.
† Calculated as cost per miles × distance.

City zones

Journey times were obtained from imputed distances, and trip costs were calculated by using an average speed of 16.7 m.p.h. throughout the city.

Estimation of Statistical Relationships

Ideally, a cost-benefit analysis of a city's transportation network would require a model of an interacting system incorporating behavioural and technological relationships. The measurement of variables in such a system, assuming data are available, may require the use of advanced methods of statistical estimation. As we have confined ourselves to a small part of such a system, we consider it meaningful to specify single equation relationships and appropriate to estimate the parameters of the equations by the method of least squares. Some of the results, obtained from analysis of data in Appendix 1, are discussed below. In using tests of significance (see pages 193–195) we have assumed that the standard textbook conditions for the valid application of these tests are fulfilled. Associated with each parameter estimate is its standard error, and also shown for each equation is the square of its appropriate measure of correlation. The key to the variables used in the equations is:

$$Y = \text{trip rate}$$
$$X_1 = \text{trip cost}$$
$$X_2 = \text{household income}$$
$$X_3 = \text{car ownership}$$

The principal hypothesis to be tested was that there was an inverse relationship between the number of car-based shopping trips and the price of making such a trip. The data used measured these concepts in terms of trip rates and trip costs for sub-region zones and city zones. (See Appendix 1, Cols 4 and 7). The following results were obtained:

1(a) *Sub-region zones*

$$Y = 53.5 - 111.2\ X_1$$
$$(8.9)\quad(26.9) \qquad\qquad R^2 = 0.487$$

(b) *City zones*

$$Y = 17.2 + 177.2\ X_1$$
$$(22.1)\ (145.2) \qquad\qquad R^2 = 0.039$$

Equation 1(a) shows clearly a significant inverse linear relationship for sub-region zones, but in the case of city zones, equation 1(b) shows a non-significant positive relationship. However, the trip cost variable accounted for only about 49 per cent. of the variation in trip rates in the sub-region zones, and in the case of city zones, as was to be expected, trip cost was a very poor explanatory variable. Two other single equation specifications were also considered, and the results (equations 2(a) (b) and 3(a) (b) below) were not altered substantially.

2(a) *Sub-region zones*

$$\log Y = 2.05 - 3.72\, X_1$$
$$(0.27)\ (0.82) \qquad\qquad R^2 = 0.530$$

(b) *City zones*

$$\log Y = 1.15 + 2.69\, X_1$$
$$(0.26)\ (1.69) \qquad\qquad R^2 = 0.064$$

3(a) *Sub-region zones*

$$\log Y = -0.552 - 2.66 \log X_1$$
$$(0.288)\ (0.56) \qquad\qquad R^2 = 0.557$$

(b) *City zones*

$$\log Y = 2.31 + 0.910 \log X_1$$
$$(0.47)\ (0.566) \qquad\qquad R^2 = 0.065$$

The low explanatory power of trip cost could be due to the lack of homogeneity in zonal delineation. Two other variables, car ownership and household income, were introduced for the purpose of making for better zonal homogeneity. Equations 4(a) and (b) establish that these two variables are inter-correlated and can be regarded as surrogates.

4(a) *Sub-region zones*

$$X_3 = 0.227 + 0.000251\, X_2$$
$$(0.017)\ (0.000006) \qquad\qquad R^2 = 0.979$$

(b) *City zones*

$$X_3 = 0.144 + 0.000289\, X_2$$
$$(0.011)\ (0.000007) \qquad\qquad R^2 = 0.977$$

The introduction of each variable in a linear fashion as a second explanatory factor yielded the set of equations 5 and 6. Non-linear specifications were also considered and the results are shown in the set of equations 7 to 10.

5(a) *Sub-region zones*

$$Y = 15.3 - 90.7\, X_1 + 0.0162\, X_2$$
$$(13.9)\ (22.7)\qquad (0.0050) \qquad\qquad R^2 = 0.682$$

(b) *City zones*

$$Y = 13.1 - 115.8\, X_1 + 0.0333\, X_2$$
$$(11.3)\ (79.8)\qquad (0.0033) \qquad\qquad R^2 = 0.754$$

6(a) *Sub-region zones*

$$Y = 6.37 - 93.6\ X_1 + 57.9\ X_3$$
$$(18.53)\ (23.8)\quad (20.7)$$

$R^2 = 0.648$

(b) *City zones*

$$Y = -0.0988 - 143.2\ X_1 + 116.9\ X_3$$
$$(10.9573)\ (77.1)\quad (10.8)$$

$R^2 = 0.775$

7(a) *Sub-region zones*

$$\log Y = 1.61 - 3.45\ X_1 + 0.000187\ X_2$$
$$(0.593)\ (0.86)\quad (0.00019)$$

$R^2 = 0.555$

(b) *City zones*

$$\log Y = 1.11 - 0.353\ X_1 + 0.000346\ X_2$$
$$(0.17)\ (1.174)\quad (0.000048)$$

$R^2 = 0.618$

8(a) *Sub-region zones*

$$\log Y = 1.34 - 3.45\ X_1 + 0.877\ X_3$$
$$(0.66)\ (0.85)\quad (0.737)$$

$R^2 = 0.566$

(b) *City zones*

$$\log Y = 0.960 - 0.811\ X_1 + 1.28\ X_3$$
$$(0.151)\ (1.060)\quad (0.15)$$

$R^2 = 0.695$

9(a) *Sub-region zones*

$$\log Y = -2.71 - 2.50\ \log X_1 + 0.684\ \log X_2$$
$$(2.65)\ (0.60)\quad (0.838)$$

$R^2 = 0.574$

(b) *City zones*

$$\log Y = -2.97 - 0.365\ \log X_1 + 1.36\ \log X_2$$
$$(0.62)\ (0.340)\quad (0.15)$$

$R^2 = 0.726$

10(a) *Sub-region zones*

$$\log Y = -0.257 - 2.46\ \log X_1 + 1.23\ \log X_2$$
$$(0.400)\ (0.59)\quad (1.16)$$

$R^2 = 0.585$

(b) *City zones*

$$\log Y = 1.64 - 0.484\ \log X_1 + 1.75\ \log X_2$$
$$(0.24)\ (0.316)\quad (0.17)$$

$R^2 = 0.767$

In the case of the sub-region zones, the overall results show that the introduction of either income or car ownership as second explanatory variables made for a slight but significant increase in the value of the correlation coefficient. However, in the case of city zones, each variable made for a very marked increase.

On balance, the introduction of income, and its surrogate, car ownership, proved not to be a useful aid to achieving *zonal* homogeneity with a view to using the Clawson methodology.

CHAPTER II

THE TOWCESTER FLOOD RELIEF
SCHEME: A CASE STUDY

In August 1969 Towcester, a small town of nearly 3,000 population in the Towcester Rural District Council area, on the A5 in Northamptonshire, suffered severe flooding after very heavy rain following many weeks of fine weather; in 1970 flooding occurred again, though this time inadequate sewerage capacity was a contributory factor. The town had long been susceptible to flooding, but drainage improvements had brought about a substantial improvement in the preceding years; it now began to look as if further improvements were needed.

Towcester RDC is a small authority, however, with a population of only 17,000. The most modest scheme that was likely to be effective was estimated to cost £275,000, of which the Ministry of Agriculture would contribute half only if satisfied that the 'total cost of alleviating flooding was justified by the benefits to be achieved from the work'. This condition implied the need for a cost-benefit analysis, and this the Rural District Council duly commissioned; the work was carried out by Dr R. F. Carter of the Local Government Operational Research Unit (RIPA), with the co-operation of Towcester Rural District Council and Northampton County Council.* Dr Carter is now with the Department of Health and Social Security (Research and Statistics Division). The terms of reference were

> 'To examine the costs of and benefits expected from a scheme to prevent flooding of the low-lying areas of the parish of Towcester occasioned by a storm of an intensity to be expected once in every five years.'

The method adopted was first to determine the costs of the 1969 flood and then – by using calculations produced by the consulting engineers of the likelihood of floods of different intensity – to predict the expected costs *which would be averted by the scheme*, and to use this as a measure of its benefit to the community. Thus the calculations anticipated floods of every kind, and not just those of an intensity that could reasonably be expected not more than once in 5 years.

---

* A more detailed account of the work was published by the LGORU in May 1971 in two reports: *Cost-Benefit Analysis of Towcester Flood Relief Scheme* and *Evaluating Flood Relief.*

COSTS

Cost presented no problems, since the proposed scheme was a straight-forward engineering job of laying a second drainage pipe and straightening out and lining with concrete the bed of an offending stream. There were no hidden or consequential costs of the kind which scientific analysis might be expected to disclose. Accordingly, the study was primarily an exercise in quantifying benefits, though as both costs and benefits arose at different times, it was necessary to reduce them to a common time basis, and this was done by the customary device of discounting.

BENEFITS

The provisional analysis of the benefits which would have to be quantified was as follows:

(1) *Benefits to the owners of public and private property*
Effect of prevention of flooding on property values, direct or indirect loss and/or damage to private individuals, industrial and commercial concerns, agriculture and schools, libraries and other public property; the relief for residents from fear of flooding; the benefit of the resulting environmental improvement.

(2) *Benefits to the community*
The benefit to the community of the avoidance of costs occasioned by the need to relieve the immediate effects of flooding, including costs incurred in respect of:
  (a) Police, local authority and welfare organizations for other emergency services including transport.
  (b) Fire brigade and Service (RAF) mobile equipment and labour for pumping, drying out, etc.
  (c) Temporary rehousing, social security payments, etc.
  (d) Emergency communications and rescue operations.
  (e) Welfare (including food, shelter and bedding, clothing, etc.).
  (f) Local community organizations and other voluntary help.

(3) *Benefits to public utilities**
The avoidance of disruption and/or damage occasioned by flooding upon the following:
  (a) Sewage disposal, main drainage and refuse collection.
  (b) GPO telephone and mail.

* In the final report (2) and (3) were combined as 'benefits to community services'.

(c) Electricity supply.

(d) Roads.

(4) *Effects on the County Plan*

The increased availability of building land within the parish. The County Plan for the parish provided for the development of approximately 130 acres (1,664 dwellings). Of this, approximately 95 acres (1,268 dwellings) would not be possible, because of refusal of planning permission, if the scheme were not undertaken. If this land was not capable of development because of the flood problem, then other land would have to be found, since Towcester was earmarked as a centre for development.

By taking advantage of hindsight we may rearrange these items in order of what proved to be their real importance, for the fourth was the determining factor in the calculation and the second and third were quantitatively insignificant. It may in fact be best to start by summarizing the conclusions and then, working backwards, to comment on the points of methodological interest that arose (Table 31).

Table 31

Total Benefit of Flood Relief Scheme

Source	Total capitalized benefit (£)
Benefits of reduced flooding to:	
1. Property	13,800
2. Community services	1,270
	15,070
Benefit of being able to develop 1,664 houses in Towcester	257,600
Total benefit of scheme	272,670
Total cost of scheme	275,000
Net benefit of scheme	−2,330

These figures assume a discount rate of 10 per cent (standard Treasury figure) and show the estimated benefit at 1970 prices in 1972. The life of the scheme is calculated as 60 years. The 10 per cent rate of discount is the standard rate accepted currently by the Treasury, though there is much argument in the literature about the rate to use in this kind of study. Similarly it is standard practice to consider a 60-year life for the scheme, although in fact any benefits – or costs – attributed more than 30 years hence have a virtually negligible effect on the answer. The remainder of the chapter comments on these figures.

The Effects on the County Plan

Under the Northamptonshire County Plan, the population of Towcester is expected to increase over the next 15 years by about 3,100 over its estimated 1967 population of 2,900 (i.e. by 107 per cent). It is intended that most of this population increase should be housed in a series of new development on land near Silverstone brook, all of which is subject to flooding. This land comprises some 134 acres (1,664 dwellings). For 95 acres (1,268 dwellings) of this, planning permission would not be granted if the flood relief scheme were not built. Hence one benefit of the scheme would be to enable this development to take place, and to measure accurately the benefit of the scheme it was essential to evaluate the costs of the alternative locations of the development. But to do this, it was first necessary to find a realistic alternative to Towcester for the development. To the planners, however, there was no acceptable alternative, measured in planning terms, because for many reasons Towcester was ideal: centrally located near main transport links, good shopping, educational and other service facilities, with sewage capacity easily expanded, and so on. On the other hand, the surrounding villages were not suitable for development because they lacked precisely the advantages that Towcester possessed, so there was no real alternative. This may have been a good argument in planning terms, but in economic terms it was less satisfactory. To say that there was no alternative to Towcester was equivalent to saying that the cost of development elsewhere must be infinite, which would be absurd.

So, because an alternative was needed against which to measure Towcester, it was agreed with the County Planning Department to adopt a hypothetical alternative. This alternative would be to assume that the development planned for Towcester would be split up into small parcels and situated in the villages in the Rural District around Towcester itself. It was clear that in practice this alternative would have been unacceptable, but in the absence of a better alternative it had to be employed.

A number of consequences followed from this decision; these consequences, and their effects on costs, are now discussed.

(1) For design reasons, houses can be built at higher population densities when built in larger parcels than when built in small ones. The County Planning Department suggested that whereas they were able to build at 12.4 dwellings per acre in Towcester, if the development was built in smaller lots they could only

achieve seven or eight dwellings per acre. This would mean that instead of using 95 acres, a total of about 181 acres would be needed. The value of the additional 86 acres absorbed would then be counted against an alternative outside Towcester. But what is the value of agricultural land? The market price cannot be taken, as this does not reflect the true value, mainly because agricultural subsidies inflate the cost of land. What is wanted is the total social benefit. This has already been the subject of research,[1] from the results of which it is possible to derive a social value of £100 per 100 acres per year in this land in 1967; allowing for inflation (i.e. converting to 1970 prices) this becomes £120 per 100 acres per year, i.e. £31.2 per acre capitalized over 60 years at 10 per cent. This figure was employed.

(2) By building all in one place, one or two farms might be completely taken up, whereas in the alternative, seven or eight farms could lose part of their land, and because of lost economies of scale in the latter case, there might be a net loss to agriculture. The former effect (the difference in value between different qualities of land) could be quantified, but the second of the two effects was much more difficult to quantify, and was not attempted.

(3) Because in almost all the possible sites for expansion in the villages the sewerage network was at or near capacity, new sewage treatment facilities would have to be provided. It is much less economical to do this by a number of small installations than in one large plant. Provision of sewerage for the 1,268 dwellings in Towcester was calculated by the consulting engineers at £141,000 (or £11 per dwelling).* By contrast, the provision of sewerage for 425 dwellings in the Wappenham Group scheme (consisting of five villages) would have cost about £258,000 (or £605 per dwelling), while provision for the 287 dwellings in the Blakesley Group scheme (four villages) would have cost about £213,000 (£740 per dwelling).† The average of these two figures is £660 per dwelling, and this figure was used in the calculation.

(4) The Towcester alternative was favoured for a number of other reasons. First, because of its already existing shopping and recreational facilities, less would have to be provided in Towcester than elsewhere, since both have some measure of elasticity. The provision of school places is less elastic, but even here there might be some saving in the consumption of land. Another point was

* But this was only the off-site sewerage: the developers quoted an average figure of £80 per house for on-site sewerage, making a total cost per dwelling of £191, or £242,000 in all.
† Figures provided by Towcester RDC from current schemes.

that it was estimated from refuse studies carried out by the Local Government Operational Research Unit that owing to present underemployment, refuse collection could be done in Towcester by the present equipment and staff of the Surveyor's Department. Putting development in the villages around would probably have entailed taking on another vehicle and crew at an additional yearly cost of £5,000. Finally, because a number of jobs would be provided in Towcester essentially for the people who would live in the projected development, putting those people elsewhere would increase travelling costs. None of these effects was quantified because it would not have been possible to do so without more definite alternatives; however, they all worked in favour of the Towcester alternative and should not be ignored.

Quantifying the Alternatives. In order to quantify these alternatives, it was necessary to make certain assumptions. The building of the 1,268 dwellings was to start in 1973, and to open at a rate of around fifty starts a year, gradually accelerating so that all the dwellings were built the end of 1986. Hence it was assumed that fifty would be built in 1973 going up to 120 in 1986. Next it was assumed that the dwellings in the outside Towcester alternative would be constructed in five groups, each about 212 dwellings, occupying 30.3 acres (i.e. seven dwellings per acre) costing £13.2 per acre, and with sewage costs at £550 per acre. The worth of the cost flows in 1972 (the year when the flood relief scheme is to be built) was about £440,000 (assuming a 10 per cent discount rate). For the Towcester alternative, the same number of dwellings (1,268) was assumed in the original 95 acres at £13.2 per acre, and with a total sewerage cost of £242,000. This gave a total cost of almost £244,000; assuming that this was all paid in the first year of the project (1973) it had a present worth in 1972 (the year when the flood relief scheme is to be built) of £182,000.

Thus on this basis there was a net present worth (i.e. benefit) to the community of building the new development in Towcester of about £440,000 − £182,000 = £258,000. If this figure was correct, it was nearly enough to justify the flood relief scheme on its own.

Benefits to Private Property

In the event the total capitalized benefit to existing property proved to be almost trivial compared with that of building the new houses. This fact was of interest in itself, since at the outset of the study the Rural District Council had supposed that it would be important, and that the justification of the scheme might prove to turn on it. Accordingly, a great deal of time was spent on factors which proved to have a small monetary value, and very little time on the factor which proved to be decisive. It was, however, of great local political importance to establish the facts, and it was perhaps an additional justification of the study that these proved to be the opposite of what was popularly supposed. The methodological problems which arose in calculating the benefit to private property were also interesting.

Methodology. In estimating the benefit to the owner of a particular property, it was important to avoid falling into the trap of double-counting. If the property suffered from the danger of frequent flooding, its value on the market would be lower than an otherwise identical property which was not so liable to flooding. If the property was actually flooded, the owner would suffer costs of various natures. But in calculating the total cost to the owner of having a property which was subject to flooding, one should not add the two effects, because one reflects the other. The house has a lower market value precisely because of the higher likelihood of incurring the costs of flooding; alternatively, the owner may have consciously accepted the risks of flooding in order to obtain a property more cheaply than otherwise. Thus to include both effects would be to introduce double-counting. However, this does mean that there were two alternative methods of estimating the benefit of removing the danger of flooding: either to calculate the total reduction in value of properties which are liable to flooding, or to estimate the effects of flooding if it occurs. These two alternatives are now briefly described.

To identify the loss of value through a liability to flooding, it is necessary to compare that property with one which is identical in all other respects except the danger of flooding, for example, its condition, position, accessibility for transport, shopping, recreation, etc. This matching of properties is extremely difficult, and although some studies, notably that of the Commission of Inquiry on the third London airport, have attempted it, the results are rarely satisfactory.

The alternative method is to identify for the property, firstly the frequency – and intensity – of flooding, and secondly, the amount of the cost incurred directly or indirectly as a result of the flooding. If this is done (a) assuming that the scheme is not constructed and (b) assuming that it is constructed, subtraction of the latter from the former will give the cost which will be averted by the scheme – in other words, this is the benefit to that property of introducing the scheme. Summing these figures over all the properties gives the total benefit of the scheme to property.

This part of the analysis fell into two stages. It was first necessary to calculate the actual cost of the 1969 flood; and then to estimate the benefit (i.e. the prevention of comparable losses) over the lifetime of the flood prevention scheme.

Calculation of 1969 Losses. Since the number of properties actually flooded was not large – about ninety houses, one hundred caravans and a small number of shops and business premises – a complete survey by personal visit was undertaken with a view to estimating loss of possessions, loss of earnings and loss of time.

The houses and caravans involved the question familiar to insurance companies of replacement value (e.g. of carpets), redecorating and of repointing brickwork. Some uninsured owners could not afford replacement and had simply done without, which raised the technical question of whether to calculate them at zero or in terms of the extent to which they were missed.

Shops and business premises were complicated by the fact that the flood took place on a Sunday, so that the only identifiable loss was that of shopkeepers' stock; though the probability of a future flood taking place on a working day had to be brought into the calculation concerning future benefit.

Finally, the loss of time confronted the research team with one of the more controversial aspects of cost-benefit analysis. Much work has been done on the monetary value that ought to be placed on time spent in different ways: working time, leisure time, travelling time, etc. It was a major preoccupation of the Roskill Commission on the third London airport and a very minor consideration in the Towcester research.

Before going on to predict future benefits on the basis of losses to the properties that were visited, it was necessary to extrapolate the results to include those that it was not possible to visit, e.g. those, especially caravans, where the owner could not be seen, those that were unoccupied at the time of the flood, or those where ownership had changed hands. This was done, in the case of private houses, by relating the previously ascertainable damage to the height of floodwater in each house (under or over 6 inches); in the case of shops and business premises by ascertained averages per foot of flooding and in the case of caravans by a simple average per van.

Tables 32a and 32b show the estimated average cost of the 1969 flood for each type of property affected and the total estimated cost for the whole of the flooded area. The 'local authority' figure was in respect of minor damage to a school and local library. The very small sum attributable to 'losses to agriculture' in the first footnote of Table 32b was in relation to a single field of growing corn.

Future Costs of Flooding

It has been necessary for the consulting engineers, using past weather data, to calculate the flood levels for storms of varying intensities, and the probability of such storms recurring over different periods. Using these figures, losses were estimated for a series of flood levels of lower

Table 32a

Estimated Costs of Flooding

Type of property	Estimated cost of flooding	Estimated man-hours to clear
Private house		
(a) flood depth less than 6 inches	£37	25 hours
(b) flood depth above 6 inches	£123	30 hours
Shops and bed and breakfast establishments*	£275 per foot of flooding	60 hours per foot of flooding
Caravans	£79	33 hours

* 'Other businesses' are not included in this estimate as each one is *sui generis*. They were calculated individually on a basis of actual 1969 costs in each particular property.

Table 32b

Total Estimated Losses, All Properties (including unoccupied ones), August 1969

Type of property	Total estimated losses (£)	Total man-hours lost†	Total economic loss (£)‡
Private houses	8,262	2,943	9,734
Shops and bed and breakfast	9,687	2,202	10,788
Caravans	3,555	1,800	4,455
Other businesses*	9,850	—	9,850
All types	31,354	6,945	34,827

Notes:

* Includes losses to agriculture, owners of caravan sites, Towcester Mill and Trading Co., the Plessey Company and the local authorities.

† Includes allowance for time during flood as well as clearing up afterwards.

‡ Total losses plus valuation of time lost 50p per hour, a figure adopted on the advice of the Department of the Environment (ex-Ministry of Transport).

intensity than that of August 1969, assuming firstly that the flood relief scheme was not built, and secondly that it was. These calculated losses are shown in Table 33.

Figure 17 shows the calculated losses for each type of storm, plotted against the probability of the storm's occurrence in a single year.* The

* Note that the probability here is the probability of the occurrence of a storm of this intensity *or worse*. Thus 1/50=0.02 is the probability in any one year of getting a storm of 50-year intensity or worse.

Table 33

Costs to Property Owners

	Return period of flood (years)	Estimated cost to property owners (£)	Range of flood intensities (years)	Annual expected value of losses in range (£)
	1	0	less than 2	22.5
	2	90	2–3	39.7
Without	3	385	3–5	84.7
the	5	889	5–10	193.4
flood	10	2,978	10–30	399.0
relief	30	11,653	30–50	211.3
scheme	50	20,116	50–60	77.5
	60	26,860	60–70	71.9
	70	33,098	70–75	34.0
	75	34,827		
				Total 1,134.0

	less than 50	0		
With			less than 50	0
the	50	0	50–60	0.2
flood	60	112	60–70	0.3
relief	70	164	70–75	0.3
scheme	75	410		
				Total 0.8

area under each curve in this figure corresponds to the total expected value of losses through flooding in a year – in other words, it is the annual cost to be expected in each case. Subtraction of the expected losses with the scheme from those without it gives, therefore, the cost averted by the scheme, i.e. its benefit.

The area under each curve was determined in sections corresponding to the types of storm considered, assuming a straight line between each pair of points. Thus for 5-year and 10-year storms, the area (see Figure 18 is

$$\frac{(0.2-0.1)\times 889+(0.2-0.1)\times(2978-889)}{2} = 193.4$$

The area for each section is shown (final column) in Table 33; without the flood relief scheme the total annual cost is £1,134, with it the cost is £0.8. The benefit to property owners is thus £1,133.2 per annum; capitalizing over the life of the scheme this yields £11,300.

One further figure was added at this stage. Several properties were either being built or were planned, and it was necessary to make some allowance for these. It was not possible to carry out a calculation like

Figure 17

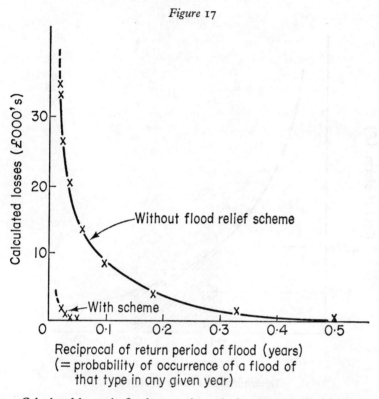

Calculated losses in floods *vs.* reciprocal of return period of flood.

that above, as damage to the properties in question could not be estimated with any accuracy. The insurance costs could not be used, as (because of a policy of spreading the load) insurance companies tend to set premiums, whether liable to flooding or not, at around the same amount. One measure was the cost of raising the buildings above flood level by means of a concrete pier. For the properties in question this came to a total cost of £7,500. If the owners were prepared to pay this, it would be a measure of the worth to them of avoiding floods. But they had not paid it, so the value must be less than £7,500. On the other hand, the value must clearly be greater than zero, or the owners would be indifferent to flooding, which they were not. Hence it must be between 0 and £7,500. There was some evidence that the true figure lay nearer the former than the latter, so rather arbitrarily a figure of £2,500 was taken, thus giving a total benefit to property owners of £13,800.

Figure 18

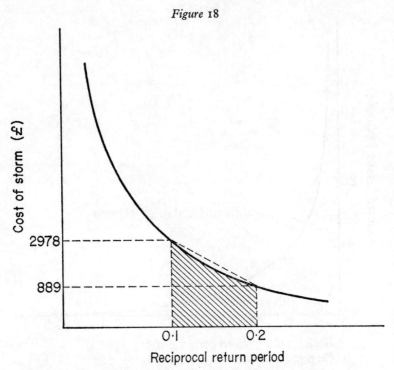

Determination of area under curve.

Benefits to Community Services

This category includes the benefits to the community and the benefits to public utilities from the original statement of scope for the study. The two were combined because both were dealt with in the same way.

Costs in the 1969 Flood. As we saw from Table 32 these were very small but they show how wide the net was cast in the search for any potential benefit of flood prevention. They included costs, additional to routine costs, of ambulance and police, out-of-pocket expenses and time of WRVS, and the cost of a temporary emergency control office set up by the County Civil Defence Officer. The total cost of all these emergency services, however, was only £368. The cost of pumping and drying, undertaken by the fire brigade, the RAF and a local hospital, was £490; and that of temporary rehousing (partly in hotels and boarding houses) and social security payments £217. In addition there were minor items for a temporary telephone line, and the issue of bedding, food and clotoing. The total of all these items was £1,643.

With regard to public utilities, calculations were made for repairs, making good or additional burdens in respect of drains and sewers, refuse collection, an electricity sub-station and roads (including losses to road users), and time and extra running costs incurred by travellers in making detours, based on traffic flows obtained from the local authority. These totalled £1,117 giving a combined total of £2,760.

Table 34

Losses to Community Services

	Return period of flood (years)	Estimated cost to community services (£)	Range of flood intensities (years)	Annual expected value of losses for range (£)
	1	0	less than 2	5.1
	2	20	2–3	6.8
	3	59	3–5	12.2
	5	109	5–10	21.8
Without	10	307	10–30	44.5
the	30	1,250	30–50	21.3
flood	50	1,880	50–60	6.9
relief	60	2,210	60–70	5.8
scheme	70	2,630	70–75	2.8
	75	2,760		
				Total 127.2
With	under 50	0	less than 50	0
the	50	0	50–60	0.00
flood	60	20	60–70	0.05
relief	70	20	70–75	0.04
scheme	75	59		
				Total 0.09

Future Costs of Flooding. It was assumed that the cost to the community services was proportional to the number of dwellings flooded, in other words that the resources employed were proportional to the number of families affected. The number of dwellings flooded was estimated for each level of flooding and the cost to community services based on the costs in the 1969 flood. The expected annual value of losses was then calculated as before. The results are shown in Table 34.

Thus the net saving to community services is £127.1 per annum; capitalized over 60 years this amounts to £1,270.

CONCLUSIONS

Two conclusions emerged from this cost-benefit study.

First, that if the alternative employed for housing development in

Towcester was a realistic one, the benefit of the scheme would outweigh the cost, taking into account the intangible benefits to the County Plan. But the alternative was a hypothetical one and might never be realized – indeed further research might suggest a better alternative in Northamptonshire itself, or outside the county altogether.

Secondly, the total benefit to property and services of the almost complete removal of the possibility of flooding was estimated at £15,070. There were, additionally, certain intangible benefits which no attempt was made to estimate. For example, the fear of flooding, which can obtrude on everyday life, and which, quite apart from the measurable economic factor of the diminished value of a house, can result in a diminution in the quality of life, although one that would obviously vary from person to person and in any event would be extremely difficult to measure. The possibility of death through flooding is by no means fanciful. Again, if there were no fear of flooding more care would be taken of land and property adjoining the stream and the visual environment would be improved.

These factors, if they could be quantified, would represent an additional bonus to the £15,070, but even so the total conceivable benefit, set against a capital cost of £275,000, would give a benefit/cost ratio of no more than about 1:18.

Accordingly if the alternative for housing development in Towcester was *not* acceptable, a decision to implement the flood prevention scheme would be a strictly political decision, in which costs could not be justified by benefits.

REFERENCE

[1] Warford, J. J., *The South Atcham Scheme: an Economic Appraisal* (HMSO, 1969).

PART V

CONCLUSION

CHAPTER 12

COST-BENEFIT ANALYSIS IN PERSPECTIVE

INHERENT CONSIDERATIONS

Attempts to evaluate the consequences of proposed action are as old as civilization itself. Individuals are constantly making such attempts. There is, for example, an old Irish song called *McBreen's Heifer*, which describes a situation of choice and resource constraint in the private sector:

> McBreen had two daughters and each one in turn
> Was offered in marriage to Jamsey O'Burn.
> Now Kitty was pretty but Jane she was plain.
> So to make up the differ, McBreen would explain,
> He'd give the best heifer he had on the land
> As a sort of bonus with Jane, understand?
> But then Kitty would charrum a bird off a bush
> And that left the lad in a horrid non-plush.
>
> Entirely bother'd was Jamsey O'Burn
> He thought that he'd give the schoolmaster a turn.
> Sez he to wed Kitty is very good fun
> Still a heifer's a heifer when all's said an' done.
> A girl she might lose her good looks any how
> And a heifer might grow to an elegant cow.
> But still there's no price for the stock d'ye mind
> And Jane has a face that the Divil designed.
>
> The schoolmaster said, with a good deal of sense,
> We'll reduce the two girls to shillin's an' pence,
> Add the price of the heifer then Jane I'll be bound
> Will come out the top by a couple o' pound.
> But still I'm forgettin' that down in Glengall
> The stock is just goin' for nothin' at all.
> So Jim thought he'd wait till the end of the year
> Till girls might be cheaper or stock might be dear.[1]

In the first stanza costs and benefits are identified. The second deals with the effect of time and uncertainty in investment appraisal. In the third an attempt is made to measure, i.e. to quantify in monetary terms, the respective benefits of the alternative choices.

It was probably not until the end of the eighteenth century that attempts were made to formulate rules for *public* decision-making in terms of benefits and costs. Jeremy Bentham was possibly the father of cost-benefit analysis in his advocacy of the principle of UTILITY as the basis for all legislation. He defined utility as

'The property or tendency of any particular thing to shield from some evil or to secure some good. *Evil* means pain, suffering or the cause of suffering. *Good* means pleasure or the cause of pleasure.'[2]

Bentham argued that 'nature has placed mankind under the governance of two sovereign masters, PLEASURE and PAIN. To them ... we refer all our decisions, every resolve that we make in life.' He postulated a decision criterion expressed in terms of 'the greatest happiness (i.e. pleasure) of the greatest number' and described the elements of a 'calculus or process of moral arithmetic' which was to be used to evaluate all proposed legislation by measuring the units of pain and pleasure which it produced. Now Bentham was essentially a pragmatist, not a head-in-the-clouds philosopher. He meant this moral calculus to be *used* as a tool of decision-making, not merely as a theoretical contribution to moral philosophy. Unfortunately, like many of the later attempts at cost-benefit analysis, the calculus broke down when faced with the problems of measuring 'intangibles' in terms of units of pleasure and pain. Still, the basic framework is generally valid today and serves to place in perspective the efforts of twentieth-century man to improve the quality of public decision-making.

His ideas were given a sharper cutting edge by a French engineer, J. Dupuit, who in an article published in 1844 first discussed the economic ideas underlying the technique which we now call cost-benefit analysis:[3]

'Legislators have prescribed the formalities necessary for certain works to be declared of public utility; political economy has not yet defined in any precise manner the conditions which these works must fulfil in order to be really useful; at least, the ideas which have been put about on this subject appear to us to be vague, incomplete, and often inaccurate. Yet the latter question is more important than the former; inquiries – be they so numerous – laws and ordinances will not make roads, a railway or a canal useful if it is not so already. The law ought to confirm the facts demonstrated by political economy. How is such demonstration to be made? Upon what principles, upon what formula, does it rest? How in a word is public utility to be measured?'

In this century the economics of cost-benefit, and in particular the concepts of social benefits and social costs, were developed by the British economist Professor A. C. Pigou. In a book[4] first published in 1920, he emphasized that decision-making involved matters of private and public welfare, that divergencies between the two were possible, and that where such divergencies existed public action would be required to eliminate them. The concepts of social benefits and social costs owe much to the work of Pigou. A good deal of the book may now appear to be a statement of the obvious, but in the political and intellectual climate of his time it was far from being so. When he was writing, for example, an industrialist building a new factory would typically take no account of the damaging effects of smoke from his chimneys on the health and convenience of people in the surrounding neighbourhood, and the conflict of private and social cost went unrecognized – or at least it was not supposed that anything should be done about it.

Nearer to our own day the use of cost-benefit analysis in the public sector has been pioneered by the Federal Government of the USA in the evaluation of water resource programmes. Its origins can be traced back to Pigou's day, and earlier, but with the passing of the Flood Control Act in 1936 the US Congress opened up a new era in the development of cost-benefit, and modern practices may be said to date from then.*

In the 200 years that have elapsed since Bentham's ideas on utility were first published, the matters for decision have become infinitely more complicated. There is now a need to identify a much larger range of interactions and repercussions of legislation and public investment, and circumstances demand more sophisticated tools for measuring the consequences of public decisions than those which Bentham possessed. Fortunately, technological progress which itself has caused many of the problems facing modern society has also sharpened many of the tools used in measuring its impact. For example, Bentham thought that the measurement of pleasure or pain depended on four factors: intensity, duration, certainty and proximity. It happens that these are the precise criteria adopted by the Wilson Committee to define a physical measure of the dissatisfaction caused by noise. Unlike Bentham, Wilson had the advantage of being able to measure noise in terms of decibels with the aid of a 'black box' (although the *cost* of noise is not yet measurable in such precise terms). Clearly, if Bentham had had the tools of modern technology, his Theory of General Utility might have made a more practical contribution to public decision-making in the nineteenth century.

The problems of modern society, infinitely complex in their nature, cannot be solved by any twentieth-century equivalent of Bentham's

---

* American economists have written extensively on this subject. Among the wealth of publications an official appraisal is given in a publication of the US Congress, House Committee on Works, *Economic Evaluation of Federal Water Resource Development Projects* (US Government Printer, 1952).

'moral arithmetic'. There will always be enough 'intangibles', 'incommensurables', and 'non-measurables' to limit the value of the computer as decision-maker and to ensure that not all problems will be solved in terms of a socially deterministic cost-benefit analysis. For some types of public decision, the tools we have are sharp; for others blunt, and for others, non-existent. But the problems do not go away because the tools are not perfect, and we must use such techniques as are available to reduce the area of purely intuitive judgement in complex matters of choice. This is what cost-benefit analysis is about. It is especially relevant in situations where choices have to be made about the allocation of scarce resources.

The Limitations of Cost-Benefit Analysis

It is not, however, argued that the objective of cost-benefit analysis is to *make* decisions or choices, but rather to *assist* in making them. It is unfortunate that the advocacy of this and other quantitative techniques is sometimes thought to imply a wish to subjugate political judgement and sensitivity, the very elements which are especially significant in public decision-making, to quantitative methods. Hence, the backlash against management techniques in general, and against cost-benefit analysis in particular, a reaction which has gained ground not only in the political sphere, but also in certain academic circles. In summing up cost-benefit analysis, it is therefore important to emphasize that the technique is not viewed as a substitute for decision-making, nor as a panacea for the problems of resource allocation in the public sector. It does not simplify the task of management by unfailingly producing the 'right' answer. Its claim to recognition lies in the truism that the quality of decisions depends on the quality of available *information* upon which the decisions are based. Cost-benefit analysis assists decision-makers by giving them *better* (not necessarily *more*) information – what use is made of the information is not the direct concern of the analyst. In public affairs, the final decision will always be political, and may in part be intuitive. But it will be a better decision if it is preceded by as much objective quantification as possible.

PRACTICAL CONSIDERATIONS

The decision-maker in the public sector is bound to be faced in the future with a growing number of urgent and complicated choices between alternatives. In central government, the increasing problems of allocating scarce resources in such a way as to achieve national objectives and priorities will demand the further development of sophisticated techniques. In local government, the recent introduction of new capital rationing procedures* gives individual local authorities more responsibility for arranging their own investment priorities. Faced with the growing pressure to provide the decision-makers with relevant information upon which to base many difficult choices, the administrator will turn more and more to techniques like cost-benefit analysis. It is therefore important that some of the pitfalls should be pointed out.

The Cost of Cost-Benefit Analysis
First, cost-benefit analysis is expensive in terms of technical skills. It requires an inter-disciplinary approach, albeit with a bias towards the quantitative disciplines. It is not sufficient merely to hire an economist and expect him to produce sophisticated analyses. Many disciplines, not least the skills of the statistician and the operational research analyst, are highly relevant in a cost-benefit exercise. In addition to these quantitative technicians, who could form the nucleus of the analysis group, it will also be necessary to second specialists with knowledge of the particular problem under examination. Cost benefit analysis may not be worth undertaking at all unless a certain range of skill is available.

Secondly, it is expensive in terms of collecting information which is often not readily available. Much is written nowadays about the need for rapid data availability and many public authorities are establishing management information systems (MIS) in order to facilitate the collection, storage, processing and presentation of data relevant to decision-making at all levels. However, a sophisticated MIS requires far more effort than the installation of a bigger and better computer which is what sometimes happens. Administrators sometimes forget that information systems already exist within their organization, some of which may never be successfully computerized. In our own research we found that a great deal of useful information was stored in people's heads and could be accessed in a way that even the best computers could not match! The basis of an information system must be a series of decisions about what information is needed and for what purposes. It is unrealistic to think in terms of a universal system which will give the analyst access to any particular set of data he may require. Nevertheless it *is* possible for basic information likely to be required in many kinds of analysis to be computerized for immediate access. For example, demographic characteristics summarized by geographical areas are used for many kinds of analyses, but are unlikely to be held by service departments. Accordingly, data of this kind should be given priority in establishing a MIS.

It is important that the analysis group should be aware of depart-

* Department of the Environment Circular 2/70.

mental information systems. Some, such as the accountancy and budgetary control systems of a local authority Finance Department, are well known and supply information to many other departments. However, data in specialist areas, e.g. social work, crime, or health, are not so readily available to the analyst and yet may be essential to particular cost-benefit studies. Without adequate arrangements to ensure that such data find their way into analysis, the use of quantitative techniques generally (and the development of cost-benefit analysis in particular) is likely to be impaired. What organizational form these 'adequate arrangements' may take is not discussed here, yet it is worthy of serious consideration in a real situation, since inter-departmental frictions are not conducive to objective analysis. Further, the public doubts about safeguarding personal information in a 'data bank society' need to be allayed. If they are not, increasing public hostility may place a heavy burden on forward planning activities.

Selection of Projects for Analysis
Shortages of staff and information make it particularly important to be discriminating in deciding which problems should be selected for analysis, and a few general rules may be borne in mind.

The first and most obvious step is to examine only those decisions which involve a relatively large investment of resources. Clearly it makes more sense to use cost-benefit analysis in an assessment of alternative housing projects than to assess the relative merits of tennis-courts and putting-greens in a public park. Nevertheless, it is as well to emphasize that this rule should not be inflexible. For example, investment in traffic management schemes rarely involves significant resource costs, yet the *benefits* may be revealed to be extremely large. However, exceptions to this general rule of selecting high cost investment decisions for analysis are relatively few. Another common-sense rule is to concentrate on those issues which have a high probability of recurring in the future. Clearly, choices between alternative housing projects recur more frequently than, say, decisions about new theatres or sports centres. If resources permit 'one-off' decisions to be studied then there is no problem, but it would seem reasonable, where technical resources are severely constrained, to concentrate, at least in the early years of building up an analysis capability, on those areas which can contribute most to the fund of experience which is essential to all analysis.

If resources are insufficient to cope with all the recurring policy issues which involve big investment decisions, two further ground rules may help. First, does it seem likely that *quantitative* criteria are conceptually feasible? If the answer to this question is 'no', there seems little point in engaging in a major cost-benefit effort. Decisions involving important visual/aesthetic considerations seem, at the moment, to fall into this category. Secondly, is the relevant information required for the analysis available, or obtainable at reasonable cost, in a given time period? If the answer to this question is 'no', then again it seems pointless to expect much in the way of results which might aid decision-making.

It is generally accepted that only a large organization can mount a major cost-benefit study within its own resources. Normally, and particularly in local authorities, it will be necessary to share expertise or possibly to undertake appraisals on a joint basis. There is, for example, a part to be played by consultant organizations like the Local Government Operational Research Unit of the Royal Institute of Public Administration,* especially when the use of highly specialist mathematical and computer techniques is contemplated.

There are, however, few kinds of expenditure by public authorities that would not benefit from the cost-benefit *approach*, even if they were not so large as to warrant the commissioning of specialist techniques. All too often decisions about investment are made in a fortuituous or subjective way, with little attempt at what could properly be called appraisal. For example, local authority spending committees tend to be influenced by such things as personal opinions unsupported by fact, or by particularly articulate advocates of a project, or by some process of 'horse-trading' whereby support is canvassed in return for a *quid pro quo*. But very often the real costs and potential benefits of apparently straightforward projects are by no means self-evident, and repercussions for either cost or benefit can be surprisingly wide.

A simple road improvement on a minor road, for instance, will increase traffic on it. This will result, in terms of cost, in increased maintenance of a surface that was probably not designed to take the volume of traffic that will now use it, including in the foreseeable future consequential improvements such as alignment, widening, safety precautions, etc.; in terms of benefit, road mileage may be saved by traffic being encouraged to take more direct routes, and better service (to which a value can be attached) will be given to certain residents, farmers and businessmen. Neither of these calculations is simple, and a subjective judgement of the balance between them is of limited value. Or again, the decision, which is constantly having to be made, about reducing or extending a bus service could involve similar calculations, but also more sophisticated ones, such as the value of the time and the saving to the pockets of members of the public and the gain and loss to different shops and other businesses – as well, of course, as profitability to the bus company. To alter traffic flows or to move a market in a town, or to install main drainage in a village, are examples of the kind of

* Whom the Towcester RDC commissioned in just such circumstances as we have in mind. See p. 209.

decisions which are often made intuitively, but where the quality of the decision could be improved by the simple process of pausing to foresee, and to evaluate, costs and benefits in the near and in the more distant future.

What is most needed is to develop cost-benefit analysis as a *frame of mind*, so that subjective discussion of the kind which is so familiar is replaced by an objective appraisal of *all* investment projects, and not only of manifestly major ones. In really minor matters this can no doubt be done, so to speak, 'on the back of an envelope', which is better than not doing it at all. Moving up the scale, into matters that require a series of minor or consequential decisions or a decision which although of major proportions ought properly to be settled within the resources of the organization, there is generally scope for 'streamlining' the methods by which decisions come to be taken. Often closely comparable decisions have had to be taken before, and an appraisal of costs and benefit made *after* the event can throw light on new proposals; internal codes of administrative practice can make quite certain that all available options are identified, and that potential costs and benefits are set out in the form of a planning balance sheet before serious discussion begins.

TECHNICAL CONSIDERATIONS

Terms of Reference

Many of the technical problems of using cost-benefit analysis have been described in the earlier chapters and some of them remain still to be resolved. One issue which has significant practical implications derives from what might be called the terms of reference of a cost-benefit appraisal. The general criterion for a cost-benefit evaluation of a project is expressed in terms of economic efficiency, i.e. its contribution as reflected in GNP plus its contribution to other benefits not so reflected. It attempts to measure the contribution of a project to social welfare as a whole, but does not evaluate internal distributional effects. Political decision-makers are only too well aware, however, that what they mean by social welfare and what the analyst may wish it would mean are often two different things. Many writers have commented on the importance of income redistribution as an objective in public decisions, and in some cases (notably those involving a regional income redistribution objective) it is feasible to specify an investment criterion which takes this into account.[5] For example, Lichfield's planning balance sheet approach* allows the decision-maker to see the effects of alternative decisions on different groups within a community. It is true, however, that the effect of many important decisions in the public

* See p. 159.

sector cannot be measured in terms of economic efficiency or income redistribution. Wildavsky has argued[6] that 'the great advantage of cost-benefit analysis when pursued with integrity, is that some implicit judgements are made explicit and subject to analysis. Yet, for many, the omission of explicit considerations of political factors is a serious deficiency' (p. 297). He claims that the political costs and benefits of a decision often outweigh any others, and sees the need for a broader based political cost-benefit calculus. Professor Alan Williams has replied that this problem can be partly solved by carefully formulating the constraints on any decision and then computing the cost (shadow price) of meeting those constraints. However, this discussion goes beyond the immediate point, which is that success or failure of a project measured in cost-benefit terms will always be a relevant, but not always *the most significant* factor, in the final decision. The analyst could well remember this when the results of his labour are – as he sees it – distorted by political considerations.

The Measurement of Benefit

There is little to be said in *general* terms about the problems of measurement. The measurement of benefit poses the greatest difficulties for the analyst and although they have to some extent been overcome in certain fields (especially transport), in others conceptual problems still persist (e.g. the 'social costs of slums') and data is virtually unobtainable. What is the analyst to do when he is faced with a situation in which he is told to *identify and evaluate* as many alternative methods as possible of achieving an objective? The identification of alternatives is, in some senses, a process which adds to the difficulties of measurement. The more alternatives, the more costs and benefits to evaluate. In most cases, some of the costs and benefits will not be capable of evaluation in money terms, or, indeed, in *any* quantitative terms. Where this happens, it is essential that the significance of measured costs and benefits is not overstated in the analysis.

Cost Effectiveness

In many cases, some quantification of the effects of investment decisions is possible in *physical* terms. For instance, many aspects of environmental quality can now be measured – air pollution and noise are probably the best known examples. While research is continuing into the problems of expressing these physical measurements in financial terms,[7] the analyst has another technique which can be useful if the problem can be specified in a particular way. This is the technique known as *cost-effectiveness analysis*, which has been described by the Treasury *Glossary of Management Techniques* as 'a method of finding (a) the cheapest means of accomplishing a defined objective or (b) the maximum value from a given expenditure'. Although this technique like cost-benefit analysis, can be used to rank projects, however, it does not provide an *absolute* measure of the value of a project; it provides merely an index of effectiveness divided by total cost to produce a cost/effectiveness ratio. This ratio, although useful for ranking projects, has a major disadvantage – it can tell us whether alternative X is better than alternative Y, but it does not tell us whether either is worthwhile. This can only be shown where costs and outputs are measured in the same units, and where a net surplus or net cost criterion can be used. For this reason, the formulation of the problem is extremely important if cost-effectiveness analysis is to be used. The technique is useful for selecting alternative approaches to the achievement of a benefit already determined to be worth achieving, i.e. the benefit is taken for granted (having been defined as politically desirable) and the object of the analysis is to ascertain the minimum cost of achieving it. In this sense, the Roskill exercise was not a cost-benefit analysis at all but a cost-effectiveness study, since it was assumed that the benefit of an airport was constant whichever site was chosen.*

Local Government Circular 2/70
Another technical issue which is likely to cause some difficulty is the selection of an investment criterion. There are several possible criteria which the analyst can use in cost-benefit analysis. Chapter 1 made brief reference to net present value and cost/benefit ratio. There are others such as minimum pay-back period and internal rate of return which are not discussed here.[8] Most of the earlier cost-benefit studies used the ratio criterion which poses problems when large disparities in magnitude occur between costs and benefits of different projects. For this reason, the net present value criterion is now generally favoured (see Chapter 1). The recent introduction in local government of Circular 2/70 procedures seem to indicate, however, that the ratio concept is likely to become increasingly relevant to local authority investment decisions. Previously, local authorities had no formal capital constraints – schemes were granted loan sanction 'on their merits' by the central government and the only constraint was the obvious one that the burden of future debt servicing might become unacceptably heavy in revenue terms. Now, however, Circular 2/70 arrangements define an absolute capital constraint for what are called 'locally determined schemes' (i.e. broadly, all capital projects except (a) education, housing, principal roads, police, social services and health, and (b) certain other larger-scale schemes). Within this constraint, authorities are free to undertake capital expenditure as they wish without obtaining formal

* See p. 66.

government approval to each and every scheme. The advantages to local authorities of such a system are apparent – more 'freedom' at the local level, etc. (one cynic has defined the 'advantage' as more freedom to spend less money!) and the satisfying feeling that local councils are making decisions and not merely recommendations. However, in the democratic tradition, with freedom comes responsibility and discipline. It is now more important than ever for local authorities to choose the best set of projects within whatever framework of local priorities is adopted. In a sense, Circular 2/70 should provide a stimulus to the development of cost-benefit analysis in British local government, but the fact that an absolute resource constraint (in the sense that access to capital funds is restricted) now operates means that it is also important to think in terms of ratios as the most appropriate investment criterion. Once the locally determined allocation has been distributed by the political process – so much for industrial development, so much for recreational open space, so much for libraries, etc. – it seems reasonable to assume that the decision-maker will be interested in pursuing projects with high cost-benefit ratios rather than those with large net present values, so that they can show that they are making the best use of every *unit* of capital available. It will be interesting to observe whether in fact the Circular has this result.

There are no simple rules telling us how to do cost-benefit analysis, and although some of the technical problems have been touched upon here, many of the theoretical controversies surrounding the technique can, indeed *must*, be ignored if it is to be of practical value to this generation. We cannot forever allow the best to be the enemy of the good. Decisions about the rate of discount for instance, a topic of fascinating interest to academic economists, cannot be allowed to monopolize the time of the cost-benefit practitioner in *local* government, obliged as he inevitably is to produce fast results. Probably the adoption of the Government test discount rate, together with the use of sensitivity analysis, is all that can be reasonably expected in a local authority cost-benefit study.

PLANNED PROGRAMME BUDGETING

One legitimate question which has often been asked about cost-benefit analysis is where it fits into the decision-making process. It is obvious that it cannot be used to evaluate every possible course of action in all major policy areas – the resources and time for such a comprehensive approach are just not available. It is also clear that if used in a haphazard fashion there are dangers of abuse and manipulation; indeed, these problems have already arisen in the United States. The answer seems to be somewhere between the two extremes, and it is now widely accepted that cost-benefit analysis finds a natural place in the decision system package known as Planned Programme Budgeting (PPB), a cursory glance at whose major characteristics will suffice to indicate the crucial role which cost-benefit analysis and other techniques have to play within it. PPB, indeed any corporate planning system, has several key features. These may be as listed in condensed form as:

(1) definition of (and assigning priorities to) objectives;
(2) identification of alternative ways of achieving stated objectives;
(3) evaluation of alternative ways of achieving objectives;
(4) presentation of results to decision-makers;
(5) implementation, feedback and review.

The first step in a PPB system is the definition of fundamental objectives and the relating of all activities of the organization to these objectives, regardless of their place in the organizational structure. The problem in the public sector is that objectives are often either not known, not generally agreed, or not amenable to quantitative analysis. Nevertheless, the exercise of defining objectives in the public sector is becoming more and more an intrinsic part of the decision-making process.

The cornerstone of PPB is the systematic identification and evaluation of alternative ways of achieving stated objectives. Identification of alternatives is a creative process arising naturally out of the setting of long-term objectives, and is a process beset by uncertainties. Nevertheless, it is a central feature of modern planning systems and provides the basic framework for meaningful plan evaluation. At this point in the system, cost-benefit analysis and other techniques come into their own. Analysis can take several different forms: it may provide estimates of the costs and benefits in money terms of alternative programmes; it may compare alternative programme costs with their associated level of effectiveness; or it may merely spell out qualitative or subjective assessments of alternative courses of action. The level of sophistication depends on many factors. It needs to be emphasized, however, that decision-makers, presented with the results of analysis within a total framework which has defined objectives and examining alternative policies and programmes for their achievement, are likely to make use of the results of analysis in a more logical and consistent manner than if they are required to make decisions on what may appear to be a series of unrelated policy proposals backed up by *ad hoc* appraisals of individual projects. In this sense, the systematic application of cost-benefit analysis has a potential for improving decision-making above and beyond its value in individual project selection.

In its present stage of development the presentation of the results of a cost-benefit analysis to the decision-makers is of critical importance.

Although the basis of the technique is to enumerate and evaluate *all* the relevant costs and benefits, there are obvious reasons why this objective is seldom achieved in practice. There comes a point in the analysis process where the marginal cost of obtaining additional information may exceed the marginal benefit which that information has for decision-making. It is not possible to define this point in general terms; it is rather a matter for the judgement of the individual analyst who in many circumstances will be operating under a time constraint which will in any case impose an artificial cut-off point in the analysis.

CURRENT CRITICISM OF COST-BENEFIT ANALYSIS

Having said this, it is necessary to reiterate something which is at the root of many criticisms of cost-benefit analysis. Professor Self, in his critique of the Roskill exercise,[9] stated:

'The cost-benefit figures are incredible, not only because of the disparate basis of the items included but because of the important items excluded.'

He was making two points: first, that it was not meaningful to attempt to consider such diverse items as capital construction costs alongside (for instance) travel costs which are based upon 'an enormous chain of speculative analysis'. His point here was that travel costs far outweighed the cost of construction yet should not have been given the same weight in the analysis, because unlike construction costs they are not valued at market prices but at prices *imputed* from observation of market behaviour. However, the fundamental (but rarely achieved) aim of cost-benefit analysis is to value all items in monetary terms, and although this objective may have drawbacks from the political scientist's point of view it is difficult to envisage any other basis upon which costs and benefits can be compared on a commensurable basis. Nevertheless, it is probably useful for the decision-makers to be presented with a *range* of values for those items of imputed costs and benefits in an analysis. This approach allows them to make their value judgements within a framework which can form a common basis for subjective judgements.

The second aspect of this part of Self's critique relates to the exclusion of important costs and benefits in an analysis. What he is really saying here is that those items which have been quantified take precedence over those which have not. In many cases, the decision-makers will be misled by an analysis which concentrates on the few quantifiable costs and benefits and ignores other items because of their 'intangibility'. This is one of the pitfalls inherent in a situation where the analysis group comprises only economists, statisticians and others oriented towards quantitative evaluation. The remedy is simply to ensure that the relevant non-quantifiable effects of an investment project are described in detail by the specialist concerned, be he educationist, social worker, or whatever. Once again, it is of paramount importance that the decision-makers are presented with information which allows them to exercise their value judgements on a rational basis. The point raised by Self on the inclusion of 'disparate' items in an analysis has particular significance in the context of the planning balance sheet. Politicians are keenly interested in information about the distribution of costs and benefits (including externalities), but theiɪ major concern has traditionally been to determine the *financial* impact of policy proposals (a concern prompted often by the Treasury at the national level and by the treasurer in local government). It would be exceptional for external benefits to particular sectors of the community to be *consistently* given higher political priority than efficiency benefits. For example, a local

Table 35

	Scheme A NPV £000			Scheme B NPV £000	
	Cost	*benefit*		*Cost*	*benefit*
Construct and let 300 houses	1,000	1,100	Construct and let 200 houses	660	720
			Divert electricity supply underground	340	680
	1,000	1,100		1,000	1,400

authority with £1m. to invest in the housing sector may be faced with two alternative housing projects on land which is crossed by electricity pylons. The (hypothetical) costs and benefits of the alternatives are shown in Table 35. Scheme A maximizes the number of houses which can be constructed on the land shows a benefit/cost ratio of 1.1 and a net present value of £100,000. All the costs and benefits considered are internal to the authority. Scheme B envisages fewer houses on the land but provides for the removal of the unsightly pylons with consequent amenity benefits to the local population. The benefit/cost ratio is 1:4 and the net present value is £400,000. The advice inherent in the figures is self-evident, yet it is more than probable that the politician would largely discount the amenity benefits because they had relatively little impact on the authority's finances. His view would depend on a value judgement about trading off 100 houses against 'a better view' – and the likely outcome in times of financial stringency would be to plump for the houses. Any analysis ought to allow presentation of a kind that would allow decision-makers to exercise judgements of this type.

COST-BENEFIT IN THE FUTURE

In Britain there is an increasing recognition of the fact that traditional accounting and budgeting methods are inadequate for the complex management tasks of government departments, nationalized industries and local authorities. To meet this deficiency, public bodies have found it increasingly necessary to develop new methods. In recent years, there has been a growing emphasis on the application of quantitative techniques in local and central government with the aim of improving the quality of information upon which to base decisions. Management accounting and cost accounting are gradually superseding traditional book-keeping methods; work study and organization and methods techniques are helping to streamline work practices and clerical routines. The advent of the computer has enabled public authorities to apply the mathematical and statistical methods of operational research, critical path analysis and so on, to many of the technical problems involved in the provision of public services. All of these developments have contributed to the achievement of a higher level of administrative and technical efficiency in public authorities. The development of cost-benefit analysis in Britain with the aim of achieving *social* efficiency in resource allocation in the public sector is now gathering momentum.

The technique has at times generated more heat than light. The extremists on both sides – critics and enthusiasts – have seldom contributed in any meaningful sense to the development of social efficiency in public decision-making. In many cases, extremism is a result of a non-understanding of the basic principles involved. Many administrators have a smattering of jargon, but opportunities for more detailed study are limited. The papers published in the learned journals are often unintelligible to the layman, whilst the surveys appearing in the professional and planning magazines are often too general to be of real benefit. It is important that this void should be filled in order that administrators and political decision-makers can be made more aware of the advantages and the limitations of the technique. Certain bodies such as the Institute of Municipal Treasurers and Accountants and the Institute for Local Government Studies have played a major role in this education process, and of course, the RIPA itself has done as much as any institution in the field. Nevertheless, it is clear that more effort is needed if the future development and application of cost-benefit techniques is to keep pace with the ever-increasing complexity of resource allocation in the public sector. The aim must be to create a dialogue between decison-maker and analyst, and in order to do this, the mystique must be removed. This does not necessarily mean that politicians need to be masters of the mechanics of quantitative analysis – it is a question of confidence. A successful general does not need to know how to fire a machine-gun or drive a tank – it is more important for him to know how to deploy such skills on the battlefield.

As cost-benefit develops, it is possible to foresee an even more important role for it in the future. Already the term is becoming increasingly familiar to the general public. It has appeared in ministerial pronouncements, parliamentary questions and newspaper columns. The saga of the third London airport site illustrates the growing significance of formal public participation in complex decision situations. It is no longer acceptable to make decisions behind closed doors – people must be given an opportunity to get involved in decision-making – at least, this is the theory behind the inclusion of statutory public participation procedures in the Town and Country Planning Act of 1968.

As an example of cost-benefit analysis in action, the Roskill exercise was of great importance in two ways: it pioneered new techniques and it added a new dimension to the planning inquiry. It has had many critics, but technically it advanced the frontiers of knowledge more than is usually recognized; for example, its methods of costing agricultural loss, air traffic movement and amenity broke new ground; while in sheer size and scope it is the biggest thing of its kind ever to have been attempted. Equally important is its probable influence on future planning inquiries. Working under conditions of radio and press publicity, it set off a national debate on fundamental values, in which its cost-benefit analysis was instrumental in posing more sharply than ever before the conflict between progress and preservation. This battle had often been fought at previous public inquiries, but never on such a scale, and never with such a wide range of weapons.

On the other hand, the Roskill analysis, in the context of this book, had two serious limitations. First, its assumption that the *benefits* brought by an airport would be constant for all four sites (an assumption only once challenged at the inquiry) meant that it became an exercise in cost minimization rather than cost-benefit comparison, though there was, of course, an internal balancing of costs and benefits in particular matters in local contexts. Secondly, the conclusion to which the analysis pointed was rejected by the Government.

This last fact does not, however, necessarily detract from its importance. The Government had to decide what to do in the most crowded corner of a crowded island, at a time when amenity was rapidly rising in the 'pecking order' of national priorities. It was the amenity lobby which had been most influential in having the original Stansted decision reconsidered, and the effect of the Roskill analysis, in spite of the fact that its logic pointed steadily towards an inland site, was to strengthen public opinion in favour of a coastal one. Indeed, Roskill provided not only an analysis but a catalyst; its cost-benefit exercise caused public opinion to crystallize, and to make clear to the

Government that a majority wanted to preserve what remains of the rural Home Counties between the two great conurbations of London and Birmingham. If one may project this experience into other areas of investment decision it is possible to see cost-benefit analysis not only as a means of justifying the selection of particular projects, but of strengthening the democratic process of finding out what people are prepared to pay for; and as areas of doubt and controversy in technique continue to diminish it will be possible to present the bill in increasingly realistic terms.

The Roskill cost-benefit analysis suffered two major disabilities. First, the factor which proved to be decisively large when evaluated in money terms, namely the cost of travelling time, was among the less tangible, and the techniques for ascribing an economic value to it were correspondingly more controversial. Secondly, a consideration which ranked low economically, namely amenity, ranked high politically. The first of these disabilities will gradually diminish, as techniques improve, though it will never completely disappear, for 'intangibles', almost by definition, will never be evaluated with complete precision; moreover in public investment, which does not produce revenue in a commercial fashion, intangibles are always likely to be an important part of the calculation. The second, however, will remain unchanged, for political considerations must in the long run be decisive, and in matters that are politically highly-charged a cost-benefit analysis must be a background aid to decision-making, rather than a conclusive argument. In the particular case of Roskill, the vital question of amenity was both political in content and intangible in character, being even more elusive and difficult to quantify than travelling time. It is indeed probable that decisions about amenity will always have strong political overtones, for it is an area in which judgement is bound to be unusually subjective, whether it is the judgement of a householder evaluating the view from his sitting-room or a Government evaluating the appearance of the Vale of Aylesbury.

The claim of cost-benefit analysis to be an indispensable tool is perhaps better substantiated in the less politically charged investment decisions which have been the main subject of this book. Is it worth spending money on a drainage scheme? (Chapter 11.) What price of admission will bring the maximum return? (Chapter 8.) What will be the effects of putting car parks in different places? (Chapter 10.) It is unlikely, though not of course impossible, that rational decisions in such matters based on cost-benefit analysis will be upset by local politics.

Cost-benefit analysis is also essential when an attempt is being made to assess hidden social costs. As we said in Chapter 9 in discussing the social costs of bad housing, there is a great deal of living accommodation in this country which is uncivilized by modern standards. 'But' runs the natural response 'can we afford to pull it down and rebuild?' Cost-benefit analysis can say, if not with precision at least with more realism than would have been possible a decade ago, what actually *is* the cost of *not* pulling it down and rebuilding.

In problems of this order – and enough of them await solution by central and local authorities – cost-benefit analysis is enlarging the scope for rational choice.

REFERENCES

1 Published by permission of Keith Prowse Music Publishing Co. Ltd.
2 Bentham, J., *An Introduction to the Principles and Morals of Legislation* (Darien, Conn., Hafner Publishing Co. Ltd).
3 Dupuit, J., 'On the Measurement of the Utility of Public Works' (translated from the French by R. H. Barback), *International Economic Papers*, No. 2 (1952).
4 Pigou, A. C., *The Economics of Welfare* (London, Macmillan, 1962).
5 MacBride, G. A., 'Policy Matters in Investment Decision-Making', *Regional Studies*, Vol. 4 (1970).
6 Wildavsky, A., 'The Political Economy of Efficiency: Cost-Benefit Analysis, Systems Analysis and Programme Budgeting', *Public Administration Review*, Vol. XXVI (December 1966), No. 4.
7 Waller, R. A., 'Environmental Quality: its Measurement and Control', *Regional Studies*, Vol. 4 (1970).
8 Quirin, G. D., *The Capital Expenditure Decision* (Homewood, Ill., Richard D. Irwin Inc., 1967).
9 Self, P., 'Nonsense on Stilts: the Futility of Roskill', *Political Quarterly* (July 1970).

INDEX

agriculture: and third London airport, 70–1; and urban expansion, 112–14
air pollution, 55–9
air transport, 102–3
amenity cost, 74–6
angling, 142, 147–53

Beacon Light District, 165–6
Bentham, Jeremy, 227–8
blight: definition of, 158
bridges, 91–3
Buchanan, Professor Colin, 65n, 180

car parking: see parking
Carter, Dr R. F., 209
Chicago, 163
Clawson, Marion, 144–5, 152, 189–200
Clyde Estuary Development Project, 102, 108
conservation, 50–63
consumer time preference, 25
consumers' surplus, 22, 39, 117
cost benefit analysis: principles of, 15; definition of, 17; origins of, 29–30; limitations of, 230–1; cost of, 231; selection of projects, 232–4; terms of reference, 234–5; criticism of, 239–40; future of, 241
cost effectiveness, 235–6
costs and benefits, identification of, 20
Coventry: urban transport, 94–8
crime rate, 170–1

diseases and air pollution, 55–9
Dupuit, J., 228
Durham University Library, 128

East Stockton, 164
Edinburgh (Turnhouse) Airport, 102–3
education: economic returns, 128–31
employment services, 131–3
environment, 50–63

flood relief scheme, 209–22

government departments, 110–12
Grafham Water, 147–53

Haringey, 167–74, 176–9
health screening, 133–5
housing, 160–74
housing quality index, 176–7

identification of costs and benefits, 20
industrial training, 131–3
information systems, 127–8
Institute of Municipal Treasurers and Accountants, 115
inter-urban roads, 89–92

Lake District, 117, 120
leisure activities, 141–53
leisure travel, 43–4
Lichfield, Professor Nathaniel, 28, 97, 114, 159
Local Government Operational Research Unit, 114, 121, 209, 233
London: public transport in, 94, 98–9
London airport, third, 65–80

M1 motorway, 30, 45–6, 85
McBreen's Heifer, 227
management information systems, 231
Manchester: urban transport in, 94–8
measurement of benefits and costs, 21–4, 235
mental health, 172
Metra Consulting Group, 108
Morecambe Bay barrage, 92, 117, 120–1
motorways: identification of benefits and costs, 39–47

National Ports Council, 109
National Research Development Corporation, 124–6
noise, 59–61, 73–4, 99–102